7457
2nd copy
338:669.21
Ref only
5-12-95
ABSTRACTS
ADDITIONS LIST

D1436908

With the Compliments

of

MKS Finance SA

&

PAMP SA

THE GOLD COMPANION

Also by Timothy Green:

The World of Gold

The Smugglers

The Adventurers

The Universal Eye: World Television in the seventies

The World of Gold Today

How to Buy Gold

The World of Diamonds

The New World of Gold

The Prospect for Gold; the view to the year 2000

With Maureen Green:

The Good Water Guide; the world's best bottled waters

THE GOLD COMPANION

The A-Z of Mining, Marketing Trading and Technology

Timothy Green

with Deborah Russell

First published in Great Britain in 1991 by:
Rosendale Press Limited, 140 Rosendale Road,
London SE21 8LG

Design and production by Pep Reiff
Typesetting by Chiltern Publishing, Beaconsfield
Colour origination by F. E. Burman Ltd., London SE1
Printed in England by Butler & Tanner Ltd, Frome, Somerset

ISBN 1 872803 02 4

"Gold is the child of Zeus
Neither moth nor rust devoureth it."

Pindar c. 522–442 *BC*

Preface

The concept for this book came from Mehdi Barkhordar of MKS Finance SA and the PAMP refinery, who has given us constant encouragement and support during the two years that it has taken to produce it. In an increasingly complex world of gold, we hope it will prove a useful guide to miners, traders and manufacturers in obtaining a broader understanding of the business, especially outside the area of their normal expertise.

While following the basic A–Z format, we have included longer essays on such varied themes as the London fixing, futures, investment, jewellery, mining, options, technical analysis and all major markets and gold producing countries to give a better introductory perspective to a topic, which is then cross-referenced to more detailed entries. On mining, besides a general essay on each gold-producing country, there are individual entries for major mining houses and mining techniques; similarly on markets the main bankers, bullion houses or refiners have their own entries. And a reader looking up delta-hedging will find not only an explanation of that technique, but cross-reference to the general essay on options.

A guide such as this, covering a variety of fields, has naturally relied upon the help of many people. At the outset, I must acknowledge the diligent work of my colleague, Deborah Russell, who put together the framework for the book, wrote many of the entries and often laboured far into the night on her word processor to piece it all together. Her specialist knowledge as a geologist and from working on the Consolidated Gold Fields annual gold survey also proved invaluable.

A great deal of essential advice has also come from our three consultants: John Baird, Jerry Arkinstall and David Bird, editor of Mining Journal's *International Gold Mining Newsletter*. I am also most grateful to my colleagues — Dr Stewart Murray, Kevin Crisp, Philip Klapwyk and Tony Sutton-Pratt at Gold Fields Mineral Services — for help with many statistics and charts, which they have kindly allowed us to use. Jessica Jacks at the RTZ Corporation also graciously allowed me to see her thesis on Options, which proved of exceptional use in writing the varied entries on that important sector of the gold business; her data base on gold loans was also helpful. Brian Marber added his own unique touch in helping me come to grips with the intricacies of technical analysis and has provided many charts.On coins, Sandra Ferguson at Spink and Son Ltd, Gina Murphy of Spink Modern Collections and Seth Hersh at Manfra, Tordella and Brooks in New York were all most helpful.

I must also add special thanks to Geoffrey Loades and Sybille Ammann of the World Gold Council in Geneva, to Michael Barlerin and his staff at the World Gold Council in New York, Jeff Toshima of World Gold Council in Tokyo and Jonie Lai in Hong Kong for help with specific queries on text or pictures of their countries, together with John Lutley at The Gold Institute in Washington D.C. Irena Podleska also helped greatly with European research.

Dr Paul Kavanagh of American Barrick Mines also offered his unique knowledge of the history of the Canadian mining industry; Ross Louthean of *Gold Gazette* in Perth, Western Australia advised us on queries there. Tom Main and his colleagues at the Chamber of Mines of South Africa provided us with much assistance. Many banks, bullion dealers and refiners have been kind not only in providing information on their own operations but in commenting on general aspects of the market. And as always, my good friend Madhusudan Daga in Bombay has advised on the entries relating to India.

A detailed reference to sources will be found at the end of this volume but in particular, acknowledgement must be made to the International Precious Metal Institute's *Precious Metals Glossary* of Precious Metal Industry Terms, Jeffrey Nichols' *The Complete Book of Gold Investing*, Paul Sarnoff's *Trading in Gold*, Terry Mayer's *Commodity Options* and to the publication *Gold Bulletin and Gold Patent Digest*.

In our own office, my wife Maureen has been both a perceptive editor of the text and a resourceful picture editor, while Pamela Burden has patiently re-typed our many revisions. Our designer, Pep Reiff, has also brought to this project the same skills she has provided on earlier projects together. Finally, the skill and patience of Hazel Powell at Chiltern Publishing enabled the many revisions to be successfully incorporated in copy-editing and type-setting. The errors, misconceptions and any omissions are, however, of my own making.

TSG
Dulwich and Lauris
December 1990

Abyssinian Gold

A gold plated alloy (q.v.) of copper and zinc.

Acceptable

A refiner, melter or assayer (q.v.) whose bars are accepted as 'good delivery' (q.v.) on the London gold market is listed as 'acceptable'.

Account/Account

See **Deferred Settlement**.

Acid Test

A technique for determining the fineness of gold by observing its reaction to specific acids.

Actuals

A term frequently used in the United States to distinguish physical commodities from futures or 'paper' contracts.

Adit

A tunnel driven horizontally into the side of a mountain or hill to gain access for exploration or mining.

Ad Valorem

The levy of customs duty, insurance premium or storage charge based on the estimated value of the gold or gold products; from the Latin 'in proportion to their value'.

Agio

The premium in exchanging one form of gold for another, or the added value on coins over their gold content. If, for example, the gold price is $400, and a one ounce bullion coin is selling for $412, the agio is 3 per cent.

Alchemy

The search for the philosophers' stone, or, more accurately, the stone of the philosophers (*lapis philosophorum*), the agent that would transmute base metals into gold. Pioneered in China in the fourth century BC, it was widely practised in ancient Greece, medieval Islam and early Renaissance Europe, laying the groundwork for modern chemistry. In addition to its transmutatory power, the stone was believed to have the properties of a universal medicine for longevity and immortality. Gold, the metal that does not corrode, symbolizes immortality. The Chinese compared the durability of gold to the much-sought immortality of the body. One of their primary goals was the preparation of liquid gold as an elixir. Alchemists included kings and popes, among them Herakleios of Byzantium, James IV of Scotland and Charles II of England. Chaucer devoted one *Canterbury Tale* — The Canon's Yeoman's — to the pursuit of the stone:

'I seye, my lord can switch subtilitee
That al this ground on which we

Alchemy. *A medieval alchemist in his laboratory seeks the philosophers' stone*

been ryding,
 Til that we come to Caunterbury toun,
 He could al clene turne it up-so-doun,
 And pave it al of silver and of gold.'

Aliquot

A small, representative sample taken from a gold bar or article for assay (q.v.) to determine its fine gold content.

Allocated Gold

Gold stored, e.g. by a bank, separately from that of other owners (i.e. not in a pool) and designated as belonging to a particular owner who is a secured creditor. Also known as **Segregated**, or **Non-fungible**.

Alloy

A mixture of gold with a baser metal or metals to lower the purity, influence the colour, or add hardness. Originally from the Latin *alligare*, to bind up.

Alloys of gold are used both for coins (q.v.) and jewellery (q.v.), and are usually made by semi-fabricators for the jewellery trade, although some jewellery manufacturers make their own alloys. The most common alloys are 22, 18, 14, 9 or 8 carat, but may be made to other standards in some countries, such as 19.2 carat in Portugal.

The colour of the alloy depends on the balance of other metals with which the gold is mixed. White shades (often used in diamond jewellery) are achieved by alloying gold with silver and nickel or palladium; red alloys contain mainly copper and sometimes zinc; green tints are achieved by varying proportions of copper and silver, nickel or palladium.

A harder alloy is made by adding nickel or a small percentage of titanium to gold, as in *chuk kam* (q.v.) jewellery. The principal added metal is known as the master alloy (q.v.).

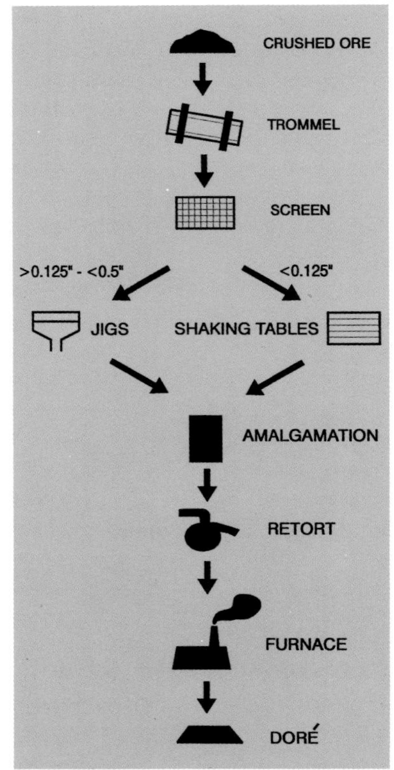

Amalgamation. *The sequence of extracting alluvial gold using mercury to form an amalgam*

Alluvial Gold

Alluvial, or placer (q.v.), gold comprises small particles or nuggets weathered away from the main gold bearing reef and usually deposited in the beds or along the banks of rivers and streams. The gold can therefore be recovered by panning, dredging or hydraulic mining, often by individual prospectors. The major gold rushes in the United States in 1848 and Australia in 1851 were prompted by alluvial gold discoveries. Such deposits remain a significant source of gold. In Brazil (q.v.) three-quarters of all gold production is from alluvial sources, and throughout much of Africa, notably Zaire, Tanzania, Guinea, Ivory Coast, Niger and Burkina Faso, virtually all gold output is of alluvial origin.

Considerable alluvial gold is also recovered in the Philippines (q.v.), Soviet Union (q.v.), China (q.v.), Indonesia and Papua New Guinea (q.v.). World-wide alluvial production exceeds 200 tonnes (6.4 million ounces) annually.

Amalgam/Amalgamation

When gold, silver and a number of base metals, such as zinc or lead, come into contact with mercury they amalgamate to form an alloy known as amalgam. The amalgamation of gold with mercury was the principal method of extracting gold from ore until the late nineteenth century, when it was largely replaced by the cyanide process (q.v.). Amalgamation was used, in particular, during the Californian and Australian gold rushes.

The ore was initially crushed in water in stamp batteries until it was reduced to fine particles, which then flowed, as a pulp, over thin sheets of copper coated with mercury; the heavier gold particles settled on the mercury to form an amalgam which could be heated in a retort, burning off the mercury and leaving gold. The process, however, was hazardous both to workers and the environment. The revival of amalgamation in the alluvial gold workings of Brazil, Venezuela and other countries in the 1980s has led to severe pollution problems.

Amax Gold Inc.

Amax Gold Inc. (Amax Gold) is an 87 per cent owned subsidiary of Amax Inc. Amax Gold has direct interests in three gold mines, the most significant being the wholly-owned Sleeper mine in Nevada. Amax also has an indirect interest in three further operations through Canamax, in which Amax Gold holds a 49.7 per cent interest, although it was proposed at the end of 1990 that this should be sold to parent Amax Inc. Sleeper produced 256,219 ounces of gold in 1989, accounting for the majority of the company's 307,387 ounces of gold production.

Amax Gold Inc.
350 Indiana Street
Golden Colorado 80401–5081
USA
Tel: (303) 273 0600
Fax: (303) 273 0703

American Barrick Resources Corporation

Formerly an oil and gas producer, American Barrick is now a major North American gold producer. This has been achieved by a vigorous programme of acquisitions and mergers. The company produced 467,837 ounces of gold in 1989 and plans to produce 565,000 ounces in 1990. Gold reserves at the end of 1989 totalled 20.8 million ounces. The company has interests in six currently operating gold mines, the most significant being the Goldstrike mine in Nevada and the Mercur mine in Utah. Goldstrike's production is forecast to rise to 900,000 ounces in 1992 and 1 million ounces in 1996.

American Barrick Resources Corp.
24 Hazelton Avenue
Toronto
Ontario M5R 2E2
Canada
Tel: (416) 923 9400
Fax: (416) 923 2457
Telex: 06318626 BRCTOR

American Depository Receipt (ADR)

Issued by a US bank, an ADR represents one or more units of a foreign security and is usually issued to simplify the physical handling and the legal technicalities governing foreign securities issues. Australian and South African mining shares traded in the United States are generally in the form of ADRs.

American Option

An American option or American-style option refers to options (q.v.) on COMEX (q.v.) which may be exercised (q.v.) at any time prior to expiration, in contrast to 'European style' over-the-counter options (q.v.) which may be exercised only on the expiration date.

Amortization

A form of depreciation whereby provision for the reimbursement of the capital investment in an asset is made over the life of the asset. This consists of regular charges and the interest accrued on those charges in, for example, mine accounts.

Anglo American Corporation

Anglo American is one of the world's leading mining and investment corporations. The company's major investments are held in or through associated companies. The main interests include De Beers (33 per cent), Minorco (39 per cent), Amgold (49 per cent), Amcoal, Amic, JCI, Rustenburg Platinum and a series of gold mines. Its gold interests include the operations of Freegold, Vaal Reefs, Western Deep Levels and Elandsrand. Freegold is the largest gold mine in the western world and produced nearly 110 tonnes of gold in its 1989–90 fiscal year. *See also* **South Africa**.

Anglo American Corporation
44 Main Street
Johannesburg (PO Box 61587
Marshalltown 2107)
South Africa
Tel: (011) 638 9111
Fax: (011) 638 3221
Telex: 4-87167 SA

Anglovaal Ltd

Anglovaal is a major mining investment house which also holds important industrial interests. One of its principal subsidiaries is Middle Witwatersrand, accounting for 22 per cent of listed investments, through which major mining investments are held. Direct holdings in gold operations are also held by Anglovaal. In 1990, gold mining accounted for 5 per cent of the company's income and represents 23 per cent of investments. Its major gold interest is in Hartbeestfontein, which produced 29.215 tonnes of gold in 1989. Other gold operations in which the com-

Anglo American Corporation. *Free State Saaiplass in the Orange Free State is the world's largest mine with output over 100 tonnes*

pany has an interest include Loraine and Eastern Transvaal Consolidated. *See also* **South Africa**.

Anglovaal Ltd
56 Main Street
Johannesburg 2001
(PO Box 62379, Marshalltown 2107)
South Africa
Tel: (011) 634 9111
Fax: (011) 634 0038
Telex: 4-86087A - SA

Annealing

The tempering of metals by slow heating to relieve internal strains built up during manufacturing processes. Strand annealing of gold wire, for example, is carried out to produce wire of guaranteed hardness along its length. Reels of wire are de-coiled through a tube heating system and re-coiled in a cold zone.

Anomaly

An anomaly is a variation in the composition of the underlying bedrock, often detected during geochemical or geophysical surveying from a statistical abnormality in the survey data. It may indicate the presence of mineralisation.

Approved Distributor

A bank or bullion dealer who has been approved to deal directly as a wholesaler with such mints as the United States Mint (q.v.)or the Royal Canadian Mint (q.v.) in the distribution of bullion coins.

Approved Refiner

A refiner whose bars are accepted as 'good delivery' (q.v.) in the spot market or on futures exchanges. Also described as 'acceptable' in the London gold market.

Aqua Regia

A mixture of concentrated hydrochloric and nitric acids, called 'royal water' by alchemists because it was the only mixture known to them which could dissolve gold.

Arbitrage

A simultaneous purchase of one form of a commodity in one market against a sale in a different market, thereby exploiting the prices applying to different locations and forms of the commodity, e.g. the purchase of tael bars (q.v.) loco Hong Kong against the sale of 12.5kg bars loco London.

Argor-Heraeus SA

Argor refinery was originally established in Chiasso, Switzerland in 1951 and was taken over by Union Bank of Switzerland (q.v.) in 1973. A new partnership was agreed in 1986 with W. C. Heraeus GmbH (q.v.) of Hanau, Germany, with UBS having 75 per cent participation. In 1988, Argor-Heraeus moved to a new refinery at Mendrisio with facilities for refining gold, silver, platinum and palladium, and the production of bars, wafers, coins, medals and semi-finished alloys.

Argor-Heraeus SA
Via Moree 4, CH 6850
Mendrisio, Switzerland.
Tel: (91) 480191
Fax: (91) 468082
Telex: 842454

Aron, J.

J. Aron is the commodities division of the Goldman Sachs group. As a New York based bullion trader they are members of COMEX (q.v.), while in London they are members of the London Bullion Market Association (q.v.). They are specialists in over-the-counter options (q.v.) trading.

J. Aron & Co.
85 Broad St
New York, NY 10004, USA
Tel: (212) 902 7600
Fax: (212) 509 1084
Telex: 6720058
Reuters: ARONGL

Ask

The price a seller asks for gold or a gold contract. Contrast with **Bid**.

Assay

The testing of gold, either as ore, bullion, coin or jewellery, to determine its fineness (q.v.) or purity. Originally done visually by scratching the gold on a touchstone (q.v.) and comparing the trace against standard marks — a method still encountered in Indian bazaars and some other parts of Asia. The technique of fire assay, however, was understood by the Egyptians, at least by 1500 BC, and that is the principal chemical method that has since been used.

In fire assaying, or cupellation (q.v.), a small sample of the gold under test is weighed on a special balance. This is placed with a quantity of lead in a small crucible — or cupel — made of bone ash, which is heated in a muffle

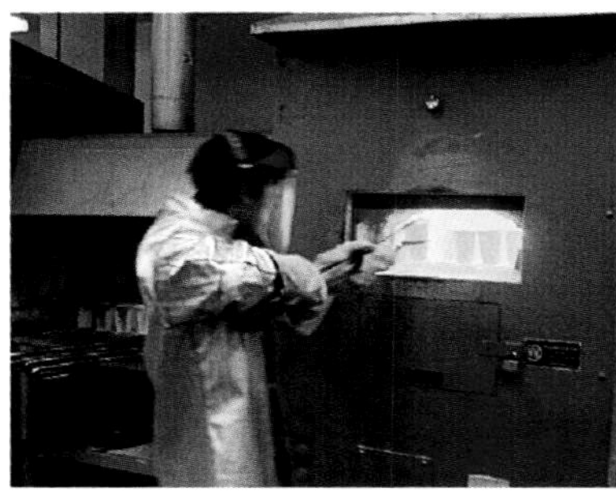

Assay. *Fire assaying samples in a muffle furnace at the Lupin mine in Canada*

furnace with a draught of air flowing over the cupel. The lead and any base metals are oxidised and absorbed into the cupel, while the gold and any silver remain as a small button. The silver is then dissolved out with nitric acid, leaving a pure gold 'cornet', which can be weighed and the gold content calculated by comparing with the original weight of the sample.

A third method of assaying, also known since antiquity although only accurately applied in modern times, involves Archimedes' principle. This

depends on the fact that the specific gravity of gold is nearly twice that of silver and more than twice that of copper. Thus if gold is debased with either of these metals, its specific gravity is progressively reduced, and the gold content can be calculated. This method is used primarily by museums and numismatists in checking ancient coins from which samples for fire assay cannot be taken.
See also **Hallmark; Refining**.

Assayer

A tester, often an officially recognised individual or company, of the fineness (q.v.) of precious metals, either in bullion form or as coin and jewellery. Each assayer has his own recognised assay mark.

Internationally, the London Bullion Market Association accepts the assay mark of fifty-four refineries in twenty-two countries on its good delivery (q.v.) list for gold, together with nineteen former assayers.

Registration of assayers and marks varies from one country to another. In France, the assay stamps recognised are those registered by individual assayers with the Chambre Syndicale des Agents de Change. In Switzerland assayers must be approved by Bureau Central du Contrôle Métaux Précieux.

Assay Office

An official or statutory organisation controlling the testing of precious metals, coin or jewellery within a country. In the United States, for example, the US Assay Office, New York, functions exclusively in the service of the US Mint to test and grade metal in coins. In Britain, independent assay offices in London, Birmingham, Sheffield and Edinburgh hallmark (q.v.) all gold, silver and platinum articles. Similar assay offices in Finland, France (Bureau de la Garantie), Ireland, the Netherlands and Sweden provide hallmark protection in Europe. In Switzerland, the Bureau Central du Contrôle Métaux Précieux in Berne exercises obligatory hallmarking of all watch cases in precious metals. Assay offices for the hallmarking of jewellery have also been established in Bahrain, Egypt, Kuwait, Lebanon, Morocco, Qatar, Saudi Arabia and Singapore, although hallmarking at these offices is not always compulsory.

Assessment Work

A legally specified amount of work that must be undertaken annually to retain control of mining rights either before any title is granted or to maintain an unpatented claim in good standing.

Assignment

Notification by the COMEX (q.v.) clearing house in New York to an option writer that an outstanding option (q.v.) has been exercised, and the writer is thus long or short of the gold futures contract following the assignment.

Atomic Weight

Gold has an atomic weight of 196.967. *See also* **Gold.**

Au

The chemical symbol for gold, from the Latin *aurum*, meaning 'shining dawn'. Aurora was the Roman goddess of dawn.

Auriferous

A geological term meaning 'containing gold'.

Australia

Gold was first discovered in Australia on a tributary of the Macquarie river near Bathurst, New South Wales, early in 1851 by Edward Hammond Hargraves. Later in the same year

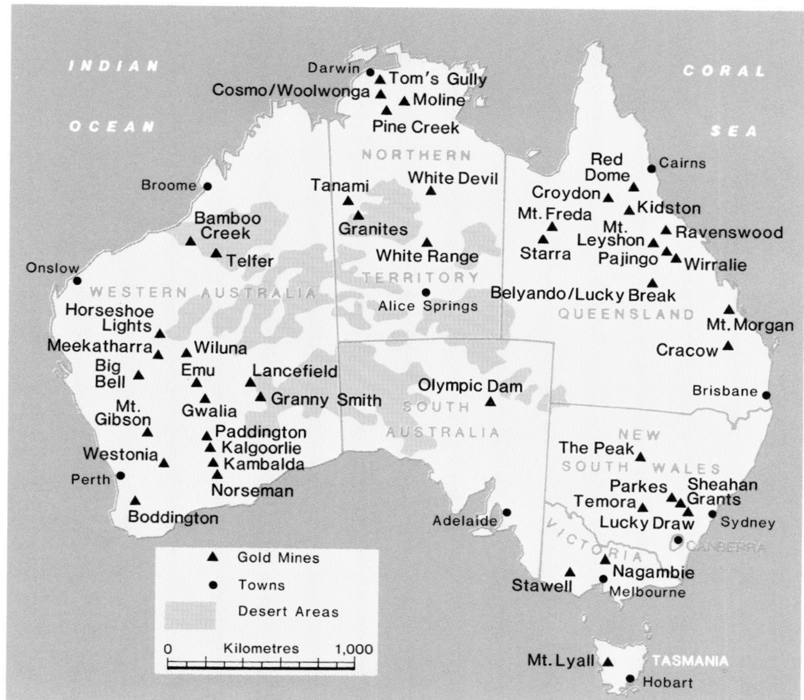

Australia. *New gold mines have been opened in every Australian state*

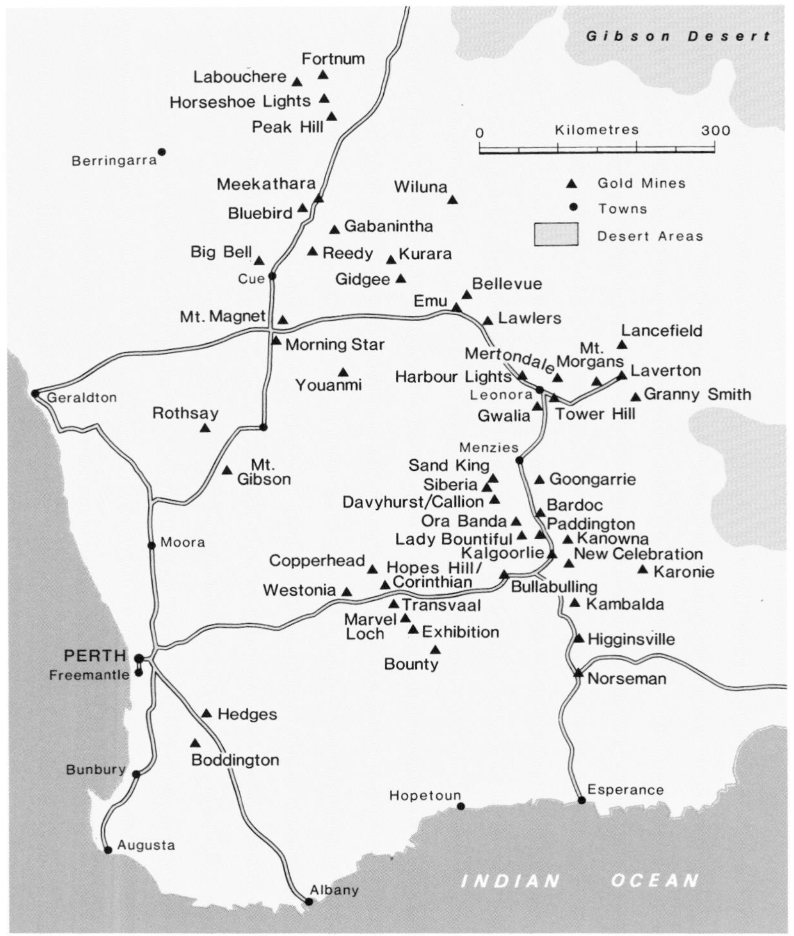

Australia. *Western Australia accounts for 70 per cent of the gold from over 100 mines, particularly the Kalgoorlie region*

further discoveries were made at Ballarat and Bendigo in Victoria.

The gold rush was relatively short-lived, peaking in 1856 when output reached about 95 tonnes. This gold rush, however, transformed both the Australian economy and the London gold market, which took 80 per cent of the gold. Despite other small gold rushes, mostly false alarms, it was not until Paddy Hannan found gold at Kalgoorlie in Western Australia in 1893 that serious production revived. Since then over 1,300 tonnes of gold have been extracted from Kalgoorlie's 'Golden Mile'. By 1903 Australian output had risen to 119 tonnes; a record not to be broken until 1988. But the richest deposits were soon worked out and, apart from a brief revival in the late 1930s after the gold price rose, Australian gold production went into almost terminal decline. By 1980 output was only 17 tonnes. Not a single mine on the Golden Mile was open and only one nearby mine, Mount Charlotte, was working.

Salvation came with the gold price rise. Exploration expenditure rose from A$30 million in 1980 to over A$200 million by 1986. New technology, notably mobile milling plants and carbon-in-pulp recovery, coupled with innovative mining finance packages, transformed the industry. Many mines were financed by low-cost gold loans, a technique pioneered by such Australian banks as Mase-Westpac (q.v.), Macquarie and Rothschilds Australia. Output exceeded 200 tonnes by 1990, 70 per cent of it coming from Western Australia.

A plethora of low-cost open-pit mines started up on the flat-weathered Pre-Cambrian shield that runs north–south through Kalgoorlie. Many pits started production in a matter of months from the locating of the ore body. An alliance between Kalgoorlie Mining Associates (KMA) and Perth entrepreneur Alan Bond began to develop the Golden Mile itself into a 'super pit', which is planned to be a mile long, half a mile wide and 1,000 feet deep. In all 105 mines were operating in Western Australia by 1990. The largest new mine is Boddington with annual output of 13 tonnes, a significant achievement on an average recovered grade of only 2.0 grammes per tonne. But this heralds the new direction in Australia; previously mines had looked for 10 grammes per tonne; new technology enabled them to accept cut-off grades down to 1.5 grammes per tonne.

The long-term future of gold mining in Australia depends on developing low-grade deposits and being able to go underground to treat sulphide ores once the easily treatable oxide ores in open-pits have been worked out. Australia's potential is enhanced by the discoveries of low-grade epithermal (q.v.) deposits in Northern

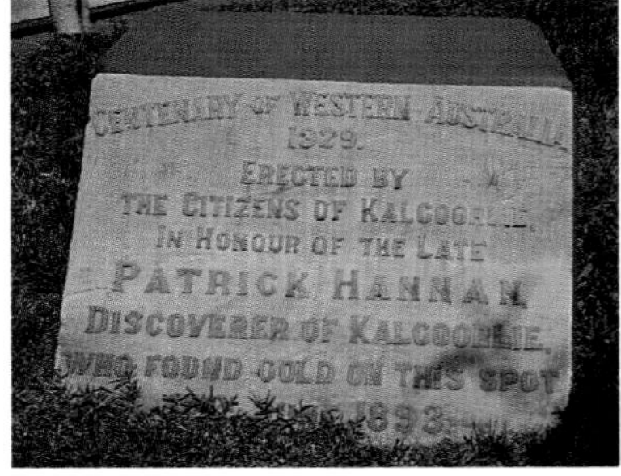

Australia. *Plaque commemorates Paddy Hannan's gold find at Kalgoorlie in 1893*

Australia: Top Twenty Mines

	Mine	Major Share Holders	Output (ounces) 1989 (actual)	1990 (estimated)
1	Boddington	Reynolds 40%/Billiton 30% BHP God 20%/Kobe 10%	421,640	450,000
2	Telfer	Newmont Australia 70% /BHP Gd 30%	255,794	310,000
3	Kambalada	Western Mining Corp. 100%	205,450	200,000
4	Kidston	Placer Pacific 70%	205,361	225,000
5	Fimiston	GMK 50%/HGAL 50%	160,361	224,400
6	Hedges	Alcoa 100%	156,602	160,0
7	Mt Leyshon	Pan Australian 100%	155,885	176,000
8	Mt Charlotte	GMK 50%/HGAL 50%	140,219	125,500
9	Meekatharra	Dominion 100%	121,838	95,000
10	Fimistn/Paringa	GMK 50%/HGAL 50%	120,433	246,100
11	Wiluna	Barrack Mines 50%/Asarco 50%	118,567	117,000
12	Big Bell	ACM Gold 50%/Placer Pacific 50%	114,882	115,000
13	New Celebration	Newmont Australia 80% /Mt Mtin 20%	110,528	110,000
14	Wirralie	ACM Gold 100%	99,831	110000
15	Starra	Cyprus 50%/Arimco 25% /Elde 25%	93,666	110,000
16	Paddington	Pancontinental 100%	3,412	85,000
17	Norseman	Central Norseman 100%	93,666	63,000
18	Mt Magnet (WMCH)	Western Mining Corp. 100%	92,239	120,000
19	Pine Creek	Renison 60%/Enterprise 40%	91,984	92,000
20	Mt Magnet (ex Metana)	Western Mining Corp. 100%	89,109	70,000
Note also:				
	Granny Smith	Placer Pacific 60%/Delta 40%	—	235,000
	Cosmo Howley	Dominion 100%	85,486	120,000
	Granites	North Flinders 100%	86,10	100,000

Queensland, which just touches the south Pacific's 'rim of fire'. The Kidston mine, now 70 per cent owned by Placer Pacific, paved the way. The mine produced 6.4 tonnes in 1989 and has produced over 34 tonnes since the start of operations in 1985. It was followed by Starra, a joint venture between Cyprus Minerals, Arimco and Elders Resources.

The historic gold mining areas of New South Wales and Victoria have also benefited. Notably at Central Norseman's Stawell, close to the original Bendigo find.

This renaissance was spurred because the profits of gold mining were tax free until January 1991. Henceforward, taxation, coupled with the fact that many of the open-pit deposits have short lives, and stricter environmental control, will curtail output again during the 1990s. Yet Australia will remain a major producer for the rest of the century.

See also **Gold Corp., Nugget, Perth Mint, R & I Bank, Sydney Futures Exchange**.

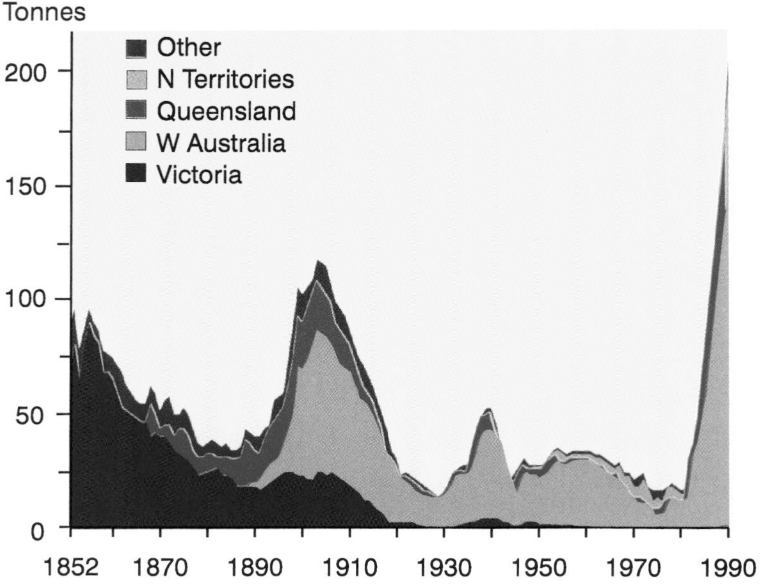

Australia. *Source: Australian Business Magazine*

Austrian Corona

Austrian gold coin. *See* **Corona; Coins.**

Autoclave

A pressurised container used on mines which are producing refractory gold ore with a very high sulphide content. Ideally the ore could be 'roasted' to unlock the gold, but burning off the sulphide poses environmental hazards. Instead, within the autoclave vessel, the sulphide ore is subjected to oxygen at high temperature and pressure to convert it into an oxide ore, which is then amenable to conventional cyanidation to recover the gold. Also known as **Bomb**.

Averaging

A buying or selling strategy based on average prices over an agreed period, e.g. a Central Bank may buy or sell gold, basis the average rate of the morning or afternoon London Fix (q.v.) during a particular month.

Back Month

A gold futures contract month that is far out: e.g. in November 1991 a back month might be December 1992, as opposed to the active (or near) month December 1991.

Backwardation

A rare situation created in the market by a shortage or tight supply, causing spot or nearby prices to go to a premium over forward quotations. Contrast with **Contango** (q.v.).

Bahrain

Offshore banking and gold trading centre in the Arabian Gulf which is also an important jewellery manufacturing centre for Saudi Arabia, especially for wholesalers from the city of Damman, just across the causeway from Bahrain. It has a well-run assay office, which tests scrap gold from Saudi Arabia, from which much of the local jewellery is made and which hallmarks jewellery for local sale.

Baht

Thai bullion bar, 990 fine, weighing 0.47 ounces or 15.4 grammes, popular with investors in Thailand. It is widely sold in gold shops in Bangkok, with main brands being from Chin Hua Heng, Seng Heng Lee and Hua Seng Heng. *See also* **Thailand**.

Ball Mill

A large, rotating cylinder used for breaking ore into smaller pieces, using metal balls as the grinding medium.
See also **Mill/Milling**.

Bank for Foreign Economic Affairs of the USSR

The bank, headquartered in Moscow, is responsible for marketing Soviet gold production world wide. The bank is an active trader in the gold market, writing options and forwards, in addition to spot sales, and has negotiated gold swaps (q.v.) with western banks. The bank has also been active in diversifying its sales by marketing kilo bars into regional markets of the Middle East and South-east Asia. The bank also trades through its Zurich branch.
Bank for Foreign Economic Affairs
Kirovski Prospect 15
107078 Moscow
Tel: 975 2127/34
Telex: 411 313

Bank for International Settlements

The Bank for International Settlements (BIS) was created in 1930 as a non-political central bank for central banks based in Basel, Switzerland. As a major pillar of the monetary structure of the western world, it has been widely used by central banks to buy and sell gold discreetly on their behalf or to act as intermediary in transfers of gold between themselves. Central banks can also swap gold with the BIS for foreign exchange. The BIS maintains its own stock of gold of approximately 200 tonnes.
Bank for International Settlements
Centralbahnplatz 2
Basel CH 1002
Switzerland
Tel: (61) 208111
Fax: (61) 2809100

Bank Leu

The oldest Swiss bank, founded in 1755, is an active gold trader in Zürich and is noted as one of the world's major coin dealers. The bank also holds important auctions of numismatic coins (q.v.). Crédit Suisse (q.v.) took a controlling interest in Bank Leu in 1990, but the bank retains its own identity in all banking and gold operations.
Bank Leu Ltd
Bahnhofstrasse 32
CH 8022 Zürich
Switzerland
Tel: (1) 219 11 11
Fax: (1) 219 36 45
Telex: 802 174 leu
Reuters: LEUG

Bank of England

The Bank of England, founded in 1694, has been the focal point of precious metal trading in London for three centuries. For much of that

Bank of England. *Gold and silver bars being weighed at the Bullion Receiving Office in the 1840s*

time, the majority of imports of gold and silver into Britain were sent for delivery at its Bullion Office. Only after the great expansion of the bullion business following the Californian and Australian gold rushes in the 1850s was the Bullion Office bypassed by brokers in the London market, weighing and storing gold independently. The Bank also had responsibility throughout the period that Britain was on the gold standard (q.v.) of buying gold and sending it to the Mint for coinage; the Bank was bound to redeem the notes that it issued in gold coin. When the gold standard was suspended in 1914 the Bank continued to take much gold, including all South African production, for Britain's reserves. After the establishment of the daily gold 'fixing' (q.v.) in London in 1919, the Bank soon became the agent for the South African Reserve Bank (q.v.) for marketing its gold at the fix; a task it continued until March 1968. During the 1960s, the Bank also acted as agent for the international gold pool (q.v.) in trying to hold the gold price at $35 in the fix. Although its pivotal role diminished with the establishment of the free market in 1968, it retains close links with the London gold market. It mounted the rescue operation for Johnson Matthey Bankers in 1985 to save the credibility of the market when the only member in its history was threatened with insolvency. And its regulatory role over the new London Bullion Market Association (q.v.) has since been enhanced. The Bank also maintains an active, if modest, trading role in gold, both for the management of UK reserves and to match its sales of new sovereigns, of which it remains the official distributor.

As a recognised IMF gold depository, it holds gold on behalf of many nations, whose central banks also ask it to act on their behalf in gold transactions. A notable Bank operation in gold was acting as an intermediary with Algeria in the complicated financial agreements for the release of the American hostages from Iran in 1981, which involved a 50 tonne transfer of gold.

Bank of England
Threadneedle Street
London EC2R 8AH
Tel: 071-601 4444
Fax: 071-601 4771
Telex: 885001

Bank of Nova Scotia (BNS)

One of North America's longest established bullion banks closely involved in the financing and marketing of Canadian gold mine output through its Toronto head office, where it is a market-maker in spot, forward and options. Bank of Nova Scotia is also a member of the London Bullion Market Association, covering European, Middle and Far Eastern clients from its London office.

Bank of Nova Scotia
Scotia Plaza
44 King Street West
Toronto M5H 1H1
Canada
Tel: (416) 367 9114
Fax: (416) 866 5053
Telex: 6219854 SCOTIA GOLD
Reuters: BNSTGL (ScotiaBank Toronto) / GOLD (Scotia Bnk Gold Tor)

Bar

(i) Gold is marketed in a wide range of bars, some of which are particular to individual countries. Their weight is always quoted in troy ounces (or metrically). For international acceptance or delivery (q.v.), however, they must conform to specific standards set by the London Bullion Market Association (q.v.) or futures exchanges and bear the marks of recognised melters and assayers. The main bars traded internationally are the 400 troy ounce (12.5 kilo) good delivery bar (q.v.) or the 1 kilo bar (32.15 troy ounces) (q.v.), such bars normally being 995 fine or 999.9 fine (q.v.). American futures exchanges normally accept 100 troy ounce (3.11 kilos) for delivery. Other bars traded regionally include:

Tael (Hong Kong) = 1.2 troy ounce or 37.3 grammes (q.v.)

Ten tolas (Indian sub-continent/ Arabian Gulf) = 3.75 troy ounces or 116.6 grammes (q.v.)

Baht (Thailand) = 0.47 troy ounces or 15.4 grammes (q.v.)

A wide variety of small bars, ingots and wafers are also marketed in weights ranging from 1 gramme to 500 grammes. Many of these are special brands or designs, such as the Fortuna (q.v.).

See also **Good Delivery**.

(ii) A placer deposit, generally submerged, in the slack portion of a stream.

Bar Chart

A type of chart commonly used in technical analysis (q.v.), typically showing highs, lows and closing prices.

Barlow Rand

See **South Africa**.

Basel Fair

The European Watch, Clock and Jewellery Fair, held for eight days in Basel, Switzerland each April, is a crossroads for gold jewellery manufacturers, designers, wholesalers and retailers. About two thousand exhibitors from seventeen countries participate.

Fair Management: Genessenschaft Schweizer Mustermesse Basel
Postfach CH4021 Basel, Switzerland
Tel: 061 686 20 20
Fax: 061 692 06 17
Telex: 962 685 smmm ch

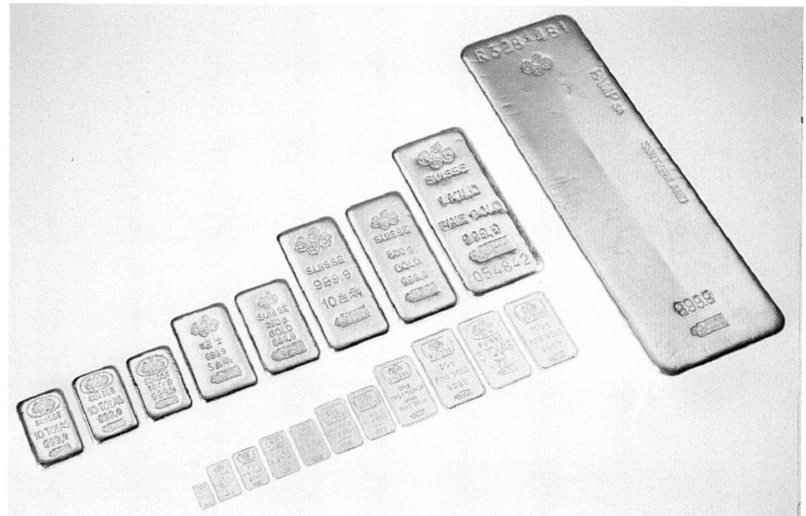

Bar. *The complete range of gold bars, 400 ounce to 1 gramme, made at the PAMP refinery in Switzerland*

Battery

The earliest machinery for crushing gold ores was called a battery or stamp mill. A battery consisted of a series of heavy iron pestles (usually five) rising and falling in an iron trough, or mortar, through which ore mixed with water flowed. The material was pounded by the 'stamps' until it was fine enough to filter through mesh screens.

Batteries were widely used in California, Australia and in the early days in South Africa but by the early twentieth century were largely replaced by multiple stage crushing equipment in ball mills (q.v.). The last stamp batteries in South Africa, for example, were built in 1918.

Battle Mountain Gold

Battle Mountain Gold expects to produce 340,000 ounces of gold in 1990. The company's principle asset is the wholly-owned Battle Mountain complex in Nevada, which produces gold and silver from the Fortitude, Surprise and Canyon Placer deposits. The operations produced 251,000 ounces of gold and 331,000 ounces of silver in 1989. Battle Mountain also owns the Pajingo mine in Australia. In addition,the company also has interests in gold operations in Bolivia, through 51 per cent owned Empresa Minera Inti Raymi, and in Chile and Papua New Guinea, through a 50.2 per cent interest in Niugini Mining. Niugini's major asset is a 20 per cent interest in the large Lihir Island late-stage development project in PNG.

Battle Mountain Gold
42nd Floor, 333 Clat Street
Houston, Texas 77002
USA
Tel: (713) 650 6400
Fax: (713) 650 3636
Telex: 763604

Bear

Someone who expects prices to fall; the term originated on the stock exchange in the eighteenth century. A bear market is a falling market. Opposite of **Bull** (q.v.).

Bear Spread

An option (q.v.) strategy combining short and long options, designed to be profitable if prices decline. One option is bought, another sold.

Benches

Steps cut back into the walls of an open pit mine to provide working areas and to allow the desired overall pit wall angle to be achieved.

Benches. *Steps cut into walls at American Barrick's Goldstrike mine in Nevada*

Beta

The volatility of the price of gold in relation to that of other commodities, bonds, stocks and housing. Gold's 'beta' is used to demonstrate how the holding of gold as part of a portfolio may smooth out its performance, in that the volatility of gold is often less than in other investments.

Bezant

A Roman gold coin, introduced by the Emperor Constantine, of 65 to 70 troy grains in weight. It was the basis of trade in the western world from the fourth to the twelfth century AD. Also known as Solidus. *See* **Coins, Numismatics**.

BHP Gold Mines

BHP Gold is a 55.7 per cent owned subsidiary of Broken Hill Proprietary Co. Ltd. The company has interests in five gold operations and a large number of exploration projects. Its assets include interests in Boddington and Telfer, two of Australia's largest gold mines. In the fiscal year to May 1990, 20 per cent owned Boddington produced 425,240 ounces of gold and 30 per cent owned Telfer produced 281,967 ounces. The company produced 300,677 ounces in the fiscal year to May 1990. A merger with Newmont Australia was proposed at the end of 1990.

BHP Gold Mines
BHP House, 140 William Street
Melbourne, Victoria 3000
Australia
Tel: (03) 609 3333
Fax: (416) 862 1850
Telex: 06-217559

Bid

The price a buyer offers for gold or a gold contract. Opposite of **Ask**.

Billon

An ingot used for coinage that is an alloy of gold (or silver) with predominating amounts of copper, tin or other base metal.

Bimetal

The term was originally applied to a gold/silver alloy, but now commonly describes gold/silver alloys which also contain platinum group metals. It is also used in semi-fabrication companies to describe rolled gold (q.v.) or gold filled products.

Bimetallic/Bimetallism

From the French *bimétallique*, it was used in the nineteenth century to describe the double standard of currency based on gold and silver. The system of bimetallism allowed the unrestricted coinage of gold and silver at a fixed price and at a fixed ratio to each other. In the second half of the nineteenth century as most nations switched from being on a silver standard to the gold standard (q.v.), after the Californian and Australian gold rushes, the bimetallic system sometimes operated during the transition period. And in some countries, notably the United States, a strong silver lobby fought a rearguard action to preserve bimetallism. The Sherman Silver Purchase Act of 1890 secured temporary retention, decreeing: 'it being the established policy of the United States to maintain the two metals on a parity with each other upon the present ratio' (16:1). The US presidential campaign of 1896 turned on the issue of bimetallism, with the Democratic candidate William Jennings Bryan of Nebraska fighting to avoid a single gold standard. In his speech to the Democratic National Convention, Bryan said: 'You shall not crucify mankind upon a cross of gold'. He was defeated; four years later the United States abandoned bimetallism for the gold standard.

Biological Leaching

A low temperature, aqueous method of treating refractory sulphide ore through pre-treatment with bacterial cultures. The bacteria catalyse the oxidation of the ore, making it amenable to cyanidation. Bio-leaching is used at the Fairview mine in South Africa and at Tonkin Springs in Nevada, USA.

Black and Scholes

Dr Fischer Black and Dr Myron Scholes are two mathematicians who, in 1973, worked out an econometrical model for options (q.v.) pricing (i.e. the premium on an option) based on data from the Chicago Board Options Exchange, which was then offering options on sixteen commodities and securities, though not on gold. The formula applies equally to gold and is the basis of most premium calculations; and a variation of it is also used for delta-hedging ratios.

Black Gold

A rare form of gold, the black coloration being due to traces of bismuth.

Blank

A blank disc of metal with milled edges used to make a coin. In the United States more commonly known as a Planchet (q.v.).

Bolivia

Bolivian gold production amounts to about 10 tonnes a year from a wide range of small deposits, particularly on the rivers flowing east from the Cordillera Real. The rivers Beni, Madidi and Madre de Dios descending from the Andes towards the Rio Madeira on the Brazilian border are worked for alluvial deposits. The main mining operation is Interaymi at Arura, in which the US mining group Battle Mountain has a fifty-one per cent share; output is around 1.5 tonnes annually.

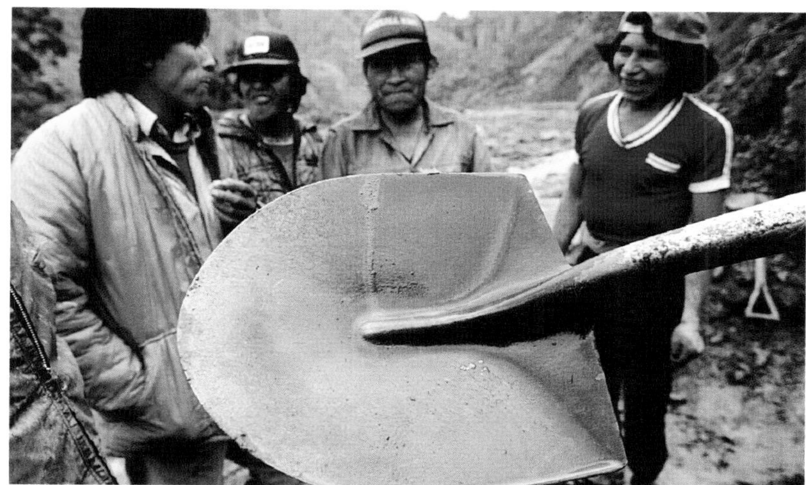

Bolivia. *Seeking gold in Bolivia, where most output is from alluvial deposits*

Bolsa Mercantil et de Futuros

The Mercantile and Futures Exchange in Sao Paulo, Brazil, was founded on 4 July 1985 and began gold trading on 31 January 1986. The Exchange offers six gold contracts:

Round Lot Gold Spot:	Unit 250 g
Gold Futures:	Unit 250 g
Gold Forward:	Unit 250 g
Odd Lot Gold Spot:	Unit 0.225g
Gold Call Options on Actuals:	Unit 250g
Gold Put Options on Actuals:	Unit 250 g

The main trading volume is in the 250 grammes Call Options. Turnover in this contract has been:

1986:	96,254
1987:	177,828
1988:	1,403,774
1989:	6,953,149

Trading hours: 10.00 a.m to 4.00 p.m.

Bolsa Mercantil et de Futuros
Prada Antonio Prado
48 Sao Paulo/ SP 01010
Brazil
Tel: (011) 239 5511
Telex: (11) 26928

Bonds (Gold Backed)

Both governments and mining companies issue gold-backed bonds as a means of borrowing money in the capital markets, although the precise formula varies. Among government bonds, the best example is the French *Rente Giscard* issued in 1973 which matured on 1 January 1988. This bond carried a guarantee that both the 7 per cent interest and the maturity value of the bond were indexed to the price of a 1 kilo bar on the Paris Bourse, if the official link between the value of the French franc and gold was severed during the lifetime of the bond. In the event, it had been, so the maturity value was based on the average Paris gold price over the last thirty trading sessions of 1987.

Gold mining companies, especially in North America, have issued bonds, usually at 7.5 per cent and often linked to gold warrant (q.v.) calls on their future production. In fact, such bonds are really an option (q.v.) to buy gold if the price should rise. But they have proved popular with small investors in Europe, who see them as a way of getting a foothold in gold, especially when the price is rising and the redemption price of the bond benefits from a higher gold price.

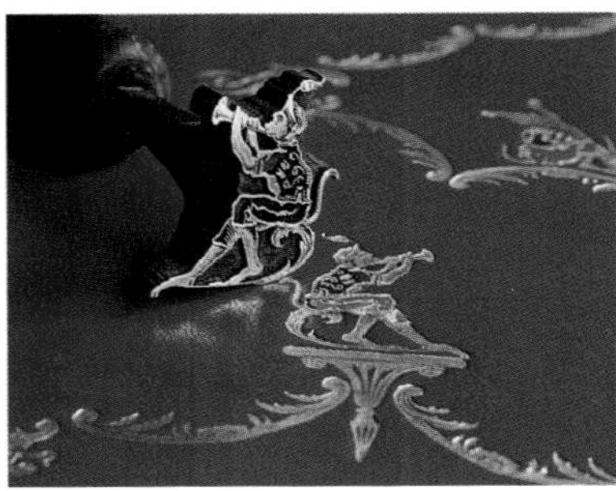

***Book-binding.** Gold being stamped into a leather book cover*

Book-binding

For more than 1,000 years extensive use has been made of gold in the binding and decoration of manuscripts and books, especially those of a religious nature. The oldest gold bindings date from the seventh century, when a fine sheet of gold, set in eight cameos in the form of a cross, was used on the front cover of the *Gospels of Theolinda*. The art of applying lacquers containing powdered gold to leather originated in the Middle East, especially in Persia, and spread through Italy to all of Europe in the early sixteenth century. Originally a light brush or pen was used to embellish book covers, but the craftsmen of Venice developed a new technique of hot gilding with gold leaf (q.v.) by means of a heated die stamp on to leather which had been treated with a mordant, or fixer, of egg white and white vinegar whisked together.

Geometrical and floral patterns adorned the books in the libraries of the Medici and Visconti and other great families of Renaissance Italy. The art reached its zenith in book-binding for many of the libraries of Europe over the next two centuries.

Borehole

A small diameter hole drilled with a diamond-impregnated drill-bit that recovers a core from the rock strata it passes through to provide geological information.

Brazil

The greenstone belts in Brazil's extensive archaean shield, similar to the Pre-Cambrian areas of Canada, South Africa, Siberia and Western Australia, host extensive gold deposits. Gold was first discovered in 1552, but significant production did not begin until the first half of the eighteenth century with discoveries in Minas Gerais, Goyas, Cuyaba and Matto Grosso. Output reached about 10 tonnes annually between 1731 and 1751, making Brazil the foremost producer and providing an important source of revenue for Portugal's South American colony. The Mineracao Morro Velho mine in Minas Gerais opened in 1835 and, with output still around 6 tonnes a year, is the world's oldest continually worked mine.

Apart from Morro Velho and some alluvial production in the Amazon tributaries, production was stagnant until the 1980s. Then the high price of gold, coupled with surging inflation, encouraged new exploration which swiftly located rich alluvial deposits, prompting hundreds of thousands of prospectors or garimpeiros to join gold rushes to the Rio Tapajos, Cumara, Alta Floresta, Rio Madeira and, above all, to Serra Pelada 270 miles south of Belem on the Amazon delta. Serra Pelada (meaning 'Hill of Gold' in Portuguese) proved one of the richest deposits of alluvial gold ever found; in 1983 alone it yielded 13 tonnes. However, increasingly hazardous working conditions as the pit deepened reduced recovery so that by 1989 output was down to 1 tonne,

***Brazil.** The main alluvial mining areas, located primarily along the major rivers*

Formal and informal production in Brazil

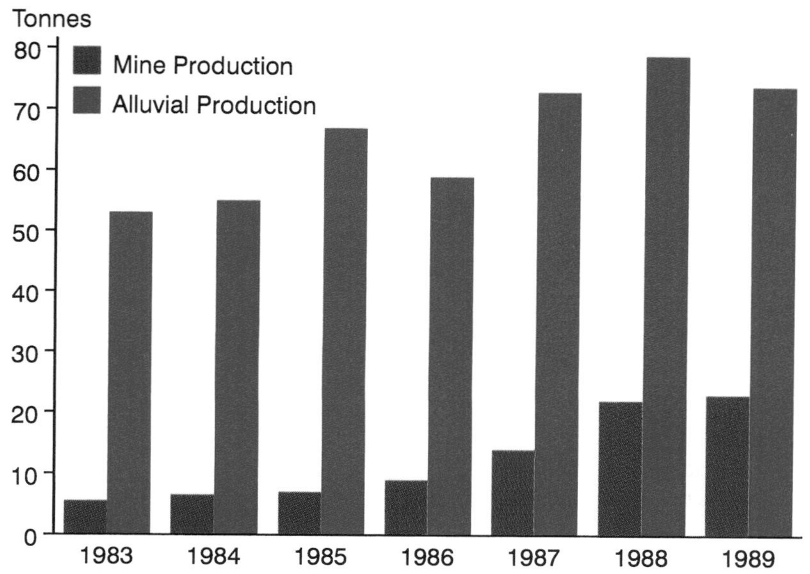

Brazil. *Source: Gold Fields Mineral Services Ltd*

mainly from the treatment of gold tailings. But other deposits, notably new finds in Roraima, meant alluvial gold still contributed nearly 80 per cent of Brazilian production of 97 tonnes in 1989. The formal mining sector, however, is expanding and mine output could reach 30–40 tonnes during the 1990s. The Morro Velho group (in association with Anglo American) opened Jacobina in 1983 and Crixas (with Inco) in 1989. RTZ's Morro de Ouro and Santa Martha mines produce about 6 tonnes annually and Amira Trading/Gencor's Sao Bento yields 2.5 tonnes. CVRD, the state-owned iron-ore company, has on-stream two mines in Minas Gerais and Bahia provinces.

But legislation forbidding foreign mining groups from holding a majority stake in Brazilian companies is limiting expansion in the formal sector, so that the major share of Brazilian output will remain with the garimpeiros (in alluvial deposits). Since their operations are also being increasingly reduced by environmental controls, and the preservation of Indian reservations in Roraima, production is likely to be maintained in the range of 70–100 tonnes annually during the 1990s.

While much of the gold was initially bought by Banco Central, the central bank, a significant private market for gold investment developed, especially during the high inflation of the late 1980s. The central bank was a regular buyer and seller into this local market to stabilise the price and to keep the parallel dollar rate under control.

Brazil: Top Ten Mines

	Mine	Major Share Holders	Output (ounces) 1989 (actual)	Output (ounces) 1990 (estimated)
1	Morro Velho	Morro Velho/Anglo American	211,868	240,000
2	Morro do Ouro	RTZ	141,460	140,000
3	Sao Bento	Amira Trading/Gencor	74,588	75,000
4	Novo Astro	CMA	64,300	65,000
5	Araci	CVRD	50,926	50,000
6	Cabacal/Sta Martha	RTZ	37,294	40,000
7	Jacobina	Morro Velho/Anglo American	23,469	40,000
8	Itabira	CVRD	15,000	15,000
9	Jenipapo	Western Mining	15,000	15,000
10	Crixas	Morro Velho/INCO	5,000	80,000

Brazil. *Seeking gold at Serra Pelada, the Hill of Gold, the richest alluvial deposit*

Commercial banks built up substantial custodial stocks of gold on behalf of multi-national and Brazilian companies hedging against rapid depreciation of the local currency. However, in 1990 the central bank initiated a new policy of paying dollars for gold in the private market and then selling the gold overseas. This resulted in considerable running down of custodial stocks, especially during the liquidity squeeze following the inauguration of President Collor.

Brazil. *Thousands of garimpeiros seek gold in the rivers of the Amazon basin*

The Bolsa Mercantil et de Futuros (q.v.) is an important exchange for spot and options trading.

Brazing Alloys

See **Solders**.

Break-Out

In technical charting, when the price breaks above or below a chart 'point' where strong resistance had been forecast on the upside or strong support on the downside.

Bretton Woods Agreement (1944)

This agreement, signed at Bretton Woods, New Hampshire in July 1944, set the framework for the post-war international monetary system with fixed exchange rates and a gold exchange standard (q.v.) under which currencies were exchangeable into gold at stable rates. It also led to the establishment of the International Monetary Fund (q.v.).

Bright Gold

(i) Liquid 'bright gold' was developed in the 1830s for the decoration of ceramics and glass. *See* **Liquid Gold.**

(ii) Bright gold plating solutions have been used in costume jewellery since the 1960s to achieve an initial sparkling finish, without too much extra polishing or 'buffing' which might damage a thin gold deposit.

See **Electroplating**.

Britannia

This 22 carat (916.6 fine) legal tender bullion coin was the first new gold coin issued by the Royal Mint (q.v.) in Britain since the Sovereign (q.v.) was re-introduced in 1817. The Britannia is struck in four sizes, containing one ounce, ½ ounce, ¼ ounce and 1⁄10 ounce fine gold, with face values of £100, £50, £25 and £10 respectively.

See **Bullion Coins, Coins**.

Britannia. *This one ounce bullion coin, struck at the Royal Mint, ws first launched in 1987*

Broker

The intermediary or middle man operating between buyers and sellers of gold, who charges a brokerage fee, or commission, for his services. Historically, the original members of the London gold market acted as brokers. Today they are usually principals dealing on their own account, except at the fixings (q.v.) when they again adopt a broker's role, charging customers a commission, or brokerage, for their services. In Switzerland,

Premex (q.v.) operates as a broker for the main Swiss banks.

Bulk Metal

A term used to describe accumulations of coins and scrap jewellery.

Bull

Someone who expects prices to rise. A bull market is a rising one. Opposite of **Bear** (q.v.).

Bull Spread

An options (q.v.) strategy comprising long and short options designed to be profitable in a rising market. One option is bought, another sold.

Bullion

The word bullion originally meant 'mint' or 'melting place' from the old French word *bouillon* (boiling), but became the generic term for refined bars or ingots of gold and silver and the trade in them. Thus, the Bullion Office at the Bank of England (q.v.) by the eighteenth century was the crossroads of most gold transactions for the London market, just as many traders call themselves bullion banks today. Although principally implying bar gold, it has been extended to cover bullion coins (q.v.).

Bullion Coin

Bullion Coin. *The Britannia, Eagle, Ecu, Maple Leaf and Nugget are the leading bullion coins*

Bullion coins, as distinct from numismatic coins for collectors, are legal tender gold coins, made by government mints and sold at a low premium to appeal to the small investor.

The concept of a one ounce legal tender coin without a declared face value was pioneered with South Africa's Krugerrand (q.v.) launched as a bullion coin in 1970 and sold at a premium of 3 per cent over its gold content. It was followed by the Canadian Maple Leaf (q.v.), Australia's Nugget (q.v.), Britain's Britannia (q.v.), the United States' Eagle (q.v.),Belgium's Ecu (q.v.) and Austria's Philharmoniker (q.v.). The appeal of the coins, marketed with heavy advertising, was widened by the introduction of ½ ounce, ¼ ounce, and 1/10 ounce versions. The bullion coin became a significant investment item in gold, taking up 14 per cent of all gold coming on to the market between 1970 and 1990.
Close to 60 million coins were in circulation by 1990. *See also* **Coins**.

Butterfly

In options (q.v.) a hedging strategy if the price is expected to fluctuate in a fairly narrow trading range. It involves the sale (or purchase) of two identical options, together with the purchase (or sale) of one option with an immediately higher exercise price, and one option with an immediately lower exercise price.
All options must be of the same type, commodity and expiration date.

Buy Signal

In technical analysis (q.v.), a pattern, such as a double bottom (q.v.), which indicates a key reversal upwards in the price and, therefore, the moment to buy. Opposite of **Sell Signal**.

By-Product

A secondary metal, such as gold, produced from a mine whose prime output is of an alternative metal or mineral. Thus gold is often a by-product of large scale copper mines, such as Bingham Canyon in Utah, USA, or of silica mining as in the Hishikari mine in Japan.
Gold may also be a by-product of low-grade scrap refining, where the main purpose is to recycle other metal.

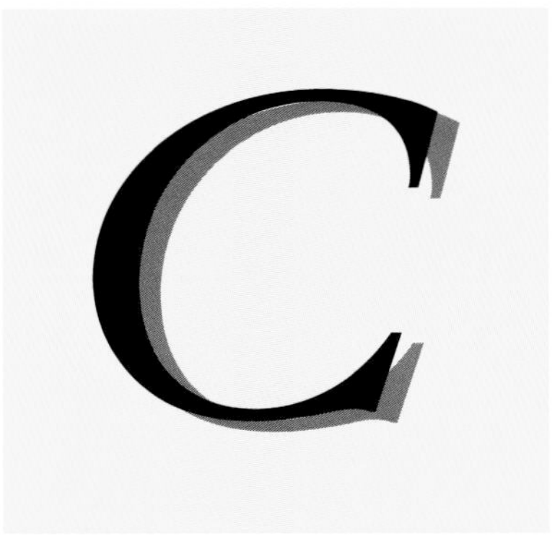

Calendar Spread

A spread in which the risk-taker buys an option (q.v.) on a gold future (put or call of a specific strike price) and simultaneously sells an option of the same strike for a differing month.

California Gold Rush

The California gold rush began after the discovery of gold in the tailrace of John Sutter's mill near the junction of the American and Sacramento Rivers in January 1848. Prospectors quickly tracked the gold back to other streams coming down from the High Sierras, identifying a belt of gold-bearing rock over 100 miles long and up to two miles wide.

The ensuing gold rush, as over 100,000 diggers made their way from all over the world to California, proved a great stimulant in the opening up of the American West. Although output peaked at 93 tonnes in 1853, when the most accessible alluvial deposits had been worked out, even today several thousand prospectors scour the American and Sacramento Rivers each year, finding small amounts of gold dust and small nuggets. *See also* **USA.**

Call Option

A contract between buyer and seller, which gives the buyer the right, but not the obligation, to buy a specified amount of gold (or other commodity) at a pre-determined (or striking) price on or before a specified date. The seller, or grantor, is obliged to deliver the gold if the buyer wishes to exercise the option and for that charges a premium. Usually abbreviated to 'call' and is the opposite of put option (q.v.). *See* **Options.**

Canada

Gold was first discovered in Canada on the Chaudiere River, Quebec, in 1823 but on a commercial scale on the Fraser River in British Columbia in 1857. This initiated a gold rush of 25,000 prospectors in the following year, who recovered about 3 tonnes. Further discoveries in the Cariboo mountains in 1862, where deep leads were tunnelled out, yielded another 6 tonnes in three years. The discoveries transformed British Columbia from a remote fur trading outpost into a viable colony. But despite other small discoveries in British Columbia and the Yukon, it was not until 1896 that major alluvial deposits were located on the Thron-diuck (or Klondike) tributary of the Yukon river near Dawson City, promoting the Klondike gold rush that yielded 75 tonnes in three years. Thereafter, although some output has always continued from the Klondike, it has not been substantial.

The real significance of Canada as a major gold producer, however, was not exploited until the development of underground mines in the Pre-Cambrian shield that covers much of

Canada. *The main gold mining 'camps' and principal mines*

Canada: Top Twenty Mines

	Mine	Major Share Holders	Output (ounces) 1989 (actual)	1990 (estimated)
1	Williams	Corona 50%/Teck 50%	494,127	550,000
2	Golden Giant*	Hemlo Gold 100%	378,369	440,000
3	David Bell	Corona 50%/Teck 50%	312,190	320,000
4	Campbell	Placer Dome 100%	267,876	236,000
5	Doyon	LAC Minerals 50%/Cambior 50%	234,690	225,000
6	Lupin	Echo Bay 100%	195,556	190,000
7	Dome	Placer Dome 100%	144,135	100,000
8	Detour Lake	Placer Dome 100%	130,080	115,000
9	Bousquet No.1	LAC Minerals 100%	110,364	87,000
10	Con	Nerco 100%	95,000	100,000
11	Timmins Div.	Giant Yellowknife 100%	92,867	75,000
12	La Ronde	Agnico-Eagle 100%	84,974	85,000
13	Hope Brook	Hope Brook Gold 100%	84,324	100,000
14	Yellowknife	Giant Yellowknife 100%	83,075	85,000
15	Macassa	LAC Minerals 100%	82,540	100,000
16	Quarter Claim	Corona 25%/Teck 25% Hemlo Gold 50%	81,576	80,000
17	Nickel Plate	Corona 100%	79,492	70,000
18	Golden Patricia	Bond Int. Gold 100%	78,759	76,000
19	Jolu	Corona 30%/Int. Mahogany 70%	75,722	75,000
20	Red Lake	Dickenson 100%	75,600	82,000

* Includes Quarter Claim production

Note also:

	Mine	Major Share Holders	1989	1990
	Bousquet No.2	LAC Minerals 100% -	—	75,000
	Premier	Westmin 50.1%/Pioneer 40% Canacord 9.9%	14,787	77,000
	Colomac	ABM Gold 100% -	—	100,000

the country, notably in northern Ontario and Quebec. The importance of the Canadian Pre-Cambrian shield is highlighted by the fact that it accounted for about 88 per cent of Canada's 1989 gold production. The Dome mine at Timmins opened as early as 1909. Gold 'camps', as Canadians call them, around Timmins and Kirkland Lake in Ontario and Val d'Or in Quebec identified quartz veining at depths of 300 to 1,500 metres which were much more accessible than the deep South African reefs (q.v.). Encouraged by the price rise to $35 in 1934, gold became the backbone of the Canadian mining industry, with output peaking in 1941 at 172 tonnes (a level not since equalled) from 146 mines. The major mines, such as Kerr

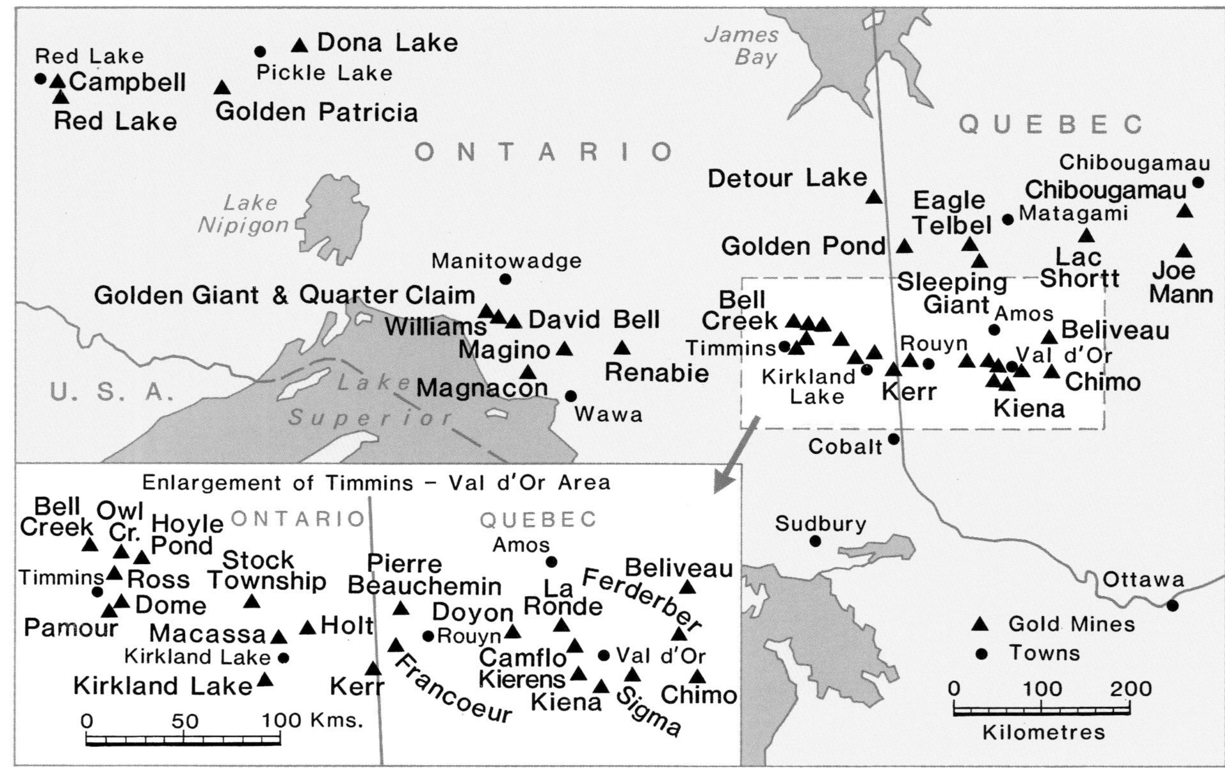

Canada. *The major gold mines of Ontario and Quebec, where most mining is centred*

Addison at Larder Lake and the Hollinger mine at Timmins, achieved annual output of close to 20 tonnes. But in the post-war period, hit by rising costs, gold mining declined sharply; the industry was kept alive after 1948 only by the Emergency Gold Mining Assistance Act (EGMA) which provided subsidy with the aim of keeping the remote mining communities alive. By 1971, 80 per cent of Canada's gold was produced under this cost-aid system. Only Campbell mine (opened in 1949 with an enviable grade of over 20 grammes per tonne) was not subsidised.

Then the gold price came to the rescue. For the first time in a generation, Canadian geologists and mining engineers paid attention to gold. Yet it was not until the 1980s that exploration paid off; output tripled from 51.6 tonnes in 1980 to 158.4 tonnes by 1989. The most significant discovery was the Hemlo field (q.v.) north of Lake Superior, whose three mines produce over one million ounces (30 tonnes) annually. The traditional mining camps, fortuitously kept going by cost-aid, also responded. The old Dome mine was modernised with a new shaft down to 1,500 metres. New mines included Detour Lake, Bell Creek, Dona Lake and Holt McDermott in Ontario and Bousquet, Doyon, Dumagami, Golden Knight and Beauchastel in Quebec. Mining also expanded in other provinces, notably with Newfoundland's first gold mine at Chetwynd, while Nickel Plate, Lawyers, Golden Bear and Premier in British Columbia finally confirmed the promise of the gold discoveries of the 1850s. The Lupin mine at Contwoyoto Lake close to the Arctic Circle in the North-West Territories, is the world's most northerly gold mine, and has a unique supply line over a winter ice road along lakes and rivers from Yellowknife 340 miles to the south.

The renaissance of Canadian gold mining brought about not only the amalgamation between such mining groups as Placer and Dome, to form Placer Dome (q.v.), but the emergence of newcomers like American Barrick (q.v.), Echo Bay Mines (q.v.), Corona Corporation (q.v.) and Teck Corporation (q.v.). And it was helped by the promotion of many smaller mining companies on the Vancouver Stock Exchange, which became the financial seed bed for expansion by channelling venture capital into gold exploration. A flow-through share financing scheme also enabled Canadian investors to write off investment in mineral exploration in Canada against other income.

Canada. *The world's most northerly mine, Echo Bay's Lupin, 56 miles from the Arctic Circle*

Canadian gold mine production

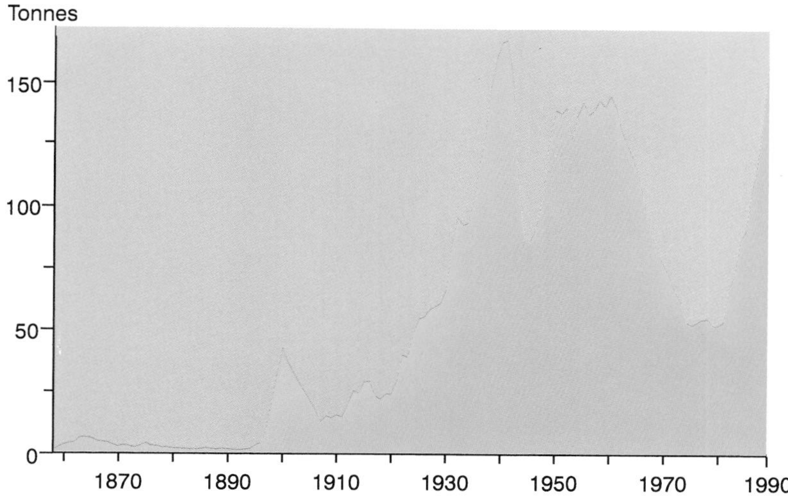

Canada. *Source: Dr Paul Kavanagh*

S

Canada's gold production is largely refined at the Royal Canadian Mint (q.v.), Noranda Minerals' Canadian Copper Refinery (including by-product gold) and by Johnson Matthey (q.v.).

The banks principally involved in mine finance and marketing gold are Bank of Nova Scotia (q.v.) and The Canadian Imperial Bank of Commerce (q.v.).

Most production is exported, usually to the United States but also to Far Eastern markets, while the main domestic requirement is for the Maple Leaf bullion coin. *See also* **Maple Leaf.**

Canadian Imperial Bank of Commerce (CIBC)

This Canadian bank has been active in gold since 1898, when its Dawson City office started buying up gold from the Klondike gold rush in the Yukon territory. They continue to buy and market not only Canadian, but US and Australian gold production. CIBC is a market maker in Toronto and is active in spot (q.v.), options (q.v.) and forwards (q.v.).

Canadian Imperial Bank of Commerce
161 Bay Street
PO Box 500
Toronto M5J 2S8, Canada
Tel: (416) 594 8300
Fax: (416) 594 8333
Telex: 0623094
Reuters: CIBG

Cap

A contract between a borrower and a lender, in which the borrower is guaranteed that he will not have to pay more than a specified maximum interest rate on borrowed money or gold. *See also* **Collar.**

Carat

The purity of gold is described by its 'fineness' (parts per 1,000) or by the carat (karat in the USA) scale (see table).

The word comes from the Greek karation, the Italian carato and the Arabic qirat, all meaning 'fruit of the carob tree'; the carob seed was

Carat Gold Scale

Carat	Fine gold	
24	1000	
	995	London good delivery
22	916	customary for many coins and for jewellery throughout North Africa and much of Asia
18	750	high quality jewellery, much of Europe
14	583.3	common usage, USA, Germany
10	416.7	lowest acceptable, USA
9	375	common usage, UK
8	333.3	lowest acceptable purity in jewellery

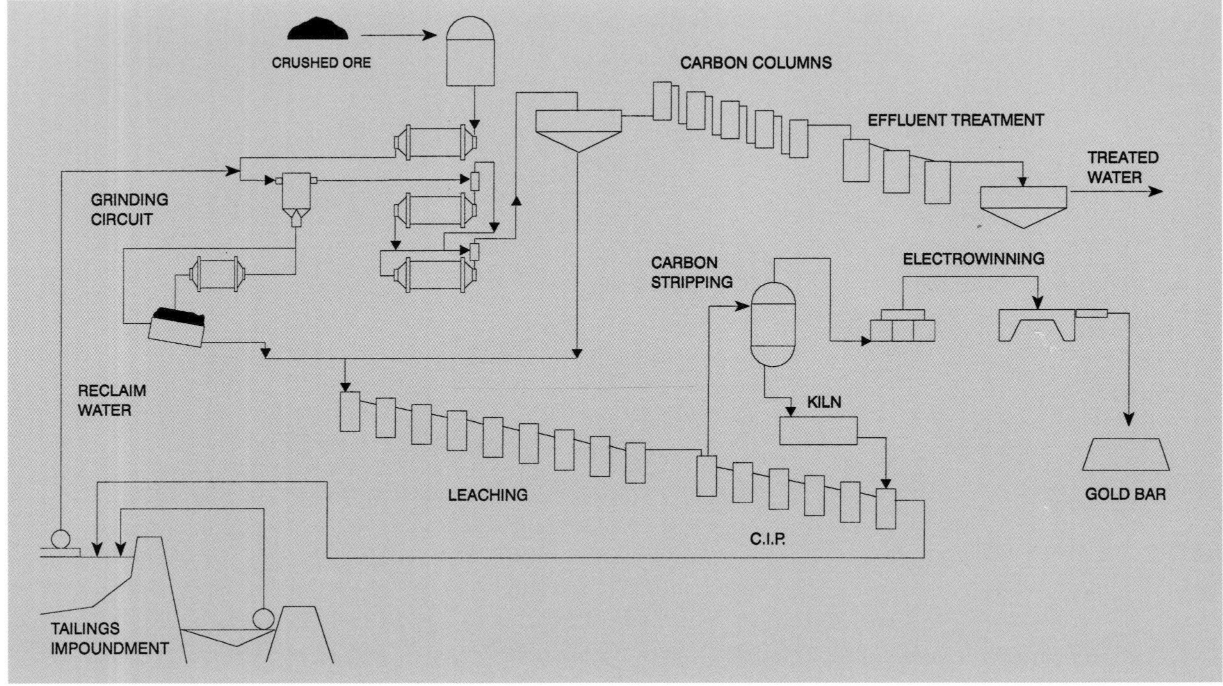

Carbon-in-Pulp. *The sequence of gold extraction from ore by the carbon-in-pulp process now widely used in Australia and the United States, particularly in open pit operations*

formerly used to balance the scales in Oriental bazaars.

Because pure gold is soft and liable to wear, it has always been alloyed with other metals. The proportion of gold is defined by the carat scale. Pure gold is 24 carat (or 1,000 fine). The proportion in jewellery varies considerably from country to country, and is preserved not only by custom but often by law. The advantage of lower caratage is that the colour of the gold can range through white, green, yellow and red hues, depending on the balance of other metals with which it is alloyed.

The validity of the caratage stamped on each piece of jewellery is often guaranteed by an official hallmarking system.

An entirely different carat scale is used for the measurement of the weight of diamonds.*See* **Hallmark.**

Carbon Adsorption

A process in which soluble complexes of gold and silver physically adhere without chemical reaction to the molecular surfaces of activated carbon particles. The process is used to collect gold and silver from the leach solution. The activated carbon is usually made from coconut shells.

Carbon-in-Leach

A process used to recover dissolved gold from cyanide leach solution after heap leaching (q.v.). The cyanide dissolves the gold from the ore into a solution, and the gold is adsorbed on to the carbon after separating the waste from the pregnant solution. The gold recovery is then similar to that described in the carbon-in-pulp process. The cyanide solution can be re-used to leach more ore.

Carbon-in-Pulp

A recovery process in which a slurry of gold ore, free carbon particles and cyanide are mixed together. The pregnant solution is passed counter current through a series of tanks containing activated carbon particles. Gold has a natural affinity for carbon and the carbon adsorbs the gold as it passes through the circuit. Loaded carbon is removed from the slurry by screening. The loaded carbon is stripped in a caustic cyanide solution under heat and pressure, prior to the recovery of the gold by electrolysis or by zinc precipitation. The carbon is treated for re-use.

Carlin Trend

North America's most prolific gold producing area, situated in Nevada and consisting of a 40 mile north-west/south-east line of low-grade epithermal (q.v.) deposits of disseminated gold currently being mined as

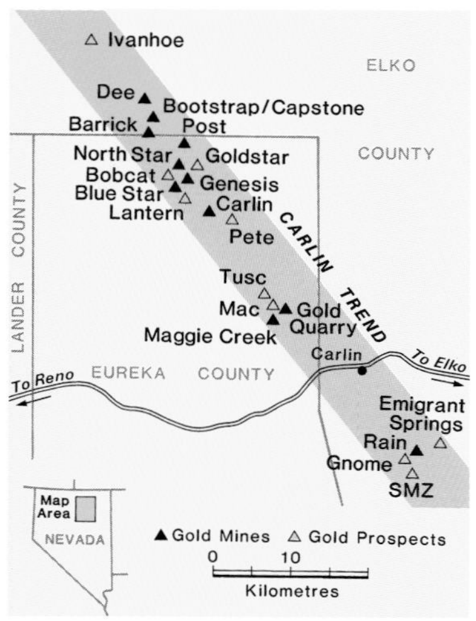

***Carlin Trend.** The low grade epithermal deposits in Nevada provide America's richest goldfield*

open pits. Significant potential also lies in the deeper higher grade sulphide deposits currently being explored in the area.The first mine was Newmont's Carlin opened in 1965, since when at least 30 new mines have started up. *See also* **USA**,.

Carrying Charges

The cost of holding gold, including warehousing, insurance and interest.

Gold Production Costs

(weighted average in US$/oz

	1988	1989
Western world	250	250
South Africa	275	277
United States	206	209
Australia	236	247
Canada	245	249
Average price	437	381

Source: GFMS *Gold 1990*

Cash and Carry

A strategy involving the physical and futures market in which a trader pays cash for immediate delivery while selling a futures contract. The gold bought for cash is eventually delivered when the futures contract matures, but the cost of holding or carrying it has been covered by the futures premium. *See also* **Futures**.

Cash Price

See **Spot Price.**

Cash Production Cost

The working costs to a mine of producing gold. The definition varies between companies and may include smelting, refining and any by-product benefit, but generally excluding taxes, exploration, depreciation, depletion expenses and financing. This cash production cost, although a benchmark of a mine's viability over the short term, is not the total cost for a mine to be sustained profitably over a long period, and to ensure shareholders a dividend.

Casting

This basic process of forming an article in a mould has many variations in gold. Jewellery is generally moulded by the 'lost wax' technique (q.v.). In the manufacture of gold bars, it distinguishes between those cast in a mould (such as good delivery bars or kilobars) and small bars and ingots, which are stamped out of a metal strip. Continuous casting allows a constant shape to be withdrawn from the bottom of a mould as the metal solidifies, so that semi-finished products such as strip and tubes can be produced.

Cellini

Benvenuto Cellini, the Renaissance goldsmith, was best known for his golden salt cellar completed in 1543

***Cellini.** His salt cellar in solid gold crafted for Francis I of France*

for Francis I of France and now in Vienna's Kunsthistorisches Museum. Cellini himself described it as: 'Oval in form, standing about two-thirds of a cubit, wrought of solid gold and worked entirely with a chisel'.

Centenario

A Mexican gold bullion coin with a face value of 50 pesos and a gold content of 1.2057 troy ounces. First struck in 1921 for the Centenary of Mexico's independence, it was issued as a standard coin until 1931. Official new mintings (restrikes) have been issued dated 1947 and are usually known as 50 pesos coins. *See* **Coins**.

***Centenario.** The Mexican 50 pesos coin, one of the most popular 'restrikes' in North America*

Gold as a percentage of official reserves

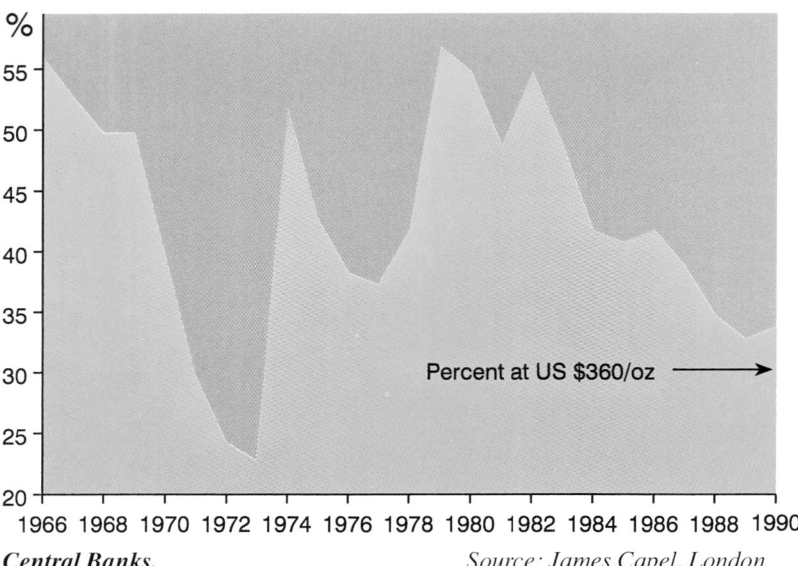

Central Banks. *Source: James Capel, London*

Central Banks

As a legacy of the gold standard (q.v.) and the gold exchange standard (q.v.), central banks hold over 29,000 tonnes of gold on their own account, while another 6,000, tonnes is deposited with official institutions such as the IMF (q.v.) and the European Monetary Co-operation Fund (q.v.). Not only is this close to one-third of all gold ever mined, but it accounts for between 35 and 50 per cent of all monetary reserves, depending on the current price (see graph). Thus gold remains an essential cornerstone of international liquidity and the action of central banks can be pivotal to the gold market.

However, after 1971 when central banks were no longer able to exchange dollars for gold at the Federal Reserve Bank of New York, their holdings have largely been immobilised. Central banks also ceased to be significant buyers of newly mined gold after the mid-1960s. Between 1948 and 1964 central banks acquired 43.7 per cent of all gold coming on the market, increasing their stocks by 7,897 tonnes; from 1965–1990 they were net sellers of just over 2,000 tonnes. The major part of this selling came from the US Treasury and the IMF through auctions in the late 1970s, but other central banks, notably in Canada and Belgium, were also sellers. Central banks, therefore, are not the main clients of the mining industry, as they were in the nineteenth and early twentieth centuries.

The balance of central bank holdings is also uneven in relation to their other reserves. Over 80 per cent of official gold holdings is in the hands of the major industrial nations; but the proportion varies. The United States has over 8,000 tonnes and Germany nearly 3,000 (excluding its tranche with the EMCF), but Japan has only 754 tonnes. In the United States gold accounts for over 70 per cent of reserves; in France, Italy and Switzerland for over 50 per cent; but in Spain and the United Kingdom for less than 20 per cent.

Despite some buying by OPEC countries in the early 1980s, and later by Taiwan, little of the reserves of newly rich nations has been switched into gold. Existing stocks are also largely frozen, except in isolated instances such as the central bank in Spain taking up part of the gold when Belgium disposed of 10 per cent of its reserves. Unless off-the-market interbank transactions can be arranged, the holdings of such countries as France or Germany are too large to be disposed of through the market place without undermining the price.

No concerted central bank activity has taken place in the gold market since the gold pool (q.v.) in the 1960s. But a number of individual central banks remain regular participants for a variety of reasons. Central banks in some gold producing nations market local production. In South Africa the mining companies must sell their output to the South African Reserve Bank, which markets the gold mainly through banks and bullion dealers in London, Zürich, Frankfurt, New York and Tokyo. The Reserve Bank increasingly uses the forward and options markets for hedging, and will, on occasion, buy back to support the price. Brazil's central bank is also active as a channel for local production, as are central banks in Colombia, Ecuador, Venezuela, the Philippines and Zimbabwe. The Bank of England (q.v.) is also a regular participant, both on its own account and on behalf of other central banks. A few central banks are also traders, or lease gold to the market for a modest interest (0.5–3 per cent, sometimes paid in gold).

This still accounts for a small part of central bank holdings, which in general are not managed as actively as currency reserves, despite the increasing attention of a younger generation of central bank governors who would like to see gold bring a better return. *See also* **Bank for International Settlements**.

Certificated Gold Stocks

Gold stored in approved exchange warehouses in the form of 400 oz 'good delivery' or 100 oz bars, from accepted refiners and smelters.

Certificates

Gold certificates have long been issued as a convenient way of confirming an investor's fully paid-up ownership of gold without going through the actual process of delivery. They were first issued in 1956 under an agreement between Bank of Nova Scotia (q.v.), Deutsche Bank (q.v.), Samuel Montagu (q.v.) and Union Acceptances Ltd (a subsidiary of Anglo American (q.v.)). Such certificates confirm the ownership of a specific amount of gold at a recognised bank or depository, deliverable on demand. It is a particularly useful way of avoiding value added or sales tax, which might be due if physical delivery were accepted. Many German investors, for example, hold certificates of gold held on their behalf by the Luxembourg branches of German banks, precisely to avoid tax. Similarly in the United States, certificates will attest to gold held in authorised depositories, often in Delaware, to avoid sales tax.

Many small gold savings schemes, initiated by banks in places as diverse as New York, Singapore and Tokyo, have also relied on certificates to guarantee investors that gold is held on their behalf.

Chain

Gold chain is both one of the oldest and one of the most popular forms of jewellery (q.v.). It is also made in a multiplicity of styles; well over 200 varieties are available, whose names may reflect their appearance (foxtail, snake, barleycorn), their geographical origin (Byzantine, Venetian, Madeira, Russian), their historical origin (curb chain, named after the German Panzerhemd or coat of mail, historical persons (Garibaldi) or a technical analogy (cable chain, which looks like an anchor chain). But in technical terms, chains are classified in seven broad groups: cable; chain types derived from cable; curb; other wire chains; pressed chains; chains made from turned parts; and fancy chains. Most chain is now made automatically by machine but the tradition of handmade chain continues where it is impractical by machine or the quantities are small, as with such picturesque styles as snail's shell and fishbone chain.

The ease with which ductile gold could be drawn into wires by early craftsmen ensured that chains, often originally a special mark of authority, were among the first jewellery fabricated. Archeologists excavating the city of Ur, dating from 2500 BC, found foxtail chains resembling plaits of gold wire that foreshadow a type of chain still made today. The first description of chain-making came in 1122 from Theophilus, who recommended using a board of oak or beechwood drilled with holes made by a red hot iron spike through which the chain could be drawn to the desired diameter and shape and then wound on a spindle. The first machines for making chain were developed in the nineteenth century, and by 1920 both foxtail and snake chain were machine made; the first fully automatic machines were introduced during the 1930s.

Although Italy now has the reputation for making low-cost machine-made chain in great quantity at factories such as Balestra, Oromechanica and Uno-a-Erre, each with several hundred chain machines, much of the pioneering work on chain manufacture was done at Pforzheim, the capital of jewellery making in Germany, at Birmingham in England and at Attleboro, Massachusetts and Providence, Rhode Island in the United States. Italian

Chain. *The broad range of 18 carat 'kihei' or curb chain available in Japan*

Chain. *Chain making at Uno-a-Erre's factory in Arezzo, Italy*

Chain. *Handfinishing of chain at Uno-a-Erre's, Italy's largest maker of chain*

design flair, expertise in improving and maintaining the machines and low labour costs have meant, however, that Italy produces more machine-made chain than any other country. Chainmaking has spread to south-east Asia and Japan, where a distinctive local variety of eighteen carat curb chain known as *kihei* accounts for nearly one-third of all jewellery fabrication. Japan has over forty companies producing chain, of whom the two largest rival Italy's biggest in chain output.

Chain is made from wires or tapes of carat gold alloy, which may be either solid or hollow to reduce weight. For hollow chain a carat gold shell is sometimes formed around a core of aluminium or soft iron wire to provide the necessary strength for manufacture, after which the internal wire is dissolved out chemically. Machine-made chain may also be made from wires that have a core of carat gold solder to aid the closing of links by soldering (q.v.). The links of chain from solid wires are soldered with copper/silver powders, usually in a controlled atmosphere conveyor furnace. *See also* **Italy; Japan; Jewellery; Pforzheim.**

Chamber of Mines and Energy of Western Australia (Incorporated)

The Chamber represents the collective interests of companies involved in mineral exploration, production and processing in Western Australia. Its membership of over 120 companies accounts for 90%, by value, of Western Australia's mineral output. Since the state accounts for nearly 70 per cent of Australia's gold production, the Chamber is closely involved with the gold industry and promotes an annual gold conference.

Chamber of Mines and Energy of Western Australia. *See also* **Australia.**

Chamber of Mines and Energy of Western Australia (Incorporated)
12 St George's Terrace
Perth, WA 6006
Tel: (9) 325 2955
Fax: (9) 221 3701
Telex: 92792 GOLCOM AA

Chamber of Mines of the Philippines,

Founded in 1975 through a merger of the Philippine Gold Producers' Association and the Philippine Base Metals Association, it is the main industry body promoting the growth and general welfare of mining, the encouragement of foreign investors and the dissemination of mining information. *See also* **Philippines.**

Chamber of Mines of the Philippines
MCPO Box 1230
1299 Makati
Philippines
Tel: (632) 817 04 43
Fax: (632) 817 68 69
Telex: (ITT) 40404

Chamber of Mines of South Africa

The Chamber of Mines of South Africa is a private enterprise service organisation founded in 1889 which promotes and protects the interests of the South African mining industry. Its ninety-eight members include the country's six major mining finance houses, other mining companies and independent mines.

The Chamber's governing body is a Council comprising two representatives from each of the six major mining houses: Anglo American Corporation of South Africa; Anglovaal Limited; General Mining, Metals and Minerals (Genmin); Gold Fields of South Africa Limited (GFSA); Johannesburg Consolidated Investment Company Limited (JCI); and Rand Mines (Mining & Services) Limited — part of the Barlow Rand group of companies.

Day-to-day policy is directed by an Executive Committee, supported by a Gold Producers' Committee and a Collieries' Committee. Chamber activities are administered by five service divisions: Operations, Health Care, External Relations, Recruitment and Corporate Services.

Services provided by the Chamber for its members include: the engaging of up to 500,000 workers annually from South Africa and other southern African states by The Employment Bureau of Africa (TEBA) which operates a network of over eighty offices; negotiation of wages and conditions of employment with representatives of numerous trade unions and officials' associations; training of miners, artisans and rescue teams; promotion of mine safety; promotion of environmental protection and land rehabilitation; conducting of wide ranging research by COMRO, the Chamber of Mines' research organisation; provision of workmen's compensation by the Rand Mutual Assurance Company; co-ordination of members' health care and administration of centralised specialist hospitals; provision of employee counselling and psycho-social services by the Chamber's Employee Assistance Programme Services (EAP); processing and marketing of all South Africa's uranium by the Nuclear Fuels Corporation (Nufcor); and refining of all South Africa's gold at the Rand Refinery (q.v.).

The Chamber also acts as the industry's central spokesman in dealings with government and provides buying, accounting, statistical, legal, economic and other services for its members. *See also* **South Africa**.

Chamber of Mines of South Africa
PO Box 809
Johannesburg 2001
South Africa
Tel. (11) 838 8211
Fax: (11) 834 1884
Telex: 4-87057 SA

Channel Sample

A continuous channel cut to a specified length in a rock exposure to provide a sample for assay.

Channel Width

The overall thickness of several closely spaced layers of reef including internal waste, particular to South African gold operations.

Charges

The costs applied to a refining lot and billed by a refiner to a shipper as the cost of refining a lot. Typical charges will include treatment, sampling, assay and refining.

Chartist

An analyst who forecasts price trends by the technical interpretation of charts of characteristic patterns of past prices. Such analysis has become significant in the gold market, especially in pin-pointing prices or chart points which are crucial support levels or break-through barriers. This work is more fully explained under Technical Analysis (q.v.).

Chase Manhattan Bank

Chase Manhattan Bank is active in spot, forwards and options through its main precious metals dealing office in New York. It is a market making member of the London Bullion Market Association (q.v.) and trades gold in Hong Kong and Sao Paulo.

The Chase Manhattan Bank, NA
1 Chase Manhattan Plaza
New York, NY 10081
USA
Tel: (212) 552 1255
Fax: (212) 552 2259
Reuters: CMAU

Chervonetz

A Russian gold bullion coin 900 fine, fine gold content .2489 troy ounces, with a face value of 10 roubles. Issued in the 1970s it achieved very few sales. *See also* **Coins.**

Chicago

Chicago pioneered futures' trading, originally known there as 'to arrive' contracts, in the 1830s. It is the home of three futures markets: Chicago Board of Trade (q.v.), Chicago Mercantile Exchange (q.v.) and the Mid-America Commodity Exchange (q.v.), which all quote, or have quoted, gold contracts since the United States legalised gold holding again in 1975.

Chicago Board of Trade

The Chicago Board of Trade (CBOT) has been operating as a futures market since 1848. The first gold contract, for 3 kilos, was launched in 1975; this was changed to 100 ounces in 1979. A 1 kilo contract was introduced in 1983. Volume on both contracts has been small in comparison with COMEX (q.v.) in New York.

Trading months: Spot, February, April, June, August, October, December

Trading hours: 7.20 a.m. to 1.40 p.m. CST. Also Sunday thro' Thursday (100 oz contract only) evening session 5.00 p.m. to 8.30 p.m. CST

Chicago Board of Trade
La Salle at Jackson
Chicago, Illinois 60604
USA
Tel: (312) 435 3500
Fax: (312) 341 3027
Telex: 253223

Chicago Mercantile Exchange

The International Monetary Market division of the Chicago Mercantile Exchange offered a 100 ounce futures contract from 1975 until 1988 when gold trading ceased due to lack of volume.

Chicago Mercantile Exchange
30 South Wacker Drive
Chicago, Illinois 60606
USA
Tel: (312) 930 1000
Fax: (312) 930 8219
Telex: 210214

Chile

The development of important epithermal (q.v.) gold deposits in the Andes mountains led to a tripling of gold production in Chile during the 1980s to 30 tonnes annually. Major new mines will bring further expansion before the year 2000. The El Indio mine, opened in 1980, revealed the exceptional grades sometimes available in Chile's epithermal region; initial grades were 358 grammes per tonne, with an additional 1,000 grammes of silver. Output in 1989 was 224,227 ounces (almost 7 tonnes) of gold. Other operating mines include El Bronce (Exxon/Callegias 113,000 ounces; 3.5 tonnes), Marte (Anglo American/Cominco/Chemical Bank 95,000 ounces; 3 tonnes), Choquelimpie (Biliton/Northgate/Citibank 89,000 ounces; 2.8 tonnes) and El Hueso (Homestake 74,000 ounces; 2.3 tonnes).

The best new prospect is La Coipa, owned by TVX Mining and Placer Dome, which is expected to produce 200,000 ounces (over 6 tonnes) of gold (and 16 million ounces of silver) in 1992. Other new mines will include La Pepa (Bridger Resources 38,000 ounces; 1.2 tonnes) and San Cristobel (Niugini Mining 50,000 ounces; 1.5 tonnes).

China

China has a long history of gold production. The Jao Yuan mine in Shandong province has been worked, on and off, for over a thousand years. Other small mines around Yiman in Shandong date from 1655. But production did not reach significant levels until the 1980s when the China Gold Company, or Gold Bureau, at the Ministry of Metallurgical Industries initiated a considerable investment programme to modernise old mines and explore for new ones. The main new mines are Xin-Cheng, close to the old Juan Yuan workings, yielding 1.4 tonnes annually with a grade of 9 grammes, the nearby Jiao Jin producing 3 tonnes at a grade of 13 grammes and Hiaojiashi, also in Shandong province, estimated at 4 tonnes. Considerable by-product is also thought to come from the Dexing copper mine. An official 1986 government report indicated 429 counties in China each with output of over 10,000 ounces (311 kilogrammes) annually.

Local authorities, collectives and individuals are also permitted to run small gold operations in areas where large scale mining is uneconomic. While Shandong province remains the main gold region, new camps have flourished in Gansu province and the autonomous region of Xinjiang both in north-western China. Output by 1990 was estimated at 80–100 tonnes annually, about half from alluvial deposits.

Policy on gold marketing, and the price paid to local miners, is set by the People's Bank of China, while the Bank of China handles overseas sales and trading on its behalf. Bank of China and its sister bank Po Seng in Hong Kong are active participants in the international gold market. Part of China's gold production is used in the Panda gold coins (q.v.) launched in 1982.

Chinese Gold and Silver Exchange Society

See **Hong Kong Gold and Silver Exchange**

Chipped Planchet

An incomplete coin blank, missing 10–25% of the metal.

Chlorination

The use of chlorine in the chemical refining of gold. *See* **Miller Process.**

Chop/Chop Mark

A small stamp or trademark used by Chinese traders to confirm the weight and fineness of gold and silver bars.

Chuk Kam

Literally 'pure gold' in Chinese, is 990 fine jewellery popular in Hong Kong. Bought on low mark-ups of 10–15% over the gold price, it is a basic form of investment jewellery. Traditional *chuk kam*, however, is soft and thus vulnerable to scratching.

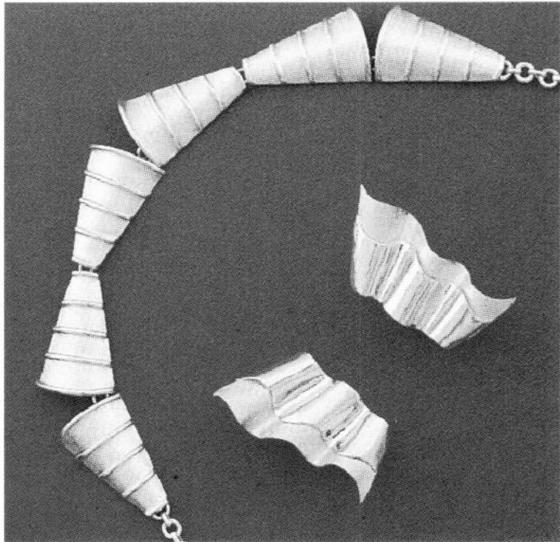

Chuk Kam. *Necklace of 990 fine 'chuk kam', with a touch of titanium for hardness, to prevent scratching*

Research, initially by Degussa, the German precious metals group, and at The Research Institute for Precious Metals and Metals Chemistry at Schwabisch Gmund, has shown that by adding one per cent titanium to 990 gold a toughened skin to the jewellery is achieved. This gold-titanium alloy is gradually being adopted by some Hong Kong manufacturers and is proving to have better wear resistance.

Cire-perdue

See **Lost Wax Casting.**

Citicorp/Citibank NA

The bullion department of Citibank, NA, a subsidiary of Citicorp, provides bullion banking, gold based financing, hedging, option and investment products to mining corporations, industrial users, central banks and other financial institutions around the world.

Bullion offices are located in New York, Tokyo, Sydney and Sao Paulo. Bullion vault facilities and custody

services are located in New York, London and Dubai.
Citibank, NA
55 Water Street
New York, NY10041
USA
Tel: (212) 291 7366
Fax: (212) 291 3514
Telex: 6801507
Reuters: CTGN

Clad Metal

See **Gold Filled; Rolled Gold**

Claim

See **Mining And Exploration Rights**.

Clean-up

The process of reclaiming any gold accumulated over the years around a reduction plant (q.v.) before its final closure.

Clearing House

The clearing house is a separate agency through which all gold contracts on exchanges are handled. The clearing house may be owned by banks or by exchange members. The clearing house for COMEX (q.v.) for example, is the Commodity Clearing Association, which is owned by full clearing members of the exchange, being those who are the strongest financially because they must stand to guarantee the contracts.

The agency is responsible for matching up the participating firms on every contract traded. This constant monitoring enables it to advise exchange members at the end of each day what their net margin requirements are based on the respective long and short positions of their clients. The clearing house also matches offsetting orders for members and issues notices to holders of short positions to make delivery. By presiding over the smooth working of the mechanics of the exchange, the clearing house guarantees every contract, thus giving the exchange its credibility.

Close Stop

A stop-buy or stop-sell order that is within the range of the recent price fluctuations in gold.

Closing Out

Liquidating or offsetting an existing long or short futures position; also known as exiting.

Cm-g/t

A concept used in South African gold mines for comparing the value of the orebody with that of the other mines or working places. It is calculated by multiplying the width of the reef (in centimetres) by the grade (grammes/tonne) over that width.

CMP/Engelhard

Leading French refiner and Paris Gold Market participant taken over by Engelhard in 1987 and now known as Engelhard SA. They have London good delivery status and are semi-fabricators of alloys for the jewellery industry and specialist electronic products. *See also* **Engelhard Industries.**
Engelhard SA
4 Rue Beaubourg
75004 Paris
France
Tel: (1) 44 61 10 00
Fax: (1) 44 61 11 91
Telex: 220271 MEPRE PARIS

Coin Gold

A gold alloy, at least 899 fine, prepared for making coins, usually with silver or copper to improve durability.

Coined Bars

The smallest gold bars of 20 grammes or less are normally no longer cast in moulds, but are punched out of rolled strips in the same way that coins are made. Coined bars, or wafers as they are called in the United States, have a high lustre finish.

Coins

The first coins containing gold were struck in western Asia Minor in the late eighth century BC.They were made from electrum, a natural alloy of gold and silver found in the rivers of the region, and had a design on one face and a punch mark or seal on the other. The introduction of pure gold and silver coins is generally attributed to the Lydian king Croesus (561–546 BC).

Thereafter gold, silver and copper coins came into increasing usage as a means of exchange. But silver was usually pre-eminent, simply because most early communities did not have

Standard Grades of Preservation Applied to Coins

	English	French	German	Italian
i	Proof	Flan bruni	Polierte Platte	Fondo specchio
ii	Uncirculated	Fleur de coin	Fdc/Stempelglanz	Fior di conio
iii	Extremely fine	Superbe	Vorzuglich	Splendido
iv	Very fine	Tres beau	Sehr schon	Bellissimo
v	Fine	Beau	Schon	Molto bello
vi	Very good	Très bien conservé	Sehr gut erhalten	Bello

Premium of Gold Coins over their Gold Content end 1989

	%
Sovereign(old)	0.00
Sovereign(new)	2.80
Britannia (1oz)	2.35
MapleLeaf (1oz)	2.35
Nugget(1oz)	2.35
Eagle (1oz)	3.15
Krugerrand (1oz)	0.70
French 20 francs (Napoleon)	0.10
German 20 marks	10.00
Swiss 20 franc (Vreneli)	9.70
USA $20 (Double Eagle)	4.45

Source: Samuel Montagu, *Annual Bullion Review 1989.*

enough gold at hand for it to become commonly used as a currency; only in such civilisations as Mycenae was gold widely used. The Greek and Roman empires used gold coinage relatively rarely, and it became increasingly debased (q.v.) as their empires waned. In the Middle Ages silver was the standard coinage, although gold coins were regularly minted in the Italian city states of Florence, Genoa and Venice that were the cross-roads of medieval trading routes.

The immense riches of the New World revealed in the second half of the sixteenth century also confirmed silver's role. Silver 'pieces of eight' (*reale de a ocho*) from the mints of Mexico City and Potosi came to dominate European coinage. Although the Americas produced some gold, no wide coin circulation was achieved until the early eighteenth century when significant gold discoveries in Brazil provided Portugal with the metal to mint its *Moedas de Oro* then used to pay for English wool. The flow of these gold coins into London was one reason that gold coinage could proliferate in Britain in the eighteenth century. It was encouraged, too, because from the recoinage of 1696 the Mint had slightly overvalued gold against silver, so that people found it more profitable to take their gold to the Mint for coinage into guineas (q.v.), while selling their silver on the market for export to India, where higher silver prices prevailed. The gold premium was confirmed by Sir Isaac Newton as Master of the Mint, who established the fixed price of gold at £3.17.10½d per standard troy ounce (equal to £4.4.11½d per fine ounce) in 1717, thus confirming the trend for the gold guinea. The guinea, originally launched in 1662, containing 8.42 grammes of gold and worth twenty-one shillings, became the first mass circulation gold coin. It was replaced in 1816, after the Napoleonic wars, by the sovereign, weighing 7.99 grammes and worth £1.

The guinea and the sovereign as legal tender coins placed Britain firmly on the gold standard (q.v.), whose basic criterion was that gold formed the whole circulation or that notes were redeemable in gold coin at a fixed price. Essentially it was a gold coin standard. Most other nations followed suit in the second half of the nineteenth century, after the gold discoveries of California, Australia and South Africa made it practical, for the first time in history, for gold to be adopted as the main circulating metal. Virtually all gold mined during the nineteenth century was turned into coin; Sovereigns in Britain, Eagles in the United States, Marks in Germany, Roubles in Russia, Crowns in Austria, Florins in Hungary and Napoleons in France accounted for over 13,000 tonnes of gold in the period of the classic gold standard prior to World War I.

The suspension of the gold standard at the outbreak of war, meant that the legal tender coin was no longer a medium of exchange, and its price was no longer fixed; it fluctuated according to supply and demand.

The gold coin business has since evolved in five main sectors:

(i) *Numismatics* (q.v.) has become a specialised sector for collectors of historic and rare coins.

(ii) *Commemorative coins* (q.v.) have been struck for such diverse occasions as the Olympic Games and the sixtieth anniversary of Emperor Hirohito in Japan (q.v.).

(iii) *Investment in coins* from the gold standard era, particularly the Napoleon, the Sovereign, the Double Eagle and the Swiss Vreneli which trade at a variable premium over their gold content, has become widespread through many bullion houses and banks. Many of these coins were melted down in the 1940s and early 1950s and premiums rose.

(iv) *A fresh category of newly minted gold coins* then opened up. Initially this took the form of re-strikes, according to demand, of such historic coins as the Austrian 100 Corona (q.v.) and the Mexican Centenario (q.v.), which enabled investors to buy gold coins at close to the spot price. They were followed by the bullion coin (q.v.), pioneered by South Africa's Krugerrand (q.v.) in the early 1970s and followed by Canada's Maple Leaf (q.v.), the US Eagle (q.v.), the Australian Nugget (q.v.) and the British Britannia (q.v.). The minting of Sovereigns was also increased so their premium came down close to those of bullion coins. The bullion coins, all from government mints, became a significant segment of gold demand in the highly inflationary days of the late 1970s and early 1980s, taking up to 15 per cent of all gold coming on the market. Forty-four million Krugerrands alone were minted. The volume of coins, however, eventually saturated the market, and the 3 per cent premium at which the mints hoped to sell to wholesalers could not always be maintained. Often bullion coins trade at little over the spot price; indeed sometimes they are marginally under or at 'melt' (q.v.). This has encouraged investors to watch the premiums on some other coins, notably the Swiss Vreneli which is in limited supply and whose premium fluctuates from as low as 5 per cent to over 20 per cent, and switch out of bullion coins into these historic coins at opportune moments, hoping to gain both on premium and price.

(v) The fifth category is *modern collector coins* (q.v.), which are proof issues of bullion coins or other well-known coins such as the Sovereign, or special limited issues by some countries. The gold coin, thus, is no longer money in the pocket whose price is fixed, but a commodity on which the investor can win or lose.

Cold Working

The processes for drawing (q.v.) gold into wire or tube or rolling (q.v.) into sheet or strip without the use of heat.

Collar

A contract between borrower and lender in which the borrower is guaranteed that he will not have to pay more than a specified maximum interest rate on borrowed money or gold, while the lender, in turn, is guaranteed payment of some minimum interest rate. *See also* **Cap**.

Collateralisation

The use of gold as collateral for foreign exchange loans was pioneered between Italy and Germany in 1974 to tide the former over a massive balance of payments deficit. That collateralisation was between their respective central banks, but this practice has evolved into more complex swap operations between a central bank and one or more commercial banks. Such deals are particularly useful in a short term foreign exchange crisis, where the sudden outright sale of the metal might undermine the price. It also enables producer countries, such as South Africa, to hold gold off the market when the price is weak. While terms vary from deal to deal, on most straightforward collateralization the central bank would receive close to 100 per cent of the market price of the gold when the arrangement was made, and would be liable for margin calls if the price fell. See **Swaps** for further explanation of the evolution of this activity.

Collector

A base metal, such as lead, used to collect and separate precious metals from impurities in the final reduction of ore or scrap to slag (q.v.).

Collector Coins

See **Coins; Commemorative Coins; Modern Collector Coins**.

Colombia

Gold production in Colombia increased substantially during the 1980s to around 30 tonnes annually, mainly due to increased alluvial operations in the north-west province of Antioquia in the Andes foothills. Dredges owned by Mineros de Antioquia and Mineros del Choco operate on the Saldana and Nechi rivers. Thousands of prospectors, known locally as *barraqueros*, work from small boats fitted with gravel pumps or use hydraulic monitors on the banks, often causing much damage to the environment. The gold is sold mainly to the central bank, Banco de la Republica, which sometimes pays a considerable premium; the gold is then sent to the United Kingdom for refining and is sold through the London market.

Coloured Golds

Alloys of gold in various colours obtained by mixing gold with other metals such as silver, copper or nickel. *See also* **Alloys**.

Commemorative Coin. *A $5 gold coin issued in the United States for the 1988 Winter Olympics*

Colours

The final traces of gold left in a prospector's pan.

COMEX

The leading gold futures and options exchange in New York.
See **Commodity Exchange Inc.**

Commemorative Coins

Gold coins or medallions struck to commemorate special events or anniversaries have achieved considerable popularity with collectors, although often sold at a substantial premium over their gold content.

Usually a few thousand are struck (often with a larger minting of silver

COMEX. *The gold trading pit at the world's premier futures market in New York*

coins), but on occasion considerable amounts of gold may be used. South Korea minted 20 tonnes of 1 oz and ½ oz 925 fine gold coins to mark the 1988 Olympic Games. The United States made 27 tonnes of 0.84 troy oz at 900 fine gold coins for the 1984 Olympics.

The record commemorative issue was Japan's 20 gramme Hirohito coin minted to mark the sixtieth anniversary of the Emperor Hirohito's reign in 1986. The initial issue of just over nine million coins required 182 tonnes and a second issue in 1987 of one million coins took another 16.6 tonnes. The discreet Japanese purchase of gold for this coin had considerable effect in strengthening the gold price in 1986. The legal tender coins had a face value of 100,000 yen, but contained 40,000 yen in gold, a premium of 150 per cent. A second commemorative issue of 3.5 million coins of 30 grammes each was made in 1991 to mark the enthronement of the new emperor Akihito.

Commercial Options

Generally long-term puts or calls on physical gold contracted between bullion dealers and industrial users and producers. *See also* **Options.**

Commodity Clearing Association

The separate corporation, owned by sixty-five leading members of the New York Commodity Exchange (COMEX) (q.v.), which monitors and clears all COMEX futures and options contracts. *See also* **Clearing House.**

Commodity Exchange Inc.

Commodity Exchange Inc. (COMEX), the world's most active metals market, was founded in New York in 1933. It has become the leading gold futures and options exchange since its gold futures contract was launched on 31 December 1974. Its precious metals volume exceeds that at all other futures exchanges put together, and it attracts world-wide participation, with many traders in Europe, the Middle East and the Far East remaining in their offices until COMEX closes. This gives COMEX unique liquidity, which in turn is much of the reason for its success; it attracts a highly diverse clientele. Trading hours reflect this; the exchange has opened progressively earlier to suit overseas clients.

Gold futures contracts volume on US and Tokyo Exchanges

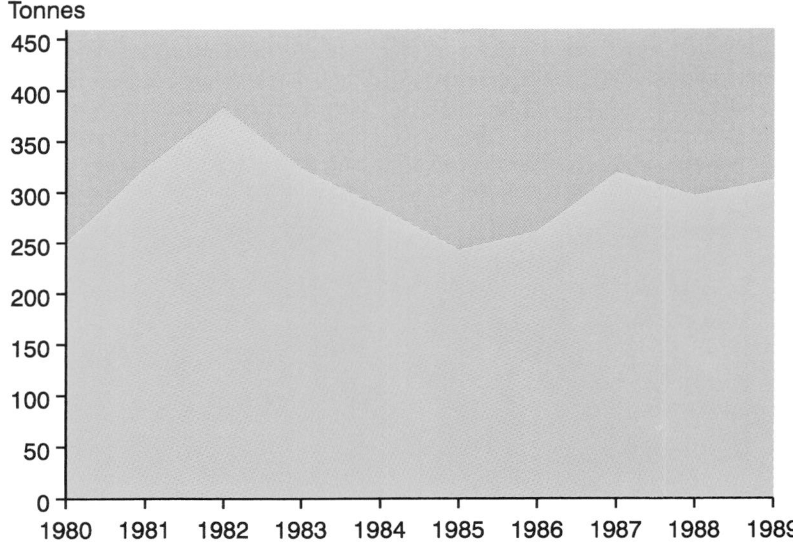

COMEX. *Source: Gold Fields Mineral Services Ltd*

The COMEX gold futures contract is based on 100 ounces of gold. Deliverable gold must be cast in one 100-ounce bar or three 1-kilogram bars by an exchange-approved refiner and assayed at no less than 995 fineness. Delivery is made in registered depository receipts issued by exchange-approved depositories in New York.

COMEX gold futures are listed on the current calendar month and the next two months and every February, April, June, August, October and December in a 23-month period. In 1990, the exchange introduced the listing of June and December gold futures out to 60 months. The extended contract provides expanded trading opportunities for hedgers and speculators.

Prices are quoted in multiples of $.10 per ounce, or $10 per contract. The last day of trading for a gold futures contract is the third last business day of the delivery month.

In 1982 COMEX launched options on gold futures, which provide the holder with the right to buy (call) or sell (put) a COMEX gold futures contract at the stated price on or before the expiration date. Options are listed for expiration for every month of the year as follows: options are listed on the nearest four of the months of February, April, June, August, October and December; shorter term options are listed in all other months and trade for a period of two months. Each option is based on the regular delivery cycle future (the February, April, June, August, October and December futures) which follows the option's expiration.

On the first trading day of any option contract 13 strike prices are listed for each put and call. Strike price increments are $10 for futures prices below $500, $20 for prices between $500 and $1,000 and $50 for prices above $1,000. New strike prices are added in accordance with futures price movements. Exercise is until 3 p.m. New York time on any business day for which the option is listed for trading with the exception of expiration dates, at which time exercise is until 4 p.m. Gold options expire on the second Friday of the month prior to the month for which the option is named.

An all-time daily gold volume record of 116,512 contracts was set by the exchange on 12 January 1990. COMEX has developed a reputation as an innovator in the financial futures and options marketplace with such products as the GAP (Gold Asset Participation) and extended 5-year gold futures contracts. In 1991 the Exchange hopes to offer 5-day gold options for trading.

Trading hours (for gold futures and options): 8.20 a.m. to 2.30 p.m. New York time.

Commodity Exchange Inc. (COMEX)

4 World Trade Center, 8th Floor

New York NY 10048

USA

Tel: (212) 938 2935/2936

Fax: (212) 432 1154

Commodity Futures Trading Commission (CFTC)

The United States government's regulatory agency for all American futures markets.

Compagnie des Métaux Précieux (CMP)

See **CMP/Engelhard.**

Complex Ore

An ore containing a number of minerals, one or more of which are of economic value, and usually implying difficulty in the extraction or separation of the valuable metals.

Comptoir Lyon-Alemand Louyot (CLAL)

Leading French refiner and Paris Gold Market participant founded in 1800, whose bars are acceptable good delivery on the London market, and semi-fabricator of a wide range of alloys for the jewellery industry and specialist electronic and dental products. It has subsidiaries in eight European countries including the leading Spanish refiner, SEMPSA.

Comptoir Lyon-Alemand Louyot
13 rue de Montmorency
75139 Paris
France
Tel: (1) 42 77 11 11
Fax: (1) 42 77 03 58
Telex: 220514 CLALF

Comstock Lode

A high grade gold and silver deposit near Virginia City, Nevada, which was the site of a secondary gold rush in 1859.

Concentrate

Ore from a mine which has been initially treated to remove certain unwanted constituents such as quartz, to increase the grade before further treatment such as refining.

Condor

An options (q.v.) strategy which provides protection on the up and down side of a relatively narrow trading range of perhaps $60. The condor involves the sale (or purchase) of two options with consecutive strike prices (q.v.), together with the purchase (or sale) of one option with an immediately lower strike price and one option with an immediately higher strike price. All options must be of the same type, commodity and expiration date.

Conglomerate

A sedimentary deposit resulting from the compression of round pebbly fragments (often of quartz), cemented in a mix of finer material. The best example is the gold-bearing conglomerate (known also as 'banket') which forms the gold reefs of the Witwatersrand Basin (q.v.) in South Africa (q.v.). The Tarkwa mine in Ghana also mines a conglomerate.

Consignment Stocks

These are gold bars, or sometimes semi-fabricated carat gold products, which are placed by a bank or bullion dealer with a client, who may be another dealer or manufacturer, against a guarantee of payment at the current price as the metal is taken out of the stock. The consignment stock system operates both domestically and internationally. A bullion dealer or semi-fabricator may place a consignment stock with a number of local jewellery manufacturers, who take the gold as they require it, thus keeping down their own inventories. On the international level, banks and bullion houses will maintain consignment stocks of bars with banks in regional markets, such as Dubai, Singapore or Hong Kong, from which clients there can buy and take immediate delivery of gold when they require it. In Dubai, bars may be released by depositories on an 'unfixed' basis — that is, they have not been priced. The consignment stock can be replenished as need be. In practice, it enables the dealer to have gold, of which he is still the owner, available in many centres for immediate delivery. The consignment stock will be part of his own, hedged, position. *See also* **Conto Deposito**.

Consolidated Gold Fields

This famous mining house was founded in 1887 by Cecil Rhodes and Charles Rudd to develop their mining interests in South Africa. As an international mining group, based in London, unlike the other main houses involved in South Africa, it evolved a world-wide network of mining links. It became the second largest gold producing group after Anglo American (q.v.), though usually holding less than 50 per cent of its associates. The principal subsidiary holdings were in Gold Fields of South Africa, Newmont Mining Corporation in the United States and Renison Goldfields Consolidated in Australia. Gold Fields also owned 100 per cent of Gold Fields Mining Corporation in the United States (which operates the Mesquite and Chimney Creek gold mines) and the conglomerate group ARC. Consolidated Gold Fields plc was taken over by Hanson plc in 1989 and ceased to exist as a separate company. Hanson has since disposed of parts of the former empire.

Contango

Contango (also known as Forwardation) was originally used on the stock exchange in London in the mid-nineteenth century to indicate the percentage a buyer paid the seller of stock to postpone transfer to the next settling day. It was also adopted on the London Metals Exchange. Modern usage particularly relates contango to the normal situation on American gold futures markets, such as COMEX, where the prices for delivery some months ahead are higher than those for near or spot delivery. The contango or percentage premium is made up of storage, insurance and financing costs, but will also reflect supply/demand for prompt delivery. Although the contango fluctuates, it is usually close to prevailing interest rates in the currency concerned. The rare and brief opposite of contango is backwardation (q.v.) when demand for immediate delivery of gold is so great that a premium actually develops for the spot commodity.

Conto Deposito (Gold Deposit Account)

A deposit placed by a bullion dealer with domestic Italian banks located in the main jewellery manufacturing centres. Purchases are made by manufacturers direct from the depositor or from the Italian bank. *See also* **Consignment Stocks.**

Conto Lavoro

Conto Lavoro, also known as Conto Lavorazione meaning 'working account', is the term used in the jewellery manufacturing industry in Italy (q.v.) to describe gold which a local or foreign wholesaler gives to a manufacturer to make up for him in payment only of the manufacturing charges. Thus the manufacturer himself does not have the cost of financing the gold. A substantial proportion of Italian jewellery is made under this system on account of American, European and Middle Eastern wholesalers.

Contract

The contract is the legally binding agreement traded on gold futures and options exchange to buy or sell a specified amount of gold at a clearly defined price on a specified date. Thus one COMEX contract, for example, is for 100 ounces of 995 gold deliverable in any of the six settling months.

Contract Month

The month when a futures contract, if it is not liquidated beforehand, becomes deliverable. On COMEX the specified months are February, April, June, August, October and December.

Core

The long cylinder of rock, about one inch (2.54 centimetres) or more in diameter, recovered by a diamond drill during exploration. The decision whether or not to develop a gold mine often depends on the grade (q.v.) of gold in these cores, which provide a three-dimensional picture of the underground orebody (q.v.).

Corner

A speculative operation by an individual or group to buy up most or all of the available supply of a stock or commodity, forcing other buyers to turn to them as the sole source at an artificially high price. In gold a corner is virtually impossible to achieve because of the diversity of supply and the existence of substantial stocks. In silver the first corner is thought to have been attempted in 1717 in anticipation, false as it turned out, of an upward valuation of silver in relation to gold. A silver corner was also tried by the Indian speculator Chunilal Saraya in 1912 and more recently in 1979–80 by the Hunt brothers and their associates; both attempts failed. An international corner in gold has not been attempted and would prove almost impossible because higher prices would bring out the huge above ground stocks. The mild relation to a corner, which can be attempted, is a 'squeeze' (q.v.) on futures markets.

Corona

The 100 Corona (Crown) is an Austrian gold coin which became popular with investors between 1950 and 1974. The coin, which is 900 fine with gold content of .9802 troy ounce, was first struck from 1908–1915 under the Austro-Hungarian empire. It was minted regularly as a non-legal tender 'restrike' with a low premium from the 1950s until the mid-1970s, when it was largely replaced by the arrival of bullion

Corona. *This 100 Corona Austrian 'restrike' was popular with investors in the 1960s and 1970s*

coins (q.v.). Investors bought the coin not only because the price was low, but because the restrikes, all dated 1915, got around regulations in some countries forbidding the purchase of coins. A coin dated 1915 could always be explained as having been in the family for generations. After the arrival of bullions, production ceased, and it normally trades at very close to the spot price or even at 'melt' (q.v.). *See also* **Coins.**

Corona Corporation

Corona Corp. is one of the largest and lowest cost gold producers in North America and has interests in eleven operating mines. Production totalled 661,291 ounces of gold in 1989, at an average cash cost (q.v.) of US$209 per ounce. The company has a large land holding in many of the major gold camps of North America and is active in exploration. In addition, Corona is developing and operating Eskay Creek in British Columbia. The most important asset is its interest in the Hemlo gold camp; it holds a 50 per cent share in the David Bell and Williams mines as well as a 25 per cent share of the Quarter Claim. In 1989, the Williams mine produced 494,000 ounces of gold and the David Bell mine produced 312,000 ounces. Corona Corp.'s gold production was in excess of 690,000 ounces in 1990.

Corona Corporation
666 Burrard St, Suite 2500
Vancouver V6C 2X8
British Columbia
Canada
Tel: (604) 669 1011
Fax: (604) 669 7177

Country Rock

A loose term to describe the general mass of rock adjacent to an orebody, as distinguished from the vein or ore deposit itself.

Cover

The balancing or protecting of a trader's open position by offsetting a sale, for example, against a purchase. *See also* **Short Covering.**

Covered Option

If the writer of an option (q.v.) already owns the gold and so can deliver if necessary, it is called a 'covered option'. By comparison a 'naked option' (q.v.) is one in which the gold is not owned. Mining companies, for example, writing put options on their production are covered.

Crédit Suisse

Crédit Suisse is one of the three leading Swiss banks and a member of the Zürich gold pool (q.v.). The bank is one of the major trading houses in physical gold bars and controls the Valcambi Refinery (q.v.). Crédit Suisse is also a market making member of the London Bullion Market Association (q.v.). It offers all bullion banking facilities and is an active trader (physical and metal account) in all bullion trading centres in New York, Hong Kong, Melbourne and Tokyo.

Crédit Suisse PO Box 590
Zurich 8021
Switzerland
Tel: 1-333 53 91
Fax: 1-333 55 15
Telex:812612
Reuters: CSGL

Cross-cut

A horizontal tunnel mined across the line of strike (q.v.) of an orebody.

Crusher/Crushing

The first stage of breaking up ore involves crushing it into small pieces, initially in a primary crusher. Primary crushing of metallic ores is accomplished by jaw and gyratory crushers. The ore then moves on for grinding in ball or rod mills (q.v.). *See also* **Mill/Milling.**

Cupellation

In the fire assaying (q.v.) of gold, the sample being tested is placed in a small crucible, or cupel (made of bone ash) in which it is heated with lead. The lead and any base metals are oxidised and absorbed into the cupel, while gold together with any silver remain as a button.

Custom Smelter

Any smelter or refinery which handles concentrates from mines or scrap from dealers and returns to them an agreed percentage of refined metal.

The smelter will charge the toll for the service, but its profit may be supplemented by any surplus metal recovered beyond the guaranteed amount stipulated in the contract. *See also* **Refining; Smelting.**

Cut-and-Fill Stoping

An underground mining method used in steeply dipping orebodies under difficult wall rock conditions. The ore is drilled, blasted and extracted in slices advancing upwards. The stope is filled with material to provide support to the country rock (q.v.) and a platform to extract the next slice. Used at Campbell mine, Canada.

Cut-Off Grade

The lowest grade at which it is profitable to mine a gold-bearing ore. *See also* **Grade.**

Cut Value

High grade assay samples from a mine exploration programme may be assigned a 'cut value' to reduce them to a more realistic level consistent with the orebody to offset any exceptional values from any chance nuggets in the samples.

Cyanide/Cyanidation

Cyanide has a natural affinity for gold, which is dissolved in it just as sugar would be in a hot drink. Cyanidation has been the principle method of extracting gold from ore since the development of the MacArthur-Forrest Process (q.v.) in 1887, which proved crucial in the development of the South African gold mining industry (q.v.). The perfection of the cyanide process largely replaced amalgamation (q.v.) with mercury which had previously been the main method of extracting gold from ore. Cyanidation has also become crucial since 1970 in gold recovery from low grade deposits through heap-leaching (q.v.).

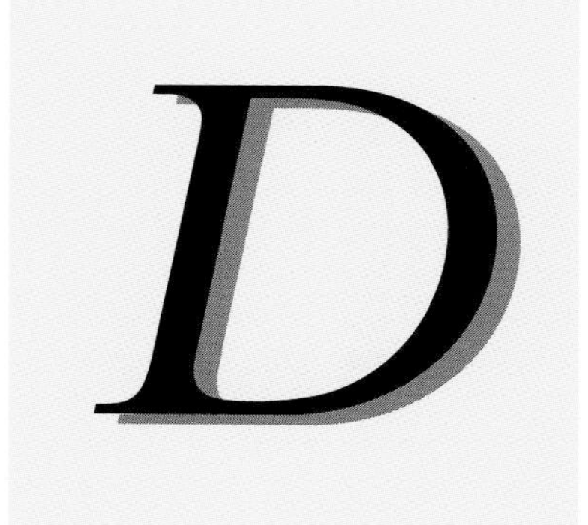

Damascene

The ornamentation of metalwork with inlaid gold or silver, which is beaten into undercut grooves. The technique, which goes back at least to the sixteenth century, originated, as the name implies, from Damascus in Syria.

Day Trader

A short term speculator on the futures markets who takes a position, but liquidates it before the close of daily trading and thus carries no overnight position.

Dealer

A trader who, unlike a broker, carries a position or stock of gold and is usually a market-maker (q.v.) quoting his clients a bid and offer price.

Debase

To degrade or lower the amount of gold or silver in a coin without changing the face value. The technique is almost as old as precious metal coins, for rulers soon realised it was possible to adulterate their coins, without changing their weight or outward appearance, by simply using more bronze or copper and less gold or silver. *See also* **Coins.**

Default

The failure of a party to a contract to meet the terms of the agreement. In particular, the failure of the buyer or seller of a futures contract to take or make delivery of the metal if required or the failure of a borrower of gold to repay the metal on the due date.

Deferred Settlement

An arrangement, much used in the London gold market, whereby settlement of both sides, of metal and money, of a spot contract is deferred on a day-to-day basis. For example, a trader buys 2,000 ounces gold spot at $400 per ounce. On the spot date, normally two working days following the deal, instead of dollars being paid and the gold being delivered, the trader's dollar account will be debited with $800,000 and his metal account (q.v.) will be credited with 2,000 ounces gold. Interest will be charged when the dollar account is in debit and paid when it is in credit. Deferred Settlement accounts are normally operated on the basis of loco London (q.v.), but are available in all markets. Thus a Middle East trader might buy 2,000 ounces in his morning from a Hong Kong trader, sell 2,000 ounces in London during his afternoon, and buy it back again from New York during his evening. All the trades pass through the one Deferred Settlement account held in London, and there is no movement of dollars or gold. This system is also known as account/account or metal account.

Degussa

German refiner and semi-fabricator that has pioneered many specialist applications of gold since its founding by Friedrich Ernst Roessler in 1843. Degussa became a joint stock company in 1873. Its liquid or 'bright gold' for ceramic decoration was launched in 1879. Now a leading manufacturer of a wide range of gold products including dental alloys (q.v.), gold potassium cyanide (q.v.), liquid gold (q.v.) and jewellery alloys (q.v.). Degussa also has refining and manufacturing plants in Brazil, Canada, Singapore and the United States.

Degussa A.G.
PO Box 1105 33
Weissfrauenstrasse 9
D 6000 Frankfurt am Main 11
Germany
Tel: (69) 218 01
Fax: (69) 218 2206
Telex: 41-222-0 dg d

Delivery

(i) The actual transfer of gold or certificates of ownership; it does not necessarily mean physical movement of the metal, for it may most often be a simple transfer of deposit receipts from a warehouse or bank to the new owner.

(ii) *See* **Good Delivery bars.**

Delivery Date

The specified time by which gold must be delivered to fulfil a contract.

Delivery Months

The months specified by each futures exchange when delivery notices (q.v.) may be given. The main exchanges, such as COMEX, list alternate months, starting with February.

Delivery Notice

The notice issued by holders of short positions on futures markets of the time and place at which they will deliver.

Delivery Period

The designated period in which holders of short positions give notice of their intention to deliver on the exchange. In a COMEX delivery month, for example, the delivery period itself starts two days after the last trading day of the previous month and extends one trading day beyond the delivery month. Heavy liquidation of long positions often takes place just prior to delivery periods to avoid the liability of having to accept gold or warehouse receipts; that is to say, the longs (q.v.) bail out a day or two before delivery may be forced upon them in the delivery period.

Delta Hedging

Delta hedging is the strategy undertaken by grantors of options (q.v.) to protect their exposure. The delta is the mechanism or mathematical formula used by option participants to measure the amount of gold to be bought or sold in order to hedge the exposure. The 'delta variable' is a measure of the probability of an option being exercised against the grantor and therefore dictates how much an option grantor must hedge to be covered or 'delta neutral'.

The delta hedge is calculated on a basic model taking into account changes in the spot price, the time to expiry and the difference between the strike (q.v.) and spot prices. As the delta changes, so the grantor will either buy or sell metal. The delta varies between 0 and 1. Deeply in-the-money options (q.v.) have a delta close to or equal to 1, because they are likely to be exercised; by contrast, the delta of a deeply out-of-the-money option (q.v.) will be close or equal to 0 as the option has little or no intrinsic value. The further out-of-the-money the options are at the time of granting, therefore, the lower the delta variable and the less the initial delta hedging. The closer into-the-money, the greater the delta hedging, with 50 per cent of the gold hedged if options are at-the-money.

In practice, how does it work? If an options dealer grants 100,000 ounces of out-of-the-money puts at a strike price of $375 when spot gold is $400, he will have sold the holder the right to sell him gold at $375. Potentially the dealer is long and must hedge. If the delta is 0.3, the dealer will immediately sell 30 per cent or 30,000 ounces into the market either spot or through a futures contract. He is now delta neutral. If the spot price then fell, increasing the likelihood of the options being exercised, the delta might rise to 0.35, calling for a further sale of 5,000 ounces. If the spot price fell below the strike price, the put options would be in-the-money, and the full 100,000 ounces should then have been sold. Conversely, if the price rose after the initial sale of 30,000 ounces, the option grantor would progressively buy back that gold as the puts fell further out-of-the-money.

Delta hedging on calls works in reverse, with the option grantor progressively buying if the calls look like being in-the-money. Thus the grantor of both put and call options will be a buyer of gold into price rallies and a seller into price falls to remain delta neutral. The rapid increase in options volume during the 1980s has meant that delta hedging can have considerable impact on the gold price.

On the other side of this exchange, the option buyer need not necessarily delta hedge, because the potential loss is limited to the premium paid for the original option. However, where a large options book is being run, the dealer himself will often be both a grantor and buyer of a range of options. Since the options are being bought not so much for price protection as for exposure to price volatility, the buyer will delta hedge. His action will be a mirror image of hedging by the options grantor, as the illustrations show. *See also* **Options**.

Demonetize/ Demonetization

In the broadest sense, the withdrawal of coin or notes from use as money, depriving them of standard monetary value. In precious metals, this happened to many silver coins in the 1870s when European nations switched from a silver to a gold standard (q.v.), and then in the 1930s to gold coins such as the US Eagle and Double Eagle in 1933 when the demise of the gold standard meant they no longer circulated as common currency.

Dental Gold

Because of its malleability and resistance to corrosion, gold has been used in dental work for nearly 3,000 years. The Etruscans in the seventh century BC used gold wire to hold in place substitute teeth, usually from a cow or calf, when their own were knocked out. The first printed book on dentistry published in Leipzig in 1530 recommends gold leaf (q.v.) for filling cavities.

This technique has not entirely disappeared. Gold leaf of 999.9 fineness is still compressed into pellets and packed into small cavities in teeth which are otherwise sound, with the aid of a hand mallet or mechanical condenser. This restoration has great durability against the chemical attack

Dental Gold. *Preparing dental gold on bridgework*

of oral fluids, but the gold must be in cavities exposed to little wear because it is soft.

Thus the main application of gold in modern dentistry is alloys, which are a mixture of gold and the noble metals platinum, palladium or silver plus copper and zinc. The aim is an alloy which is easy for the dentist to manipulate, but is strong, stiff, durable and resistant to tarnish and corrosion. These alloys are used for inlays, crowns and bridges. The gold content of the alloy will vary from 620–900 fine according to the precise application. A typical crown and bridge alloy may contain 62–78 per cent gold, with silver, platinum and palladium added to make at least 75 per cent noble metals, plus copper and zinc.

The rising cost of gold has meant a proliferation of inferior alloys, with gold content as low as 30 per cent, and a reduction of national and international standards of approval. Some palladium-based alloys, with as little as 2 per cent gold, have been produced. Gold alloys are also being ousted by a resin-bonding technique for bridges.

Gold demand for dentistry has consequently fallen, especially as some governments, notably in Germany, have tightened up on social security insurance payments for gold dental work. Fabrication of dental gold products, which is undertaken mainly by a handful of manufacturers in Japan, the United States, Germany, Italy and Switzerland, requires no more than 50 tonnes annually. There is considerable informal and unrecorded consumption, however, in Asia and Latin America where dentists buy their own gold to make alloys or even melt down gold coin.

Depletion

The exhaustion of a natural resource, such as an orebody.

Deposit

A natural occurrence of a useful mineral in sufficient quantity to invite further exploration. There is a continuing need to discover new mineral deposits as an economic deposit is a depleting resource.

Exploration must locate promising mineral deposits and, once identified, provide sufficient information about the geology of a deposit; in particular, its geometry and grade (q.v.) must be measured in order to determine whether a deposit is economic to mine and extract the mineral(s), and upgrade to an orebody (q.v.).

Depreciation

Spreading the costs of capital items over their expected life.

Deutsche Bank

A leading German commercial bank with its head office in Frankfurt (q.v.) that has been in precious metal trading since the nineteenth century, including disposing of much silver from Germany in the 1870s after the country switched to the gold standard. In more recent times Deutsche has been the main bank for physical bullion and coin distribution in Germany, notably with Krugerrand marketing in the 1970s before the introduction of value added tax on coin sales. It is a major international market-maker in gold, and is also active through its Luxembourg branch with gold investors, and is a member of the London Bullion Market Association (q.v.). Deutsche Bank is also a market maker in Hong Kong and New York.

Deutsche Bank AG
Taunusanlage 12
D-6000 Frankfurt 1
Germany
Tel: (69) 724 0548
Fax: (69) 71505099
Telex: 412711

Development

(i) The initial stages of opening up a new mine. The preparation of the deposit for commercial production including installation of plant and machinery and the construction of all related facilities.

(ii) The tunnelling to open up, prove the location and value, and allow the extraction of ore.

Diamond Drill

A type of rotary rock drill which cuts a core. *See* **Core.**

Diggings

An early mining term, dating at least to the sixteenth century, and particularly relating to alluvial gold-fields. It was commonly used in the Californian and Australian gold rushes (q.v.). In California those near rivers were known as 'wet diggings', those higher up as 'dry diggings'.

Dilution

The effect of waste or low grade mineralized rock, mined as part of normal mining practices in extracting an ore. This lowers the grade of the mined ore. *See also* **Grade.**

Dishoarding

The selling back of physical gold, either for reasons of political or economic distress or simply for profit, has become a regular feature of the gold market. Historically the motives were usually distress, because the gold price was fixed. Many of the French aristocracy who fled to London from the French revolution in 1789 flooded the market there with gold coin. Equally, gold came out of Russia in the years after the revolution and, more recently, from Vietnam after the American withdrawal in 1975, Iran after the Shah's overthrow and Kuwait after Iraq's invasion.

But on an international scale it has been price fluctuations that have precipitated dishoarding in the twentieth century. Dishoarding from India in the early 1930s was caused not only by economic distress but by the gold price rise to $35. The wide fluctuations in the gold price since 1970 have also prompted profit-taking on gold, rather than distress selling, from the Middle East and south-east Asia where gold bars or high carat gold jewellery sold on a low mark-up are traded in when the price rises sharply. Notably in 1974, 1980 and 1986 as much as 150 tonnes of gold was swiftly dishoarded in these regions. This reversal of the normal trend of imports can have considerable impact on the market very quickly. The first signpost of dishoarding is when the local price in such markets as Taiwan, Indonesia, Egypt or Saudi Arabia goes to a discount on the London price; if it remains for more than a week or two, actual shipment of metal back to refineries in Europe will begin. *See also* **souks.**

Doré Bullion. *A doré bar comes out of the smelter at the Lupin mine on the Arctic Circle*

Double Eagle. *The Liberty type Double Eagle, struck from 1877–1907*

Double Eagle. *The St Gaudens type Double Eagle, struck from 1907–1933*

Disseminated Ore

Ore in which small particles of valuable minerals are spread more or less uniformly through the deposit. (This is distinct from massive ore wherein the valuable minerals occur in almost solid form with very little waste matter included.) The Carlin Trend (q.v.) in Nevada is a classic example.

Dollying

A technique used by alluvial gold miners to hand crush ore with a mortar and pestle in order to free the gold for panning or washing out.

Dominican Republic

One of the world's largest open-pit gold mines, Pueblo Viejo in the Dominican Republic, was opened in 1975 by Rosario Resources Corporation. The mine had a high grade doré bullion, with a peak annual production of over 12 tonnes of gold and 50 tonnes of silver in the early 1980s, since when output has declined.

Doré Bullion

1. An impure alloy of gold and silver produced at a mine which will be refined to high purity metal. The median for gold doré is 65% gold and 35% silver.

2. In US usage, doré bullion is synonymous with base bullion: crude lead with recoverable silver, with or without gold.

Double Bottom/Double Top

Double bottoms and double tops are two of the basic patterns to look out for in charts in technical analysis (q.v.). A double bottom occurs when the price falls twice to the same level and fails to penetrate; it is regarded as a signal of good support. Equally, a double top occurs when the price twice rises to the same level but fails to penetrate; this signals considerable resistance to the price moving yet higher. And either may indicate a reversal in the recent trading pattern, possibly the switch from a bear to a bull market or vice-versa.

Double Eagle

The Double Eagle was the $20 legal tender gold coin, minted in the United States from 1849 until 1933. The coin was 900 fine, with a fine gold content of 0.9675 troy ounces. Like the smaller $10 Eagle (q.v.), the Double Eagle was initially minted with a Liberty head on the face, but from 1907 until 1933 this was replaced with the figure of St Gaudens. The coins usually trade now at a premium, and some of the coins, from years in which few were minted, are collectors' items.

Doubloon

See **Escudos.**

Drawing

Gold's ductility enables a single ounce to be made into 50 miles of thin gold wire. This process is called drawing. It can be done manually by using special leather padded pliers to pull strips of gold through a guage clamped in a vice. But usually drawing is done mechanically by passing long strips of gold through dies designed to make round, square, rectangular or triangular wire. Multi-die machines operating at high speed progressively draw the gold through smaller and smaller openings to the required size.

Drawing. *A multi-die machine draws gold into wire for chain making*

Dredging

A mining method for placer deposits used particularly for gold in the United States (Alaska), Canada (Yukon), the Soviet Union and Brazil. A dredge consists of a number of items of machinery mounted on a floating platform, the dredging apparatus itself, the treatment plant and tailings disposal apparatus. The dredging apparatus might be a bucket-line dredge, a bucket-wheel dredge or cutters with hydraulic suction. The dredge sometimes floats in its own specially created pond to recover shallow, unconsolidated ore. The ore is recovered by the dredging mechanism, concentrated and the tailings disposed of at the rear.

Dredging. *In Russia, dredges work on the Siberian rivers excavating gold bearing sands to depths of 150 feet from rich alluvial deposits*

Dresdner Bank

A leading German commercial bank, with head office in Frankfurt (q.v.) which is an international market-maker in gold. It was particularly noted as a large buyer at the International Monetary Fund (q.v.) and US Treasury gold auctions in the 1970s for institutional and central bank clients. Dresdner is active through its Luxembourg affiliate, is a member of the London Bullion Market Association (q.v.), and trades through its offices in New York and Hong Kong.

Dresdner Bank AG
1 Jurgen-Ponto-Platz
D-6000, Frankfurt 11
Germany
Tel: (69) 2630
Fax: (69) 2635966 or 2636166
Telex: 41231
Reuters: DRGF

Dressing

The preparation of ores by sorting, cleaning and concentrating before actual precious metal recovery.

Drift/Drive

A horizontal tunnel driven along, or parallel to, the strike of the orebody, for the extraction or exploration of ore.

Drilling

Drilling occurs on a mineral deposit at the exploration, development and production stages of a mining operation.'Blasthole' drilling, which involves drilling holes in which to place an explosive charge to break the rock, occurs during development and production. This may be to break waste rock or ore either on the surface in an open pit or underground.

In exploration, drilling is an important method of delineating a deposit. In the early stages, the term 'scout' drilling is often used. Drilling not only provides information about the main features of the deposit, but also provides information about the surrounding rock for mine design. Once a deposit has been outlined by drilling on a regular pattern, further detail may be determined by increasing the density of drill holes through 'infill' or 'step-out' drilling. This allows an increase of confidence in the initial stage of exploration.

Three methods of drilling are commonly used in mineral exploration: diamond, rotary and percussion. 'Diamond' (or core) drilling uses a hollow diamond studded bit that cuts out a cylindrical core of rock. The column of rock is extracted from inside the drill rod for geological examination and assay. The drilling medium is usually water. Rotary and percussion drilling break the rock into chips using rotary or percussion (or combination) methods of penetration. The rock chips are continually flushed up the hole (usually outside the drill pipe) and are collected in sequence for geological examination and assay. Rotary and percussion drills are faster and cheaper than diamond drills. 'Reverse circulation' drilling is a type of rotary drilling that uses a double-walled drill pipe. Compressed air, water or other drilling medium is forced down the space between the two pipes to the drill bit, and the drilled chips are flushed back up to the surface through the centre tube of the drill pipe.

Dry Blowing

In alluvial (q.v.) gold mining, the use of air currents to separate small particles of gold from other dust, dirt and small pieces of rock.

Dubai

This port in the United Arab Emirates, has been a major regional gold and silver market since the early 1960s, serving the Arabian Gulf countries and, primarily, India and Pakistan. The trade is mainly in 999 ten tola bars (q.v.) of which Dubai is the prime distribution point. Imports peaked at 259 tonnes in 1970, then declined to a low of 2 tonnes in 1980, reviving again in the mid-1980s to reach 162 tonnes in 1989. While the re-export business is pre-eminent, Dubai is also a substantial jewellery manufacturing and wholesaling centre.

Ducat

Ducats were gold and silver coins widely circulated in Europe from medieval times. The first were issued about 1140 by Roger II of Sicily, as Duke of Apulia; the word ducat came from *ducatus*, or duchy.

The most famous early versions were minted in Venice, where the gold ducat issued by the doge Giovanni Dandolo in 1284 weighed 3.56 grammes. The Venetian gold ducat circulated widely not only in Europe but along the trade routes to the Levant. Ducats of varying values were struck in Germany, Austria and the Netherlands. The Austrian mint has even made re-strikes of Austro-Hungarian 1 and 4 Ducat coins in recent times.

Ducat. *The Venetian Ducat, which circulated widely on major trade routes from the 13th century*

Gold imports to Dubai

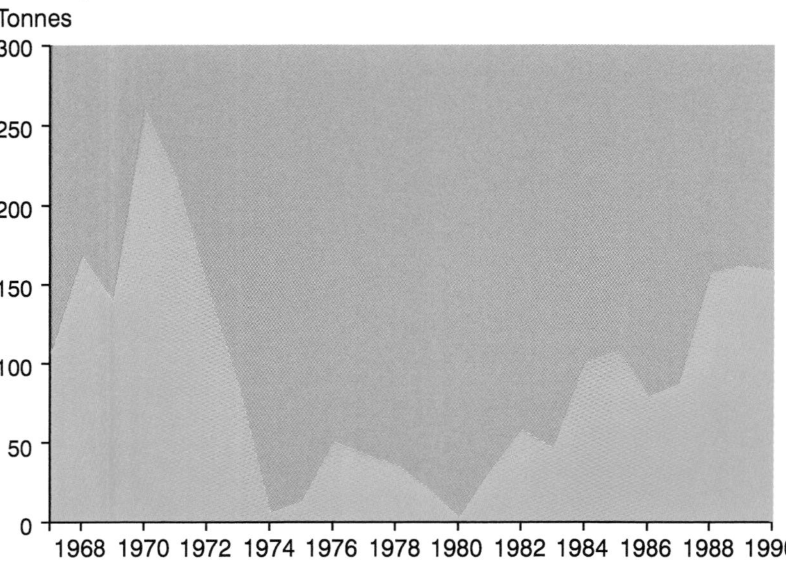

Dubai. *Source: Gold Fields Mineral Services Ltd*

Dump

Also known as Spoil. The waste material which has been extracted during the mining or treatment of ore and discarded in a large heap on the surface. *See also* **Tailings; Slimes.**

Dump Leaching

A form of leaching where the run-of-mine ore is loaded directly on to the leach pad without prior crushing.

Dyke

An igneous rock intrusion.

Eagle

(i) The first legal tender US gold coin, bearing the national emblem of the bald or white-headed eagle, was originally authorised by Alexander Hamilton at the Continental Congress to be struck at a new mint in Philadelphia. In practice only silver coins were minted in the early years of American independence, because gold was slightly undervalued and people primarily took silver to the mint for coinage. The first $10 Eagle was struck in 1795; it was 916 fine, with a fine gold content of 0.515 troy ounces. This was minted until 1804. The $10 Eagle was reissued in 1838 at 900 fine, with a fine gold content of 0.48375 troy ounces. From 1866 it was again reissued as a Liberty Eagle, and from 1907 until 1933 with an Indian Head on the face. A $2.50 Quarter Eagle was also issued from 1840 and a $5 Half Eagle from 1795. The $20 Double Eagle (q.v.) was first struck in 1849, the year after the California gold rush. These various eagle coins formed the main gold coin circulation in the United States until it went off the gold standard in 1933.

Eagle (i). *$10 Eagle, Indian Head type, minted 1907–1933*

Eagle (i). *$5 Half Eagle, Indian Head type, minted 1908–1929*

(ii) The Eagle was re-launched by the United States Mint as a one ounce legal tender bullion coin (q.v.) in 1986. The coin, like its predecessors, carries the eagle head; it is 916 fine and has a nominal face value of $50, that is to say, much less than the value of the gold it contains. Half ounce, quarter ounce, and one-tenth of an ounce coins were also issued. The novelty led to the sale of nearly 3 million ounces of the coin in each of the first two years, but demand then declined.

The coins are distributed by the US Mint to authorised banks and bullion dealers.

Eagle (ii). *The one ounce American Eagle gold bullion coin, first minted 1986*

Echo Bay Mines Ltd

One of North America's major gold producers with interests in twelve operating mines. Production totalled 717,000 ounces of gold in 1989, at an average cash cost (q.v.) of US$220 per ounce. Operations include the wholly-owned Lupin mine, a 25 per cent interest in the Round Mountain operations, the world's largest heap leach mine, and the wholly-owned Cove/McCoy operations where production is expected to rise to 320,000 ounces of gold in 1990. Echo Bay is expected to produce 900,000 ounces of gold in 1990.

Echo Bay Mines Ltd
10180 101st St
Edmonton,
Alberta T5J 3S4
Canada
Tel: (403) 429 5811
Fax: (403) 429 5899
Telex: 037-41510

Ecu. The half ounce Belgian legal tender coin, first minted 1987

Ecu

(i) Series of Paneuropean and European Community commemorative coins struck at the Paris Mint from 1972, initially honouring important European statesmen such as Jean Monnet, Paul-Henri Spaak, Winston Churchill, Edward Heath and Konrad Adenauer. Later 1 Ecu coins of 1.4790 troy ounces at 0.920 fine were issued from 1979.

(ii) Half ounce Belgian legal tender coin first minted in 1987, with a face value of 50 European Currency Units.

EFP

The abbreviation for 'exchange for physical' (q.v.).

El Dorado

A legendary golden city, traditionally linked with Lake Guatavita in Colombia.

Electric Furnace

Several types are used in the precious metal industry, e.g. the electric induction furnace is used to produce silver, gold and platinum group alloys, and the electric arc furnace is used in ore smelting.

Electrolysis/Electrorefining/ Electrowinning

The recovery of gold by electrolysis is important both in the initial stages on the mine and in final purification in the refinery.The original process of electrolytic refining was developed by Dr Emil Wohlwill (q.v.) in the late nineteenth century. His process is based on the solubility of gold, but the insolubility of silver, in an electrolyte solution of gold chloride ($AuCl_3$) in hydrochloric acid. Impure gold or doré (q.v.) is cast into anodes of about 100 ounces each which are suspended in porcelain cells, while the cathodes are thin strips of pure gold. By passing an electric current from anode to cathode through the electrolyte solution, the anodes are gradually dissolved and the gold therein is deposited on the cathodes; any silver, not being soluble in the solution, is precipitated to the bottom of the cells. The gold coated cathodes are removed, melted and cast into bars.

The initial process can produce gold up to 999.5 fine, with further treatment bringing it up to 999.9. The disadvantage of the process is that it ties up gold in the cells for two days or more, and if gold of only 995 is required, it will usually be refined by the chemical Miller process (q.v.).

Electrolysis is also used on gold mines using carbon-in-pulp (q.v.) recovery for 'electrowinning'. The gold (and any silver) is separated from the carbon into a solution of sodium cyanide and caustic soda, which is placed in electrowinning cells through which a current is passed. The gold, still with silver, is deposited on steel wool cathodes, from which it can be melted off as gold foil ready for fire-refining into doré ready to go to the refinery.

See also **Refining.**

Electronics

The use of gold in electronics is based on the combination of its electrical conductivity, its ductility and its total freedom from corrosion or tarnishing at either high or low temperatures. Its near-perfect corrosion resistance means gold provides an atomically clean metal surface which has an electrical contact resistance close to zero, while its high thermal conductivity ensures rapid dissipation of heat when gold is used for contacts. It is the gold plating of contacts for switches, relays and connectors that accounts for most of the 120–140 tonnes of gold required annually by the electronics industry. After jewel-

Electrolysis. *Gold-coated cathodes being removed from their cells after electrolysis to produce 999.9 fine gold*

Electronics. *Gold plated contact and connectors are an essential part of modern electronics in everything from computers to television*

lery and, in some years, coin, electronics is the biggest fabricator of gold.

The production of gold potassium cyanide (GPC) (q.v.), otherwise known as plating salts, accounts for about 70 per cent of all electronic use. Contacts are normally electroplated with a very thin film of GPC. Prior to the gold price rise from $35, when gold was cheap, plating thicknesses were often 20 microns, but they have since been sharply reduced to 2½ microns or less, while the contacts themselves have become dramatically smaller. However, the scale of the modern electronics industry means overall gold use has not been reduced.

Gold plated contacts are used in everything from washing machines to computers to telecommunications. The ordinary touch-tone telephone contains thirty-three gold contact points. Gold plated connectors are an integral part of plugs and sockets for cable terminations, integrated circuit sockets, computer backplates and printed circuit boards. The more sophisticated the equipment and the greater the degree of reliability required, the more gold plating is used in connectors.

This means that in telecommunications, especially satellites, computers and, above all, in defence systems, gold is indispensable. The American space programme has made particular use of gold connectors in spacecraft to conduct the subtlest of low voltages.

Gold's other main electronic use is in fine wire or strip to bond or connect parts of semi-conductors such as transistors and integrated circuits to ensure reliable connections between components. This 'bonding' wire is specially refined up to 'five nines' (999,99) and has a typical diameter of one hundredth of a millimetre. A special merit is the ease with which it can be bonded into position in tiny circuits. A third use is 'thick' and 'thin' film used in microcircuitry, in which the circuit is printed on a ceramic base using an ink-like paste containing gold. Originally, 'thick' film left a deposit of about 18 microns; 'thin' film cuts this by more than one-third.

The high price of gold in the early 1980s caused the electronics industry both to use gold more selectively and sparingly and to look for alternatives. Most manufacturers, however, found there was no practical substitute; nothing quite combined the properties of gold. So fabrication demand has stabilised and fluctuates largely in tandem with a boom or recession in electronics.

The fabrication of electronics products is concentrated essentially in Japan, which accounts for about 40 per cent, and the United States with about 30 per cent; only Germany and the United Kingdom, each with about 7 per cent, make any other significant contribution, although South Korea is coming up. The electronics industry in Asia largely imports the products it needs from Japan.

Electroplating

The coating of a gold potassium cyanide (q.v.) solution on a base metal by means of electrolysis. Electroplating is widely used in the electronics industry (q.v.) to coat contact points, but also has many decorative applications in the plating of costume jewellery, watches, cigarette lighters and pens. It is also used in aerospace, where a thinly deposited layer of gold reflects heat from jet or rocket engines. The gold plating is often as thin as one thousandth of a millimetre.

Electropolishing/ Electrostripping

The polishing of jewellery after it has been cast (q.v.) to remove the metallic appearance and provide a bright surface.

Electrum

A very pale yellow, natural alloy of gold with 20–50 per cent silver, found in the rivers of Asia Minor and used by the Egyptians as early as 5000 BC for gold artefacts and by 3100 BC as standardised gold bars used for exchange. Early coins were also made of electrum. Around 2000 BC the Egyptians mastered the technique of separating out the gold and silver. In modern terminology it may describe any gold alloy where the

Enamelling. *Gold cloisonné enamel medallion of an archangel, created about AD 1000*

proportion of silver is enough to affect the colour.

Enamelling

The technique of bonding enamel with gold has been known for at least 3,500 years and remains widely used today. Among the earliest examples are Minoan and Mycenean jewellery from the late fifteenth century BC in which dark blue enamel was fused into depressions in gold sheet, a form of enamelling known as *repoussé*. There are two other categories of gold/enamel work; *cloisonné*, in which the enamel is contained within strips of gold set perpendicular on a gold base, and *à jour*, in which the enamel is set in a framework of gold.

Enamelling. *Enamelling a modern gold earring in the workshops of De Vroomen Design in London*

Engelhard Industries

This leading producer of speciality chemical products, engineered materials and precious metal management services has its headquarters in Edison, New Jersey. Originally founded by Charles Engelhard Sr in 1902, the company owns four refineries on the London Good Delivery List (q.v.): Engelhard Corporation in the USA, Engelhard of Canada Limited, Engelhard Limited in the UK and Engelhard SA in France. It also has a London based metals trading company, Engelhard Metals Limited, which provides a comprehensive range of financial services. It is a fabricator of a wide range of industrial precious metal products,carat alloys and liquid golds from facilities in France, Italy, the United Kingdom and the United States. *See also* **CMP/Engelhard.**

Engelhard Corporation
Edison
New Jersey
USA
Tel: (201) 205 6000
Fax: (201) 632 9253

Envelope

In technical analysis (q.v.), an envelope is a band drawn 2½ per cent above and 2½ per cent below the thirteen day moving average. On intra-day European trading a break out of the top or bottom of the envelope is taken as a signal only of a short term over-bought or over-sold condition and not as a longer term trend.

Epithermal

Epithermal is used to describe gold deposits found on or just below the surface close to ancient vents or volcanoes, formed at low temperature and pressure. An epithermal deposit is deposited at shallow depth. The gold has become concentrated as mineral-rich hydrothermal fluids pass through the heated rocks of a volcanic system, then, when the mineralisation cools on the surface, it often forms very rich orebodies; almost a golden cap sitting on top of a volcano. This has often undergone weathering and the gold is spread over the surrounding area, although grades may still be spectacular. The El Indio mine in Chile and the Hishikari mine in southern Japan, both of epithermal origin, have produced grades of over 100 grammes per tonne.

Epithermal deposits are located particularly in the broad arc of volcanic rocks swinging round the Pacific Basin from Chile to Fiji (where the Emperor mine has been worked since 1932), to New Zealand (the Waihi mine), on to touch eastern Australia, then Papua New Guinea, Indonesia, the Philippines and finally Japan. The exploitation of these epithermal deposits in the Pacific provides the gold mining industry with its biggest technical challenge over the next century as the areas of mineralisation are sometimes still active and in 'hot rocks'. The best potential is in Papua New Guinea (q.v.); in addition to two existing epithermal mines, Bougainville and Ok-Tedi, three more world class mines, Porgera, Lithir and Misima, are developing.

Escudos

A Spanish gold coin popularly known as a doubloon, widely circulated in Latin America and Europe from the sixteenth to the eighteenth centuries. The eight Escudos weighed 27.07 grammes at 0.96 fine.

European Monetary Co-operation Fund

This fund, EMCF for short, is maintained by the participating nations of the European Community, each of whom deposits 20 per cent of their gold reserves with the Fund in return for currency units known as 'ecus', which count as a reserve asset. The Fund holds nearly 3,000 tonnes of gold and in calculating the issue of ecus values it at the full market price averaged over the preceding six

Escudos. *An eight escudos coin minted in Spain in 1805 in the reign of King Charles V*

months (unless the current day's price is lower, when it is adjusted downwards). Thus gold is part of the 'basket' determining the amount of ecus in the European system.

Evaluation

The initial engineering estimate of the economic worth of a mineral deposit.

Excess

Futures and forward contracts require a margin (q.v.) deposit as good faith that the contract will be honoured finally. Excess is any additional amount in the investor's account over the basic margin requirement.

Exchange

The major exchanges for gold trading, including futures and options, are COMEX in New York, Hong Kong Gold and Silver Exchange, Bolsa Mercantil et de Futuros in Sao Paulo, Tokyo Commodities Exchange, Sydney Futures Exchange and Singapore Monetary Exchange (all q.v.).

Exchange for Physicals

Exchange for physicals, or EFP, is a regular futures market (q.v.) transaction, in which a futures contract is switched ahead of time for physical or spot gold. There is an active EFP market with dealers quoting bid and offer, usually COMEX active month (q.v.) against loco London spot (q.v.). The device is used in the professional market by traders who wish to adjust positions in different markets without making outright purchases or sales or, in other words, without changing their net positions. The EFP can also be a trading instrument in its own right.

Exchange Options

Options (q.v.) which are offered on an exchange, as opposed to over-the-counter (q.v.) options granted by an individual bank or bullion dealer, which are tailored to each client's needs. Exchange options offer a standard contract, which can be traded on the exchange many times before it expires. The most successful exchange option has been the one launched by COMEX (q.v.) in New York in October 1982. A COMEX gold option is actually on a gold futures contract; it provides the holder with the right to buy (call) or sell (put) a COMEX gold futures contract of 100 ounces at the exercise (strike) price on or before the expiration date. Contract months are the nearest four of the following contracts: February, April, June, August, October and December. (See COMEX for further option contract specifications.) Volume on COMEX has easily exceeded other options contracts launched on the American Stock Exchange and the Mid-America Commodity Exchange (q.v.). The Bolsa Mercantil et de Futuros (q.v.) in Sao Paulo, however, has built up very substantial volume with its 250 grammes option contract, launched in 1986, which had a turnover of nearly seven million contracts in 1989. While exchange options are used by many professionals, they also attract speculators because of the high leverage.

Exchange Stocks

The physical gold bullion owned by members or customers of members of an exchange such as COMEX (q.v.), which is actually lying in approved exchange warehouses, and is available for delivery if need be. In practice, because delivery takes place on a relatively small proportion of futures contracts, exchange stocks will be small (often less than 20 per cent) compared with the 'open interest' (q.v.) on the exchange.

Exercise

On COMEX (q.v.), the conversion of an option (q.v.) by the holder into the appropriate underlying futures contract. Generally, the exercise by an option holder of his right to buy (call) or sell (put) gold at the agreed striking price (q.v.).

Exercise Price

See **Options; Strike Price.**

Exhaustion

The complete removal of economic ore reserves from a mine.

Expiration Date

The last day on which an option (q.v.) can be exercised (q.v.).

Exploration

The exploration for new gold deposits can be divided into two basic categories:

(i) *Grassroots exploration,* often by individual prospectors or 'junior'

Exploration. *Core samples from exploratory drilling near Kalgoorlie, Western Australia*

mining companies, to locate new orebodies. The prospect of Canada's huge Hemlo gold deposit (q.v.), for example, was identified by two experienced prospectors and a geologist, David Bell (after whom one mine was eventually named), in 1980. Their initial work was followed up by two Vancouver-based 'juniors', who took options in 1981 on two key blocks in the heart of the strike zone. Once they had shown the full potential of the orebody, they sought out joint-venture partners in major mining houses, which led to:

(ii) *Definition exploration;* highly detailed exploration to define the exact size and shape of the orebody, and later the possibility of extensions to it. This stage may take two or three years. In Hemlo's case it was nearly five years from initial prospecting to the opening of the first mine. All mining companies have substantial exploration budgets which must be targeted to find metals which may be in demand five or even ten years ahead. In gold's case the stagnant price after World War II until the early 1970s meant that gold exploration took a small place in most exploration budgets — if any place at all. And it was only in the late 1970s that mining companies, for the first time in a generation, turned towards gold. Encouraged by the high prices in the early 1980s, gold exploration became the vogue, so that by 1986, 80 per cent of the exploration budgets of mining companies world wide were devoted to the search for gold. That led to the virtual doubling of output, and a weaker price, and by 1990 mining companies were diversifying exploration out of gold back into base metals.

Exploration Licence

See **Mining And Exploration Rights.**

Extraction

The mining and removal of ore from a mine.

Extrinsic Value

The price of an option (q.v.) less its intrinsic value (q.v.). All the premium of an out-of-the-money (q.v.) option is extrinsic value.

See also **Intrinsic Value; Time Value.**

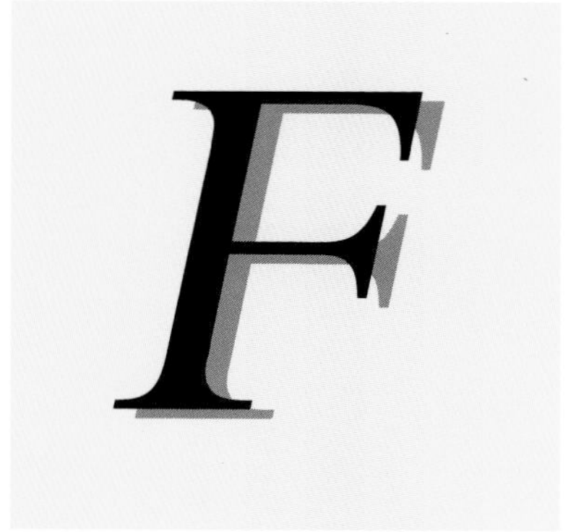

Fabergé

Carl Fabergé, a Russian of French Hugenot extraction, was one of the greatest goldsmiths. He took over his father's jewellery firm in St Petersburg (Leningrad) in 1870 and spent the next 30 years creating exotic masterpieces in gold, not only for the Czars, but for kings and bankers from all over Europe. The house of Fabergé eventually employed 500 craftsmen, but Fabergé himself did the designs. His intuitive feeling for a combination of many coloured golds, using different alloys to give a range of yellow, green, red and white, was allied to a technical mastery that gave him enormous freedom in design.

Fabricated Gold/Fabrication

Gold that has been manufactured beyond the casting stage, including jewellery (q.v.), coin (q.v.), dental (q.v.), electronics (q.v.) and other industrial uses. Fabrication is the major element in the demand for gold, normally absorbing over 80 per cent of new gold supplies coming to the market annually from mines. An annual report of fabrication demand was made each year from 1969 to 1989 by Consolidated Gold Fields (q.v.), and since then by Gold Fields Mineral Services Ltd (q.v.). (See Tables, page 50.)

Face Value

The nominal value given to legal tender coin or currency. Historically, under the gold standard, gold coins were used as a medium of exchange at their fixed face value. But many modern bullion coins or special issues have a face value which may be more or less than the actual value of the coin in terms of its gold content. The one ounce Britannia bullion coin has a face value of £100, less than half the value of the gold within; the US Eagle one ounce bullion coin has a face value of only $50, one-fifth or less of the value of the gold. By contrast, the Japanese 20 gramme Hirohito coin issued in 1986 had a face value of 100,000 yen, but contained only 40,000 yen worth of gold. *See also* **Coins.**

Fault

A rock fracture zone along which there has been relative displacement of the two sides. The fault may provide a channel for the passage of mineral-bearing solutions and the deposition of minerals such as gold or silver.

Feasibility Study

A definitive financial and engineering estimate or calculation of all costs, revenues, equipment needs and production likely to be achieved when a mine is developed.

Fabergé. *The splendid easter egg containing the Imperial Coronation Coach, created by Fabergé in 1897 for Tsar Nicholas II*

The study is used to define the economic viability of a project and to support the search for project financing.

FIFO

An accounting term meaning 'first in, first out'. The opposite of LIFO: 'last in, first out'. Both are used in valuing inventories of precious metals.

Filigree

The delicate tracery in gold or silver wire twisted and soldered into patterns that was first used in Egypt as early as 2500 BC. This style of jewellery is still found in Syria, especially from goldsmiths in Aleppo. It is also a speciality in Portugal and is used by designers throughout Europe.

Fill or Kill Order (FOK)

On futures exchanges, an order which must either be executed immediately by the floor broker (q.v.) or cancelled.

Gold fabrication by region

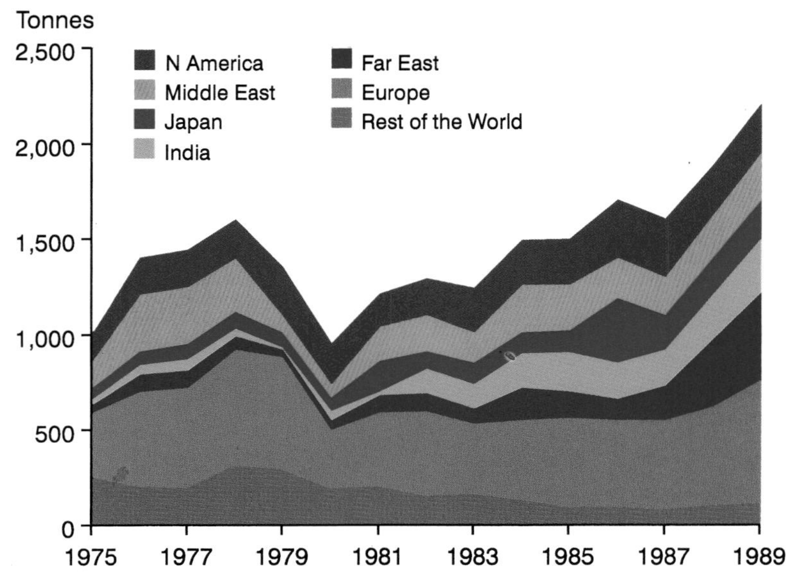

Fabricated Gold. *Source: Gold Fields Mineral Services Ltd, Gold 1990*

Summary of gold fabrication

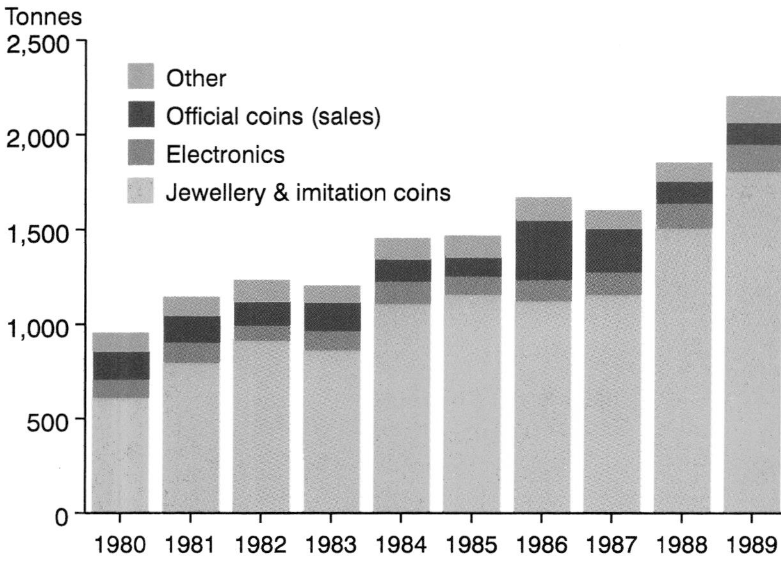

Fabricated Gold. *Source: Gold Fields Mineral Services Ltd, Gold 1990*

Final Settlement

In refining, the agreed date when the refining contract is completed and the final documents are issued by the refiner. It can also mean the date on which a refiner considers his profit on a particular contract has been earned.

Fine, Fineness, Fine Gold

This refers to the gold content in 1,000 parts of a bar or alloy. A normal 'good delivery bar' is 995 parts pure gold, and 5 parts other metals or impurities. The gold market accepts bars only up to a purity of 999.9 (four nines), but in electronics a bonding wire of 999.99 (five nines) is used. The fineness is usually stamped along with the refiner's or assayer's mark. Fineness is also expressed in

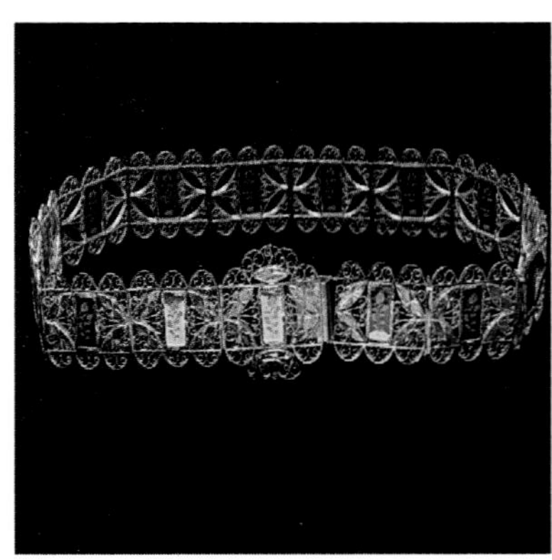

Filigree. *The delicate tracery of filigree on a modern gold bracelet*

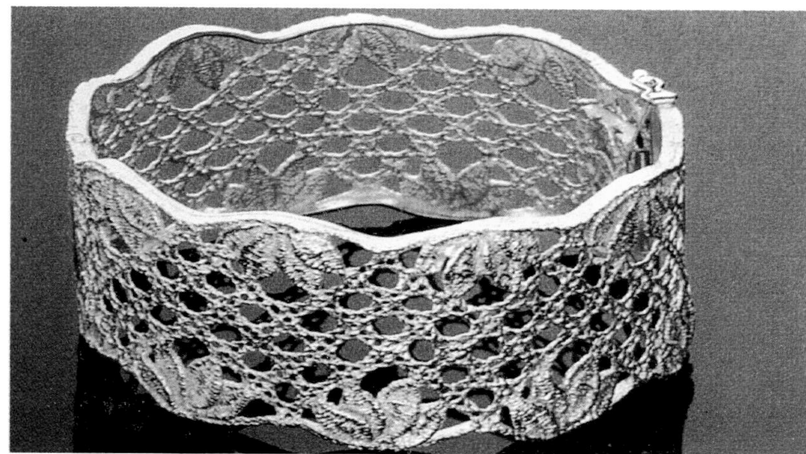

Filigree. *Out of fashion for many years, filigree makes a comeback in this necklace. It is particularly popular in Portugal*

carats, especially in the jewellery trade.

Fine Ounce

The description of a troy ounce of gold that is assumed to be 995 pure, unless otherwise specified.

Fine Weight

The weight of gold contained in a coin or bullion as determined by multiplying the gross weight by the fineness.

Fines

In the refining of a type of scrap gold known as 'sweeps' (q.v.), 'fines' refers to the metal which can be ground to a fine powder for chemical refining.

Fire Assay

The basic method of assaying gold ores, bars or scrap by placing a small sample of the gold under test, which has been weighed on a special balance, with a quantity of lead in a small cup or cupel (q.v.) made of bone ash. This is heated in a muffle furnace with a draught of air flowing over the cupel. The lead and any base metals are oxidised and absorbed into the cupel, while the gold and any silver remain as a small button. The silver is then dissolved out with nitric acid, leaving a pure gold 'cornet', which can be weighed and the gold content calculated by comparing with the original weight of the sample. Also known as **cupellation**. *See also* **Assay.**

Fixing

In the London gold market, the price of gold is 'fixed' twice daily at 10.30 a.m. and 3.00 p.m. at the premises of N. M. Rothschild & Sons, whose representative acts as chairman of the 'fix'. The fixing is attended by five bullion houses: Mocatta & Goldsmid, Sharps Pixley, N. M. Rothschild, Samuel Montagu and Mase-Westpac (who took over the seat formerly held by Johnson Matthey Bankers). The first fixing took place on 12 September 1919, when the price was agreed at £4.18.9d ($20.67), initially as a way of marketing South African gold. 'The principle to be maintained with regard to the sale of gold in the free market in London,' a contemporary instruction noted, 'is that everyone attending the Gold Fixing is entitled to buy or sell gold on equal terms with everyone else present at the Gold Fixing. It is also agreed that only one price shall be quoted and shall represent the price at which all supplies can be absorbed.'

That principle has been the strength of the fixing, because it means that large volumes can be bought or sold at one price. The advantage of a clearly posted price has encouraged mines, central banks, fabricators or investors to do their business on the fix because it is undisputed, especially at times when the gold price is volatile.

At the fix, five participants sit at desks in a special room at Rothschilds each with an open

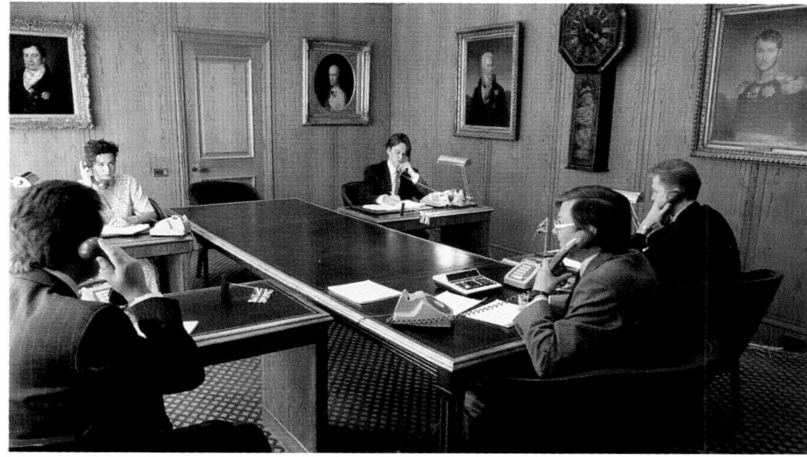

Fixing. *The London gold fixing held at N. M. Rothschild & Sons at 10.30 a.m. and 3 p.m. It began originally in September 1919*

telephone line to his own trading room. Each trader has a small Union Jack flag beside him with which he can stop the session by declaring 'flag up' while he confers with his trading room. The chairman suggests an opening price and, after conferring briefly, each trader indicates if he is a seller, buyer or has no interest. If no seller appears at the opening bid, the price will be moved up, perhaps by 15 cents or more; if no buyer, it is moved down.

Once sellers and buyers appear, the chairman asks for 'figures please', and each states how many bars are offered or required. When selling matches buying, the price is 'fixed'. Commission is by agreement; payment is two working days after the contract date. Actual turnover is not revealed, but may vary from zero to more than 20 tonnes. The price was quoted in sterling from 1919 until 1968, when it was changed to US dollars. The fix normally takes five or ten minutes; the longest in living memory, 2 hours 26 minutes, took place on 23 May 1990 when a Middle East bank came into the fix offering about 15 tonnes.

Several local markets also have their own fixing but none enjoys the position of world-wide benchmark that London holds.

Fizzer Cell

An electrolytic cell with a semi-permeable membrane used for gold refining.

Flag

A flag (also known as a pennant) is one of the basic patterns or signposts to watch out for on charts in technical analysis (q.v.). A flag is a short-term consolidation in a bull or bear market. In a bull market a flag occurs when prices consolidate for a period not exceeding three weeks then continue to rise. Conversely, in a bear market, a flag occurs when prices momentarily consolidate then continue to fall.

Foil. *Gold foil acts as a radiation shield in space on Apollo lunar module*

Flat

'Being flat' and 'flat position' refer to a trader's net gold position, meaning that his books show that any holdings are balanced by liabilities.

Floor Broker

The broker actually working on the floor of a futures exchange, in the trading pit for gold or another commodity, executing orders relayed to him from his brokerage house by runners or clerks. On COMEX, gold floor brokers each have a number on a green badge so that their counterparty in the open out-cry forum has only to note that down when a trade is done. Floor brokers also stand on specific steps according to the delivery month they are negotiating: February step, April step and so forth. Floor brokers often trade for their own account, as well as acting for commission houses. *See also* **COMEX.**

Flotation

Flotation is a process for separating out minerals from ore that depends on the adhesion of minerals (such as copper and zinc) to air bubbles in a solution of crushed ore and water. This creates a metal-rich concentrate on the surface which can be skimmed off.

Gold is recovered in this way (usually with pyrite) in the re-treatment of tailings (q.v.) in South Africa.

Flow-Through

A refinery's total through-put of precious and base metals.

Flow-Through Shares

A share-financing scheme introduced by the Canadian government in 1983 to stimulate mining by enabling a private or corporation investor to write off investment in mineral exploration within Canada against other income. Within three years US $550 million was raised by this scheme, of which three-quarters went into gold exploration. The flow-through shares in fact helped many small mining companies who would never have been able to raise other financing. But many projects came to nothing and the tax-break was later phased out.

Flux

A chemical compound such as silica, used to remove impurities in metal smelting and refining. The molten mixture of impurities forms a slag.

Foil

Sheets of foil, less than 0.15mm thick, are used in space programmes as a radiation shield. The lunar modules of the US Apollo flights were shrouded in foil.

Fool's Gold

Pyrites of iron sulphide which is gold-like in appearance and can delude amateur prospectors.

Footwall

In mining, the lower side of an orebody (q.v.), often the floor of the stope (q.v.).

Fortuna

Gold ingots in sizes from 1 gramme up to 50 grammes produced by the Pamp refinery (q.v.) in Switzerland. The bars, depicting the Roman goddess of Fortune emerging from a conch shell (the symbol of plenty), have been marketed in diamond, oval and pear shapes as well as the traditional ingot form. They have achieved substantial sales in the Middle East and have done much to widen the small bar market.

Forward Contract

A transaction in which two parties agree to the purchase and sale of gold at some future date, commonly 1 month, 3 months, 6 months or 1 year hence, but any date may be traded in the professional market. The premium on a forward transaction expressed in US$ will reflect current Euro-dollar interest rates less an allowance for current gold interest rates.

Forward contracts are an integral part of many swap (q.v.) arrangements, in which a central bank, for example, sells gold spot while simultaneously entering a forward contract to buy it back.

Forward Premium

The difference between spot and forward or futures quotations, which will depend both on money and gold interest rates and on carrying charges. *See also* **Gold Forward Rate Agreement.**

Footwall. *Hydraulic drilling on a footwall in the southern section of Freegold in the Orange Free State in South Africa*

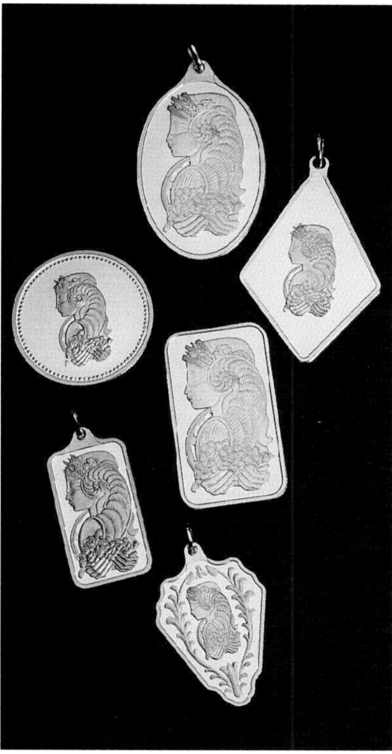

Fortuna. *An assortment of Fortuna bars produced by the Pamp refinery in Switzerland*

Four Nines (999.9)

The highest purity of gold bullion or coin that the market will accept is 999.9 parts per thousand gold. Gold wire is made to five nines (999.99) but this is for the electronics industry.

France

The French have a reputation for being the world's greatest investors in gold, but it is one that was won largely before 1970 in the aftermath of two world wars which swept across their country in a generation, leading to repeated devaluations of the franc. Gold kilobars and coins became for many the basic form of saving. And while General de Gaulle ruled France, it was supported by his famous remark at a press conference in 1965: 'There can be no other criterion, no other standard than gold.

Yes, gold, which never changes, which can be shaped into ingots, bars, coins, which has no nationality and which is eternally and universally accepted as the unalterable fiduciary value par excellence.'

Such promotion encouraged the French to amass a private holding estimated at 6,000 tonnes, with a market value in 1900 of around US$75 billion, accounting for close to one-quarter of all savings deposits in France.

But the eagerness for gold has waned since de Gaulle; the younger generation in a prosperous, politically stable France has little time for gold investment, except some short-term trading, especially in options in which Société Générale in particular runs a large book. Volume on the Paris gold market (q.v.) has declined and it is no longer a pace-setter for gold prices. But the stock of gold remains, mostly privately and secretly held, but subject to sales tax of 6 per cent if it is sold.

At the official level, too, France is gold minded; the central bank, Banque de France, has 2,546 tonnes (excluding its tranche with the European Monetary Fund), the third largest official holding.

See also **Bonds, Comptoir Lyon-Alemand, CMP, Napoleon, Paris Gold Market.**

Frankfurt

As the financial capital of Germany, Frankfurt is the centre of gold trading. This is concentrated principally in the hands of the two major commercial banks, Deutsche (q.v.) and Dresdner (q.v.). A daily gold fixing is held at 12 noon to set a DM price for 1 kilo and 12½ kilo bars for the interbank market in Germany exempt from value added tax. But tax regulations in Germany have meant that the focus of much German gold business has been switched to the Luxembourg gold market (q.v.), where the German banks maintain a significant presence. Commerzbank, for instance, has its main office for gold not in Frankfurt but Luxembourg.

Free Coinage

Under both the gold standard (q.v.) and the silver standard, people could take either metal to the mint and receive in exchange coins of equal weight at no cost. In practice, if either metal was slightly under-valued, they would take that metal for minting and sell the other in the market. In Britain, for example, gold was slightly under-valued after the 1696 recoinage and thereafter was taken to the mint for coin, while more highly valued silver was sold as bars for export to the east. By comparison, in the early years of American independence, silver was slightly under-valued and so it was taken to the mint. In the one case Britain got a gold coinage, and in the other the United States a silver coinage forming the main circulation. Free silver coinage ceased once countries switched to the gold standard, and free gold coinage was also generally suspended in 1914 at the outbreak of World War I.

Free Gold

An alternative description of alluvial (q.v.) or placer gold.

Free Milling

Term applied to ores which contain 'free' gold (or silver) which can be liberated by crushing and gravity separation or amalgamation without roasting (q.v.) or other chemical treatment.

Fundamental Analysis

Analysis of the precious metal markets which concentrates on basic supply/demand factors. *See also* **Technical Analysis.**

Futures/FuturesExchanges/ Futures Markets

The concept of futures and futures markets, involving a legally binding contract for the delivery of a specified quantity of a commodity at a specified time in the future at an agreed price, originated in Chicago (q.v.) in the 1830s. The intention was to try to even out prices and give

Gold futures contracts volume on US and Tokyo Exchanges

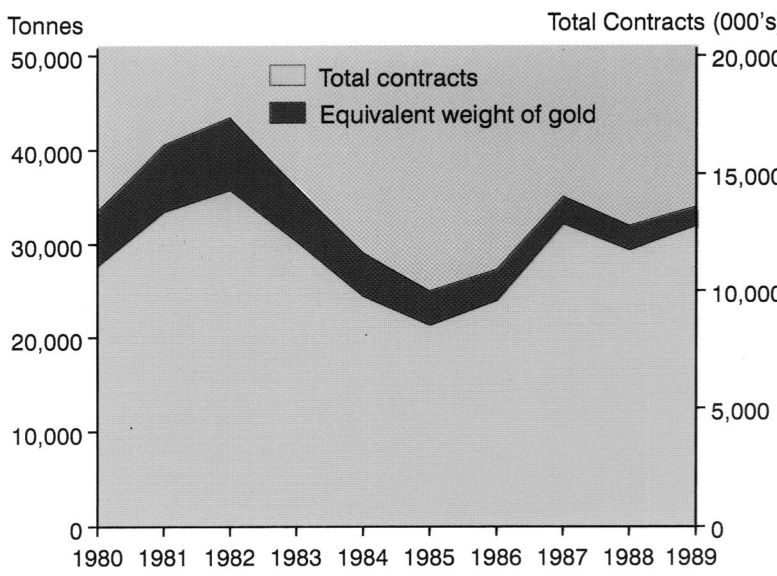

Futures. *Source: Gold Fields Mineral Services Ltd*

farmers, in particular, some way of hedging their crops well before harvest. They were known as 'to-arrive' contracts, and were for agricultural commodities as diverse as soybeans, wheat and pork-bellies.

After the American Civil War, the Chicago Board of Trade (q.v.) formalised this into the first real futures markets with standardised contracts. Thus the concept of trading futures contracts soon came naturally to Americans and the custom spread to New York.

Gold futures contracts came on the scene much later, simply because no one traded gold while the US was on a fixed price gold standard (q.v.) until 1933. Then, for a generation, Americans were forbidden to buy or trade gold. It was not until 31 December 1974 that the first gold futures contract was traded in New York on the Commodity Exchange (COMEX) (q.v.). Other American exchanges, including Chicago Board of Trade (q.v.), followed suit. In fact, there was also a trial run for gold futures with a 400 ounce contract on the Winnipeg (q.v.) exchange in Canada launched in 1972 prior to the relaxation of American legislation. But it was the American exchanges, and above all COMEX, that brought a new dimension to international gold trading. COMEX had the advantage because of its close affinity with New York's banks and financial institutions, which immediately gave it a worldwide clientele; the Chicago exchanges still tended to cater to Americans of the mid-west more attuned to trading pork bellies than gold.

The attraction of gold futures, while on the one hand providing miners with a means of hedging their forthcoming production and on the other of offering refiners or jewellery manufacturers the chance of hedging their inventories, was also that it provided many other investors or speculators with a cheap and highly efficient way of getting into gold. And, since most futures contracts are liquidated ahead of maturity, there are no problems of delivery, insurance, storage or re-assay upon sale that go with the physical metal. The further attraction is that gold futures contracts can be bought on margin (q.v.) of as little as 10 per cent. This gives the opportunity to 'leverage up' (q.v.) to larger amounts, because an initial claim on $1 million in gold can be achieved for as little as $100,000.

The futures markets thus offered an entirely new concept of gold; it was something to trade, on which to make money; not just a metal to be used in jewellery or physically hidden away as coins or small bars against a crisis. The volumes traded annually may be greater than conventional gold markets. Since 1978, when futures trading took off in the United States as the dollar weakened and inflation rose, the volume on the US exchanges has rarely fallen below 10 million contracts annually, involving over 30,000 tonnes of gold (almost as much as is held in all official government reserves) and nearly a third of all gold ever mined.

A fresh dimension has been added by the launching of gold futures trading on the Tokyo Commodity Exchange (TOCOM) (q.v.) where annual turnover exceeds 2 million contracts.

Trading is by open out-cry throughout the working hours with specific pits for each commodity on the exchanges, and most floor brokers (q.v.) limited to trading specific pits. Much of the trading is by hand signals. The hand pushing forward, five fingers outstretched, means selling five contracts; beckoning means buying. Abbreviations abound: 'Sell 2 August at market' means 'sell two August lots at the current market price'; 'Sell 1 December 395 stop' means 'sell one December contract if the price falls to $395'.

The techniques of futures trading have also evolved their own language of 'market orders' (q.v.), 'stop order' (q.v.), 'market-if touched' 'straddles' (q.v.) and 'switches' (q.v.). The premium or contango (q.v.) on a futures contract will comprise notional costs of storage and insurance (perhaps 0.5 per cent) plus the financing costs for gold over the agreed months to delivery, which will vary with interest rates but might typically be 9–10 per cent on an annualised basis.

Most exchanges have six delivery months (q.v.), usually February, April, June, August, October and December.

Futures exchanges normally have separate clearing houses (q.v.) which match and monitor all turnover and keep track of additional margin that must be posted according to daily price movements.

See also entries on all individual futures exchanges as indicated (q.v.), and futures markets terminology and techniques as indicated (q.v.).

Futures Commission Merchant (FCM)

The legal term for a US commodity brokerage house handling futures exchange (q.v.) business.

Gangue

The waste rock surrounding and/or within an ore which must be separated for the extraction of the mineral.

Gencor

A major South African mining investment house, with a broad diversity of other interests. The mining division, Genmin, accounted for 41 per cent of the company's income in 1990. It also holds a 50 per cent interest in Genbel, its mining investment and exploration arm, accounting for a further 29 per cent of income. Other assets include interests in Sappi and Malbak. Gencor administers 13 operating and developing gold mines, including Buffelsfontein, Beatrix and St Helena. In the financial year to June 1990, Buffelsfontein produced 14.64 tonnes of gold.

Gencor,
6 Hollard St
Johannesburg 2001
(PO Box 61820, Marshalltown 2107)
South Africa
Tel: (011) 376-9111
Fax: (011) 838-4716
Telex: 4-85830

Geochemical Exploration

A method of mining exploration (q.v.) which analyses variations in the chemical composition of rocks, soils and sediments.

Geophysical Exploration

A method of mining exploration (q.v.) which analyses such physical properties of rocks or minerals as magnetism, electrical conductivity and radioactivity.

Germany

See **Degussa; Dresdner Bank; Deutsche Bank; Frankfurt; Heraeus; Pforzheim.**

Ghana

Formerly the Gold Coast, Ghana has been an important source of gold for more than two thousand years. The Phoenicians and Carthaginians probably reached there in the 5th or 6th centuries BC in the search for gold.

By the 9th century gold trade with 'the gold coast' was well established, and by the 18th century it was a major source of supply to the London market.

There are three main types of gold deposits: vein and lode, auriferous quartz-pebble conglomerate and placer. The development of these deposits by modern mining methods from the end of the 19th century expanded output so that when Ghana became independent in 1961 it ranked fifth in world output at 34 tonnes. But production by the mining group, Ashanti Goldfields Corporation, which is owned 55 per cent by the government and 45 per cent by Lonrho, subsequently declined due to the lack of foreign exchange for modern equipment at their Obuasi mine. Ghana's output fell to 12 tonnes annually. Since 1985 financing arranged through the World Bank has enabled Ashanti to deepen two shafts and install a carbon-in-pulp treatment plant.

The State Gold Mining Corporation operates two underground mines at Tarkwa and Prestea and a multi-dredge placer operation at Dunkwa, which are also being expanded. In recent years, the country has undergone a rejuvenation of gold production. In 1988, the country witnessed the start-up of its first new mine in forty years when Southern Cross Mining (70 per cent) and the State Mining Corp. (30 per cent) opened the Konongo heap leach mine. Then towards the end of 1990 the Bogosu open pit mine and mill was opened. The mine is owned by Billiton (65.5 per cent), Sikaman (15.5 per cent), International Finance Corp. (9 per cent) and the government (10 per cent) and is expected to produce about 130,000 ounces (4 tonnes) per year. Sikaman also has a 34 per cent interest in the Kwabeng alluvial project which also began production at the end of 1990 and is expected to produce 25,000 ounces (0.78 tonnes) of gold per year. With expansion Ghana's output could reach 15–20 tonnes annually in the 1990s.

Gilding

Covering with a thin layer of gold an ornament, watch case or cigarette lighter, or such bathroom fittings as taps, usually by electroplating (q.v.).

Globex

Technically advanced computational, international clearing system pioneered by Reuters and the Chicago Mercantile Exchange. Scheduled for launching in Spring 1991.

Glory Holes

Holes from which unusually rich deposits of gold-bearing ore are extracted.

GOFO

Since July 1989, twelve market makers have contributed to the GOFO page on Reuters their rates for lending gold (against US dollars) and at 10 a.m. a mean is calculated automatically giving the market, in effect, a gold LIBOR (London Interbank Offered Rate).

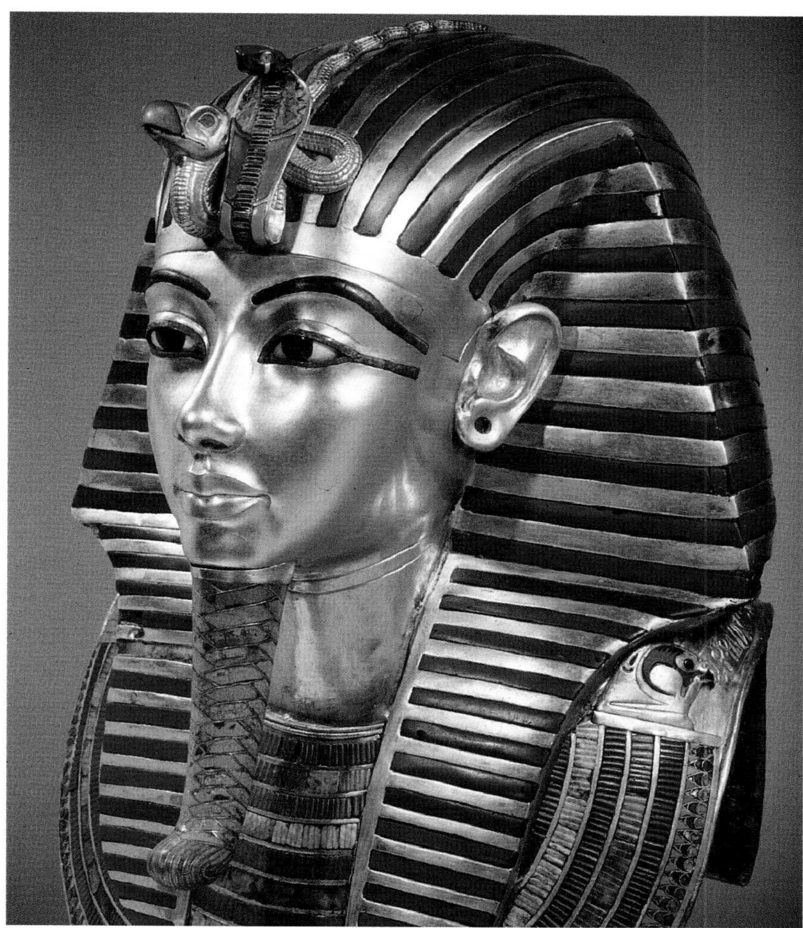

Gold. *Mask of beaten gold from the tomb of King Tutankhamun, 1361–1352 BC*

Gold

A yellow, noble metal, noted for its malleability, ductility, and resistance to corrosion. The chemical symbol is Au, from Aurora or dawn.

It can be beaten into leaves only 0.00001mm thick, one ounce drawn into 50 miles of thin gold wire, and is dissolved by cyanide and by aqua regia (q.v.), a mixture of nitric and hydrochloric acid. It has been used for ornamental purposes and as a medium of exchange for over 5,000 years.

Its occurrence in the Earth's crust is 0.005ppm, and just over 100,000 tonnes is estimated to have been mined.

The main properties of gold are:

Atomic number:	9
Atomic weight:	196.967
Melting point	1,063°C
Specific gravity (the sixth heaviest metal)	19.32
Hardness (Brinell)	25
Tensile strength	11.9

Goldbeater

Craftsman who makes gold leaf or gold foil by hammering. *See also* **Gold Leaf.**

Gold Bullion Standard

Britain's compromise return to the gold standard in 1925 was initiated by Winston Churchill, then Chancellor of the Exchequer. Gold coin did not circulate freely and notes could be redeemed only for 400 ounce good delivery bars. The real mistake of this attempt to revive the gold standard was that sterling was maintained at the traditional gold price of £4.4.11½d, which had prevailed since 1717. This was a considerable over-valuation after the trauma of World War I which gave the pound far too high an exchange rate against the dollar. It lasted for only six years until Britain abandoned gold in 1931. *See also* **Gold Standard.**

Gold (III) Chloride (Auric Chloride)

A trivalent salt of gold that is used as a toner in photography and, when dissolved in hydrochloric acid, as an electrolyte in the Wohlwill process (q.v.) for refining gold.

Gold Coast

See **Ghana**.

Gold Coins

See **Coins**.

Gold Control Act

Indian regulations introduced in 1962 which prohibited individuals from holding unwrought gold and allowed goldsmiths to keep only 100 grammes as stock in trade, while licensed traders were not subject to any restrictions. A bureaucratic army of officials was employed to administer the Act and also issue gold to authorised users in dental, medical and electronics uses. The Act was repealed in June 1990.

GoldCorp Australia

The marketing organisation which operates the Perth Mint (q.v.), now renamed the Western Australian Mint, in Western Australia and handles the selling of the Nugget bullion coin (q.v.) and the platinum Koala and silver Kookaburra coins. One of GoldCorp's main aims is to promote Australia as a gold producer. GoldCorp is a wholly owned subsidiary of Gold Corporation, set up and guaranteed by the government of Western Australia in 1987. The Western Australian Mint in Perth is also a Gold Corporation subsidiary.

GoldCorp Australia
Perth Mint Buildings
310 Hay Street
East Perth, Western Australia 6004
Tel: (9) 421 7222
Fax: (9) 221 3812
Telex: GOLDAA 197171

Golddealers Luxembourg a.s.b.l.

Founded on 27 April 1983, the association grew out of the Luxembourg gold fixing, which had been established on 17 March 1981. The main aim is to promote the Luxembourg gold market and to provide the members with all possible information about the precious metals market. Since its foundation, Golddealers Luxembourg has organised some 30 different conferences, seminars, meetings and annual 'European Precious Metals Conferences'. The association has some 90 members from both Luxembourg and abroad.

Golddealers Luxembourg a.s.b.l.
P O Box 1657, L-1016
Luxembourg
Tel: (352) 46-0512
Fax: (352) 460507
Telex: 3764

Gold Deposit Forward Rate Agreement (GODFRA)

See **Gold Forward Rate Agreement.**

Gold Deposits

Central banks wishing to make a small return on their gold holdings may deposit part of their reserves with the main market-makers for a set period in return for a modest interest (usually paid in gold) of between 0.5 and 3 per cent. The current interest rate levels are posted in the Reuters Gold Forward Rate Agreement (q.v.) page. This central bank gold provides the market with considerable extra liquidity; as much as 200–300 tonnes may be on deposit at any given moment. The facility has been used mainly by small central banks, but considerable caution in new deposit agreements was exercised after it was revealed that a number of the central banks faced substantial losses on gold deposited with Drexel Burnham Lambert, the New York investment bank which collapsed in 1990.

Gold Equivalent

In mining company reports or refinery agreements, production of silver, and sometimes other metals, is converted into the equivalent ounces of gold using the current ratio of silver–gold prices. For example, with silver at $5 per ounce and gold at $350, 70,000 ounces of silver would be credited as 1,000 ounces of gold.

Gold Exchange Account

A kind of bank account frequently operated by semi-fabricators for their customers who supply them with fine gold ahead of delivery of alloyed products. When the alloys are delivered, the equivalent gold is deducted from the account, thus removing financing costs for the semi-fabricator.

Gold Exchange Standard

This half-way house return to the gold standard (q.v.) was born out of the Genoa monetary conference of 1922, under which central banks kept part of their reserves in such key currencies as sterling and dollars, which could still be exchanged for gold. It did not include the right for ordinary citizens to cash in notes for coin at a fixed price, implicit under the true gold standard. Central banks, too, soon found danger; some, notably in Europe, kept sterling in their reserves, thinking it was as good as gold, until Britain suddenly went off the gold standard completely in 1931 and they found, to their cost, it was not. The only remaining link to gold was through the dollar, and that, too, was finally severed in 1971 after which central banks could no longer trade dollars at the Federal Reserve for gold.

Gold Fields Mineral Services

Research company owned by Gold Fields of South Africa (q.v.), Newmont Mining Corporation (q.v.) and Renison Goldfields Consolidated, which produces and publishes the annual gold market surveys formerly published by Consolidated Gold Fields plc (q.v.).

Gold Fields Mineral Services Ltd
Greencoat House
Francis Street
London SW1P 1DH
Tel: (071) 828 8040
Fax: (071) 233 5096
Telex: 916352 G FMSG

Gold Fields of South Africa (GFSA)

A major South African mining and finance house. The company concentrates its efforts on investment in the exploration for, and mining and processing of, metals and minerals in southern Africa. The principle asset and major source of income is the substantial portfolio of investments, mainly in gold mining companies, which in June 1990 accounted for 74 per cent of group assets. No less than 32 per cent of the total investments were accounted for by Driefontein. The Driefontein operation is one of South Africa's major gold mines and produced 52.06 tonnes in the year to June 1990.

Gold Fields of South Africa
75 Fox Street
Johannesburg 2001
(P O Box 1167, Johannesburg 2000),
South Africa
Tel: (011) 639-9111
Fax: (011) 639-2101
Telex: 450043

Gold Filled

Gold filled and rolled gold (q.v.) refer to products in which a layer of carat gold alloy is bonded to another metal. The process is also known as rolled gold plate, gold plate or gold overlay; in France it is known as *plaque laminé* (q.v.). It should not be confused with the decorative coatings through electroplating (q.v.). Standards in certain countries regulate the description. In the United States, for example, gold filled can describe only an alloy of 10 carats or more which must comprise at least 1/20 by weight of the total metal content of the article. If it is less than 1/20, it must be designated rolled gold plate or gold overlay. Under all definitions it is widely used in costume jewellery, while gold filled sheet is used in cigarette cases, lighters and cuff links, gold filled tube in pens, pencils or lipstick cartridges, and gold filled wire in the basis of optical frames and rings.

Gold Flashed (Gold Washed)

An exceptionally thin film of gold, less than 7-millionths of an inch thick, electroplated on a base metal.

Gold Forward Rate Agreement (GOFRA)

A hedging instrument used by producers who, having drawn down gold loans (q.v.), can lock in forward gold interest rate exposure. The GOFRA hedges against the combined effect of moves in both US dollar and gold interest rates with settlement in dollars. The GOLFRA (Gold Lease Forward Rate Agreement) restricts itself to gold interest rates with settlement in gold. The increased activity of the central banks in lending gold to the market means that they too have exposure to gold rate volatility and the GODFRA (Gold Deposit Forward Rate Agreement) is tailored to their particular activities.

Gold Funds

Funds which specialise in gold, gold shares and sometimes other precious metals. In practice, most of these funds are in mining equities and are often actually forbidden, as in Britain, to invest in the metal itself or, in the case of some American funds, are limited to 10 per cent of the portfolio in gold. The 40 listed American precious metal funds held assets of $3.6 billion in 1990 which included approximately 9 tonnes of gold, valued at $115 million with gold at $400, or 4 per cent in actual metal. The number of American funds including gold in their portfolio increased after the 1987 stock market crash, because the funds already holding gold suffered less than those with no gold. In Canada there are nine precious metal funds.

Gold Institute

International association based in Washington DC that includes miners, refiners, bullion suppliers, manufacturers of gold products and wholesalers of gold investment products. It was founded in 1976 and has nearly a hundred members from North America, Europe, Japan and Australia. Its aim is to promote the common business interests of the gold industry as a whole by providing members with current statistical data and other relevant information, while alerting them to potential changes in the operating climate for the industry. The Institute also provides information on gold to the media and public and acts as an industry spokesman.

The Gold Institute
Suite 240,
1112 Sixteenth Street NW
Washington DC 20036
USA
Tel: (202) 835 0185
Fax: (202) 835 0155

Gold Leaf

Gold Leaf has been used for decoration of tombs and statues, cathedrals and temples, fine books and picture

Gold Leaf. *Railings at the Palais Royale in Paris being decorated with gold foil*

frames since Egyptian times. It is still often preferred for adorning the domes or ceilings of public buildings (such as the Canadian Houses of Parliament in Ottawa and the State Capitol in Denver, Colorado or the Metropolitan Opera House in New York) because its resistance to corrosion means it will outlast paint by many years.

The craft of beating gold into a wafer-thin leaf only three-millionths of an inch thick evolved in antiquity because it required neither heat nor mechanical devices. Many mummies and their cases in Egyptian tombs, such as King Tutankhamun's in 1352 BC, were overlaid with gold leaf as fine as any made today. The technique of gold beating has changed little. The gold beater stands before a granite block set on a block of wood or tree trunk in the ground; the resiliency of the wood base gives bounce and rhythm to his hammering. Gold is initially rolled into ribbons one-thousandth of an inch thick, then cut into 1¼ inch squares and placed in squares of seaweed paper, encased in turn in parchment paper. This packet, called a 'cutch', is then squeezed in a press to compress the paper. The 'cutch' is beaten with a seventeen pound hammer until the gold is in four inch squares. These are then placed on ox skins, coated with brime, a powder-like substance made from volcanic ash, brushed on with the hind leg of a Russian hare. This new packet, a 'shoder', is beaten for two hours with a nine pound hammer, then divided again into a 'mould' wrapped in parchment, which is beaten with a seven pound hammer. In all, about 82,800 blows are necessary to reduce the gold to three-millionths of an inch thickness. The gold is then so delicate that it can be cut only with a malacca reed shaped into a cutting tool or 'wagon' which is slid across the gold.

Today, only a handful of craftsmen in Britain, France, and the USA still practise the technique.

Gold Lease Forward Rate Agreement (GOLFRA)

See **Gold Forward Rate Agreement.**

Gold Libor

See **GOFO.**

Gold Loans

Gold loans provided a considerable part of the capital for the gold mining boom of the 1980s. Mining companies borrowed gold, sold it spot giving them immediate cash flow, while selling part of their future production forward to repay the loan and interest. Since the gold could often be borrowed at between 3 and 4 per cent, it was a much cheaper way of raising finance than borrowing money and easier than going to the equity market which was disillusioned with gold shares after the stock market collapse of 1987. The number and scale of loans put considerable pressure on the gold price in the peak year of 1988 when 84 new loans involving over 150 tonnes were taken out. The vogue for loans originated in Australia, but soon spread to the North American mining industry. The two largest loans were by Newmont Mining for 31.1 tonnes and American Barrick for 33 tonnes. Such loans helped push up gold lending rates and encouraged central banks to deposit gold with the market because of the improved return.

Thereafter, the net effect of loans declined as the mining boom waned and paybacks began, but they have been established as an important element in mine financing. Defaults, because proposed mine projects did

Gold loans to the mining industry

Tonnes
200
150
100
50
0
-50
Number of loans
New draw downs
Known pay backs
Draw downs less pay backs
1981 1982 1983 1984 1985 1986 1987 1988 1989 1990

Gold Loans. *Source: RTZ Corporation plc*

not mature, were few and small scale.

Gold Overlay/Gold Plate

Alternative terms for rolled gold (q.v.) in which the weight of the carat gold alloy is less than 1/20th of the whole article. *See also* **Gold Filled.**

Gold Plating

See **Electroplating.**

Gold Pool

The gold pool was an alliance between the central banks of Britain, Belgium, France, Italy, the Netherlands, Switzerland, the United States and West Germany from 1961 to 1968 to try to maintain the gold price at $35 an ounce. The Bank of England operated for the pool through a direct line to the fixing (q.v.) in London, selling from their combined reserves if the price threatened to breach $35.20 and buying back for the pool account when it was weak. The pool finally collapsed in March 1968 when the run on gold, after the Tet offensive in Vietnam undermined confidence in the dollar, overwhelmed its resources. The pool lost nearly 3,000 tonnes of its combined reserve of 24,000 tonnes, including 1,000 tonnes between 8 and 15 March 1968, when the London gold market was closed temporarily. When it re-opened two weeks later the pool had been disbanded and gold was left free to find its own level.

Gold Potassium Cyanide

Gold potassium cyanide, normally known as GPC or PGC, is the most important gold source in electrolytic gold plating. The salt, $KAu(CN)_2$, is generally obtained by anodic dissolution of gold in an aqueous solution of potassium cyanide and subsequent crystallisation. It usually contains about 68 per cent fine gold, and has the appearance of a white powder which dissolves in water. Well over 100 tonnes of GPC is manufactured annually for use both in the electronics industry for plating contacts or connectors and for decorative plating of costume jewellery, watches and pens.

Gold Price

See **Fixing; Price of Gold.**

Gold Producers' Association Ltd

A marketing organisation formed in 1954 by mines in Western Australia to market gold on behalf of its members by inviting bids on a weekly basis from international banks and bullion dealers bidding a margin on the 10.30 a.m. Tuesday London fixing. During 1990 the Association processed about 50 tonnes of gold, approximately 23% of Australia's production.

Gold Producers' Association
7th Floor, 12 St George's Terrace
Perth
Western Australia 6000
Tel: (09) 325 2955
Fax: (09) 221 3701
Telex: GOLCOM AA92792

Gold Reflective Glass

Gold's ability to reflect heat has led to the increasing use of glass coated with a thin film of gold in modern buildings. One ounce of gold suffices to cover one thousand square feet of glass, which not only reflects summer heat, but helps to retain it in winter. The Royal Bank of Canada

Gold Reflective Glass. *The Royal Bank of Canada building in Toronto has 77.7 kilos of gold in its windows, cutting cooling and heating costs*

building in Toronto, for example, is sheathed in reflective glass using 2,500 ounces (77.2 kilos) of gold. The use of reflective glass has reduced cooling and heating costs by as much as 40 per cent in some buildings.

Gold Reserves

The official reserves of central banks (q.v.) contain over 29,000 tonnes of gold, while a further 6,000 tonnes is held by such institutions as the International Monetary Fund (q.v.), the European Monetary Co-operation Fund (q.v.), and the Bank for International Settlements (q.v.). This amounts to close to one-third of all gold ever mined, and in value accounts for between 35 and 50 per cent of all international monetary reserves, depending on the gold price.

Gold Rushes

The impetuous rush to a rumour of gold is a relatively modern phenomenon, first seen in Brazil in the early eighteenth century, but really characterised by the great alluvial rushes of the nineteenth century, first to California (q.v.), then to Australia (q.v.), and finally the Klondike (q.v.). They involved thousands, even hundreds of thousands, of ordinary men throwing up their jobs, homes and families and dashing off halfway round the world in search of an elusive metal. 'The rush and struggle is awful and the only chance is to fly off at the first sound', wrote one prospector. 'The mischief is that you hear many wonderful stories that prove false.' Yet these invasions had a dramatic effect upon the opening up not only of the American West, but of British Columbia and the Yukon in Canada, and the rush for gold helped to transform Australia from a remote penal settlement into a viable nation

The fact was not lost on Joseph Stalin in the 1920s in his ambitions to open up Siberia; learning from the

Gold Rushes. *Gold diggers who joined the rush to California after 1848*

American experience, he encouraged Russian prospectors to go east. The catalytic effect of gold rushes in opening up an economy is by no means over. In Brazil, Indonesia, the Philippines, Papua New Guinea and Venezuela the discovery of rich new alluvial deposits in the 1980s has brought another era of gold rushes (often with catastrophic effect upon local rivers and forests) sometimes engaging, as in Brazil, as many as 200,000 diggers.

Most gold rushes, however, are relatively short lived. After three to five years the main alluvial deposits, easily workable by an army of prospectors with little more than shovels, are worked out, and more serious miners have to move in with heavier equipment. But such rushes can produce remarkable amounts of gold in a short time; 93 tonnes was dug out of California in 1853, and Brazil's rushes in the 1980s have yielded up to 80 tonnes annually.

Gold/Silver Ratio

The number of ounces of silver that can be bought with one ounce of gold. Historically, while both were monetary metal, the ratio was fairly constant, although it might vary from continent to continent. In Mexico and South America, where silver was mined, it was 1:17; in Europe it was 1:15 and in India and China it was 1:13 or even 1:12. That variation determined flows. Since silver was more highly valued in the east it was exported there from Europe from the sixteenth century to pay for goods, while gold largely stayed in Europe.

After the general demonetisation of silver in the second half of the nineteenth century that constant alliance broke. The gold/silver ratio was as wide as 1:90 in the 1930s. Although it came back momentarily to 1:17 in 1980 in the Hunt Brothers' attempt to corner the silver market, it has fluctuated widely since World War II in a range from 1:30 to 1:90. Although there is no logic to the modern ratio, speculators do play the ratio, selling gold, buying silver and vice versa at what are seen as crucial chart points in technical analysis (q.v.).

The ratio between the gold and silver price 1980–1990

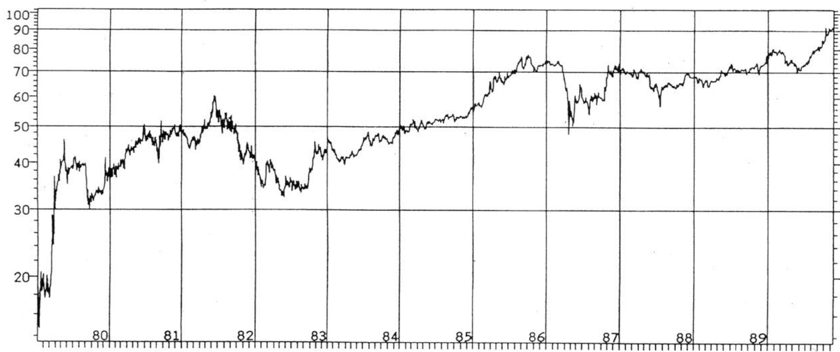

Gold/Silver Ratio. *Source: Brian Marber & Co.*

Goldsmiths (Worshipful Company of)

The Worshipful Company of Goldsmiths in London received its first royal charter on 13 May 1327, although an organised body of craftsmen in gold existed as early as the 12th century. As a guild it rigorously controlled the craft, particularly confirming that gold used in plate, jewellery and coin of the realm was up to standard. It is the oldest hallmarking authority in the United Kingdom. All British made articles approved at the Assay Office at Goldsmith's Hall are stamped with a leopard's head hallmark (q.v.). At the annual Trial of the Pyx (q.v.), which dates from 1282, the Goldsmiths' Company tests samples of gold (and silver and cupro-nickel) coin of the realm. The company's technical advisory service provides assistance throughout the industry.

The Worshipful Company of Goldsmiths of London
Goldsmiths' Hall, Foster Lane
London EC2V 6BN
Tel: 071-606 7010

Gold Standard

The monetary system with a fixed price for gold, and with gold coin either forming the whole circulation of currency within a country or with notes representing and redeemable in gold, has always been known as 'the gold standard'. Internationally, completely free import and export of gold was included with all balance-of-payments deficits settled in the metal. The gold standard was supposed to discipline an economy. Gold flowed out of a country in deficit, leaving less for internal circulation, thus controlling prices and making exports more competitive. Equally, a country in surplus imported gold and its economy expanded.

Britain went on to an unofficial gold standard in 1717 when Sir Isaac Newton, then Master of the Mint, established a fixed price of £3.17.10½d per standard (22 carat) troy ounce, equal to £4.4.11½d per fine ounce. Although silver, which had previously formed the major circulation in the country, was not officially demonetised, it circulated little after that. Britain adopted a formal gold standard in 1821 at the end of the Napoleonic wars, after the introduction of the Sovereign (q.v.) as the main circulating coin. The rest of Europe, however, remained on a silver standard until the 1870s, when the great flows of gold available from the United States and Australian discoveries made it practical for it to be adopted as the main metal circulating. Germany switched to gold in 1871, Scandinavia in 1874, the Netherlands in 1875, France and Spain in 1876 and Russia in 1893. The United States remained on a bimetallic system of gold and silver until 1900 when the Gold Standard Act confirmed the supremacy of gold. Eventually 59 countries were on the gold standard, with China on silver as the only main exception. Its heyday was short. At the onset of World War I in 1914, most countries suspended gold payments, preferring to husband their reserves for essential war needs. Many never returned. Britain went off the gold standard in 1919. Although attempts were made to revive the gold standard during the 1920s, gold coin circulation was limited and many central banks began to keep part of their reserves in key currencies, such as sterling or dollars, which they could still exchange for gold. Thus the gold exchange standard (q.v.) was born.

Britain itself went on the gold bullion standard (q.v.) in 1926, which had a fixed gold price (still £4.4.11½d per troy ounce, as in 1717) but notes were not convertible into gold coin and could be exchanged only for 400 ounce good delivery bars. Britain went off this standard in 1931 and most European countries followed suit in the early 1930s. The United States went off gold in March 1933, when private holding and export were forbidden. Only the export of gold to recognised central banks and governments was permitted. This created the dollar–gold exchange standard under which dollars could be traded for gold at the Federal Reserve. This system was confirmed by the Bretton Woods Agreement (q.v.) in 1944 and lasted until 1971.

Gold Warrants

Gold warrants originated in 1986–87 when they were mostly related to gold mine issues. Now being widely issued by Swiss, American and Japanese banks and securities houses, a warrant gives the buyer the right to buy gold at a specific price (usually dollars) on a specified value date, normally one year or eighteen months hence. The buyer pays a premium for this opportunity. The warrants can usually be sold back at any time, and in practice buyers do not normally expect to take delivery. Warrants are essentially options (q.v.), but some investors prefer to take this paper rather than trade in the complexities of options trading.

The Golden Constant

The title of a book by Professor Roy Jastram analysing the purchasing power of gold over four centuries which he found to be remarkably 'constant'. 'Gold maintains its purchasing power over long periods of time, for example, half-century intervals', Professor Jastram observed. 'The amazing aspect of this conclusion is that it is not because gold eventually moves towards commodity prices, but because commodity prices return to gold.'

(Roy W. Jastram, *The Golden Constant*, New York, John Wiley & Sons, 1977.)

Good Delivery Bar

The ultimate seal of approval on a gold bar is that it is up to the exacting 'good delivery' requirements of the London Bullion Market Association (LBMA)(q.v.). A good delivery bar must contain 350 to 430 troy ounces of gold with a minimum fineness of 995, and must bear the stamp (or 'chop' (q.v.)) of one of the 49 firms world wide who are approved melters and assayers (q.v.). The LBMA also specifies that the bars must be of good appearance and easy to handle and to stack. The good delivery bars are the medium for international trading and the spot gold price itself always relates to these bars.

Good Till Cancelled (GTC)

An order to a broker or a dealer to be held until it can be filled (i.e. by the right price being achieved), or until it is cancelled.

GPC

See **Gold Potassium Cyanide.**

Grab Sample

A sample taken at random, assayed to determine if valuable elements are contained in the rock or lot of material.

Grade

The amount by mass of metal or mineral in an ore, usually expressed as troy ounces per ton (oz/ton) or grammes per tonne (g/tonne) for precious metals and as a percentage or parts per million for other minerals.

(i) *Reserve grade* — estimated grade of an orebody based on the reserve calculation.

(ii) *Cut-off grade* — the lowest grade of mineralised material considered economic. Used in the calculation of ore reserves in a given deposit and for determining waste from ore in mining,

(iii) *Mill (head) grade* — the grade of mined ore going into a mill for processing. Usually lower than reserve grade because of dilution,

(iv) *Recovered grade (yield)* — the actual grade recovered from an ore, determined after processing.

Grain

(i) One of the earliest units of weight for gold; one grain being the equivalent of one grain of wheat taken from the middle of the ear.

1 grain = 0.0648 grammes or 0.002083 troy ounces

15.43 grains = 1 gramme

480.6 grains = 1 troy ounce

24 grains = 1 pennyweight.

(ii) Spherical particles of gold grain widely sold in the jewellery trade for alloying (q.v.); grain alloy is also an initial material for the lost wax casting method (q.v.) The grain is made by pouring molten gold into water, but the grains are not of uniform weight and do not correspond to those in (i) above.

Granulation

The decoration of the surface of jewellery with tiny granules of gold, a technique first perfected by the Etruscans by the seventh century BC.

Gravel Pump

Gravel pumps are used extensively in the recovery of alluvial gold (q.v.) from the beds of rivers in such countries as Bolivia, Brazil, Colombia and Venezuela. The pumps are mounted on small boats, like miniature dredges, and suck through a mixture of medium-sized gravel and water.

Gravity Separation

The separation of gold from waste material by virtue of different densities. Used when gold is free milling (q.v.), such as in alluvial gold recovery. Used at the Howley mine in Australia, operated by Metana Minerals.

Greenstone

A type of compact igneous rock, with high chlorite levels caused through alteration. Commonly associated with auriferous deposits.

Grey Gold

An alloy (q.v.) containing palladium and/or nickel and silver to make it whiter; often called white gold.

Grinding

The final stage of reducing ore to the fineness of flour in grinding mills. *See also* **Mill/Milling.**

Gross Value

A theoretical calculation of the value of gold in an ore, arrived at simply by relating the grade of an assay sample to the current market price. However, since it does not allow for mining, refining costs or losses in those processes, it is the roughest of guides.

Gross Weight

The total weight of a gold bar, coin or shipment of scrap, as opposed to the weight of the fine gold therein. For example, a one ounce gold coin of 916 fine will have a gross weight of 1.092 troy ounces.

Guinea. *George III 'Spade' Guinea, 1798, so called because of the distinctive spade-shaped shield on the reverse*

Guinea

British gold coin with a nominal value of £1, first issued in 1663 and named after gold from Guinea in West Africa 'in the name and for the use of the Company of Royal Adventurers of England trading with Africa'.

The coin was unofficially revalued at £1.1.0d (twenty-one shillings) at the recoinage of 1696, a value confirmed in 1717. The Guinea became the legal tender coin circulating for the next one hundred years and symbolised Britain's shift to the gold standard (q.v.).

Payments in Guineas were largely replaced by notes during the Napoleonic wars; the last was minted in 1813 and in 1817 it was replaced by the Sovereign (q.v.) containing slightly less gold and valued at £1.

Gutter

In alluvial mining (q.v.) the lowest and richest part of the deposit is called the gutter.

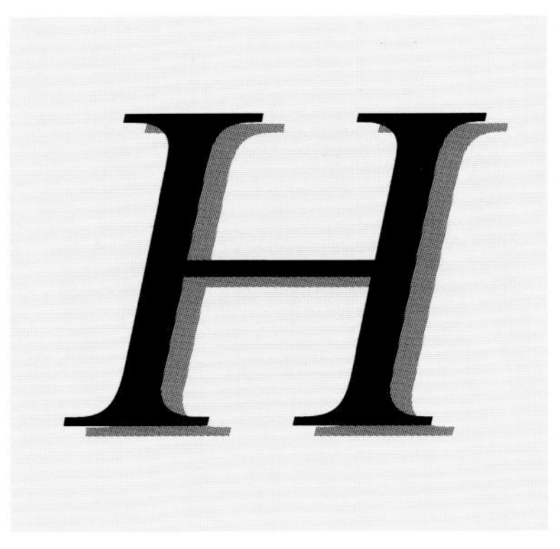

Halbzeug

The German term for semi-fabricated gold products, such as sheet, tube or wire.

Hallmark

A mark, or number of marks, made on gold, silver or platinum jewellery or plate to confirm that its quality is up to the correct legal standard. In much of Europe that would be 18 carat for gold; in Britain the legal standards are 22, 18, 14 and 9 carat. The concept of the hallmark originated in England in the thirteenth century and systematic hallmarking began in 1300. Shortly thereafter it came under the control of the Worshipful Company of Goldsmiths (q.v.) in London, who still operate one of four authorised assay offices hallmarking jewellery in Britain. Indeed, strictly speaking, 'hallmark' means the mark of the Goldsmiths' Hall in London, but the term has taken on a broader connotation. Britain maintains some of the tightest regulations concerning hallmarking. Assay offices (q.v.) in London, Birmingham, Sheffield and Edinburgh check all carat gold production weighing over one gramme and their hallmarks (see box) are a guarantee of consumer protection. In France, every piece of jewellery weighing more than one gramme must be submitted to the Bureau de la Garantie in Paris for checking and stamping. Similarly, all jewellery in Finland, Ireland, Sweden and the Netherlands is monitored by government assay offices.

Elsewhere in Europe, the jewellery industry is left to police itself, each manufacturer is supposed to stamp every item with an identifying mark for his company and the gold content.

Government hallmarking is not exclusively a European preoccupation. The British and the French both introduced it to countries that they administered in colonial days, so offices may be found in Morocco, Egypt, Lebanon and Kuwait, and

***The Sponsor's Mark.** — The initials belong to the article's maker or sponsor*

***The Quality Mark** — certifies the qualityof the gold and indicates its carat quality*

***The Assay Office Mark** — shows where the gold was tested for quality. Birmingham has an anchor; Sheffield a rose; Edinburgh a castle; and London a leopard*

***The Date Letter** — a letter of the alphabet which changes every year and indicates in which year the article was made, e.g. 1986 was an 'M', 1987 an 'N' and 1988 a 'P'*

Hallmark. *Hallmark symbols used at the Assay offices in Britain*

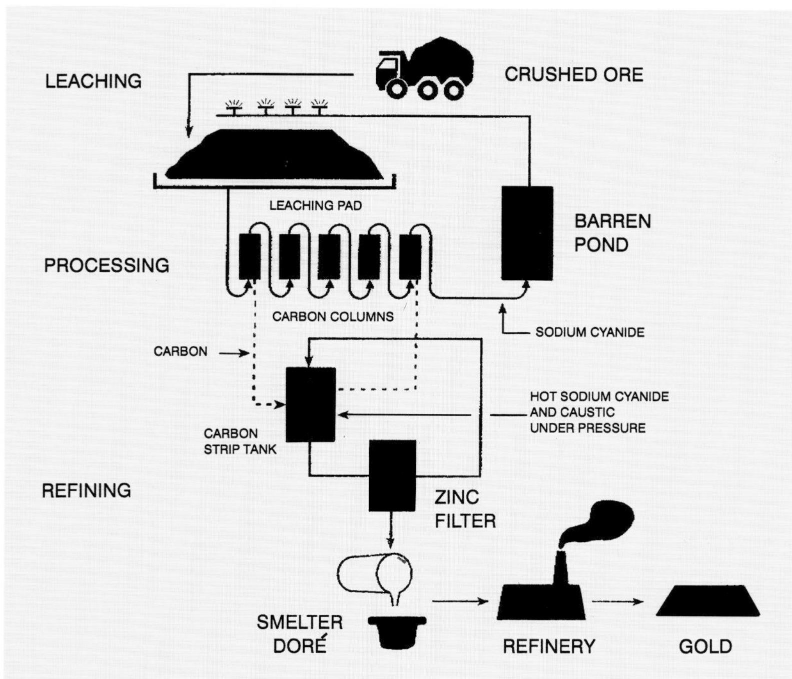

Heap Leaching. *The extraction of gold using heap leaching and carbon recovery*

have opened more recently in Bahrain, Qatar and Singapore.

Handy and Harman

US refiner and semi-fabricator, whose cash gold price is widely used as the 'wholesale' price in the jewellery trade in North America.

Handy and Harman
850 Third Avenue
New York NY 10022
USA
Tel: (212) 752 3400
Fax: (212) 207 2614

Hangingwall

The upper side of an orebody, often the roof of the stope.

Hard Money

Historically this phrase was used to mean, quite literally, money that was hard, like gold or silver, as opposed to paper notes. That term is still used today, especially by the 'hard money' lobby in the United States, spearheaded by the National Committee for Monetary Reform, that would like to bring back gold as the monetary standard. A broader definition now embraces 'hard currency', which comprises such major currencies as the dollar, the Deutschmark, sterling, the Swiss franc and the yen which are seen as 'hard' in comparison with the rapidly depreciating paper of some developing nations and for that reason have the appeal that hard money had in earlier times.

Haulage

Large tunnel in a mine through which ore and waste are removed to the shaft or surface, usually by a diesel or electric locomotive or a conveyor system.

Head and Shoulders

Important pattern in technical analysis (q.v.).

Head Grade

See **Grade.**

Heap Leaching

The successful application of heap leaching to the extraction of gold from low grade deposits was one of the main factors in higher output during the 1980s, especially in the United States. It is a low cost process which extracts a soluble precious metal or copper compound by dissolving the metal content from the crushed ore. Ore is heaped onto open-air leach pads with a base of asphalt or impervious plastic sheeting. A sprinkler system is then laid along the top of the ore pile through which a solution of dilute cyanide is sprayed. The cyanide percolates down through the heap for several weeks, leaching out the gold. This solution, now enriched with gold, drains off the bottom of the pad into what is known as 'the pregnant pond', from which it is pumped to the recovery plant.
Heap leaching of gold was pioneered in the United States in 1973 at Placer Development's Cortez open pit in Nevada, and proved on a larger scale at Pegasus Gold's Zortman Landusky mine in Montana. Although it is low cost, recovery rates average only 65–70 per cent, significantly less than with conventional milling (q.v.). But it has enabled low grade ores, which otherwise might not be economically viable, to be processed. In the United States, where heap leaching is used

Heap Leaching. *Spraying cyanide on leach pads at the Zortman-Landusky mine in Montana*

most extensively, half of all production is won by this method.

Heavy Gold Electroplate

Electroplating (q.v.) on which the gold deposit must be at least 1/10,000th inch thick.

Hedge/Hedging

The strategy of securing against a loss by entering into contracts that balance each other out, or protect from sudden price fluctuations. The main *raison d'être* of forward sales, futures and options is for such protection, whether by a mining company selling output forward or writing put options (q.v.) to protect against a price fall, or a fabricator who will need gold in six months buying a futures contract or call option (q.v.) to insure against a price rise. Hedging, in short, is all about insulation from the variable winds of the market. Hedging techniques using the futures and options markets have become extremely sophisticated. *See also* **Forward Contract; Futures; Options.**

Hemlo

The biggest new gold field discovered in Canada this century is at Hemlo in Ontario, north of Lake Superior. Developed during the 1980s as three mines — David Bell, Golden Giant and Williams — Hemlo produces over 30 tonnes annually. The unique feature of the Hemlo field is that it is a very thin disseminated orebody averaging 9.5 grammes per tonne sandwiched between sedimentary and volcanic rock. Ninety per cent of the reserves are in a single 'horizon' from the surface down to 1,500 metres along a strike length of two kilometres. *See also* **Canada**

Hemlo Gold Mines

The main interest of Hemlo Gold is the Golden Giant mine, one of North

Hemlo. *The headgear and mill of the Williams mine, Canada's largest*

America's largest and lowest cost producers, and one of the three mines in the Hemlo gold camp of Ontario. Gold production in 1989 was 378,379 ounces at a production cost of about US$130 per ounce.
This is well below the industry average, reflecting the high ore reserve grade. Annual production is expected to reach 400,000 ounces over the next few years.

Hemlo Gold Mines
Suite 4500,
Commerce Court West
Toronto, Ontario, M5L 1B6
Canada
Tel: (416) 982-7116
Fax: (416) 982 7423
Telex: 6524231

Heraeus

German refiner and semi-fabricator, founded in 1851; a pioneer in the refining and use of platinum, which remains an important part of its world-wide precious metal activities. In gold, Heraeus manufactures a wide range of jewellery alloys (q.v.) and specialist products in the electronics, decorative and dental fields. Heraeus has a joint-venture refinery, Argor-Heraeus (q.v.), in Switzerland, and precious metal manufacturing facilities in such countries as Belgium, Canada, Australia, Hong Kong, Japan, South Korea, the United Kingdom and the United States.

Heraeus Holdings GmBH
Postfach 1561, D-6450 Hanau
Germany
Tel: (6181) 351
Fax: (6181) 33591
Telex: 415202 - 0 hud

High Grade

(i) In mining, ore which is above the average grade (q.v.) of the mine. High grading is used to mean that the miner is taking out too much high grade ore for a normal, balanced, long-life mining operation. Such high grading took place, for example, in Australia prior to the introduction of a tax on gold mine profits, to maximise output and profits before they were liable for tax. High grading can also mean workers in mines with very high grade deposits or nuggets, stealing chunks of rich ore; this has been a particular problem on some mines in Latin America and the Philippines.

(ii) In refining, precious metal over 800 fine, or sweeps over 200 fine.

Hirohito

A special 20-gramme coin in 999 gold, with a legal tender face value of 100,000 yen but with a gold content worth 40,000 yen, issued by the Japanese government in 1986 to mark the 60th anniversary of Emperor Hirohito's reign.

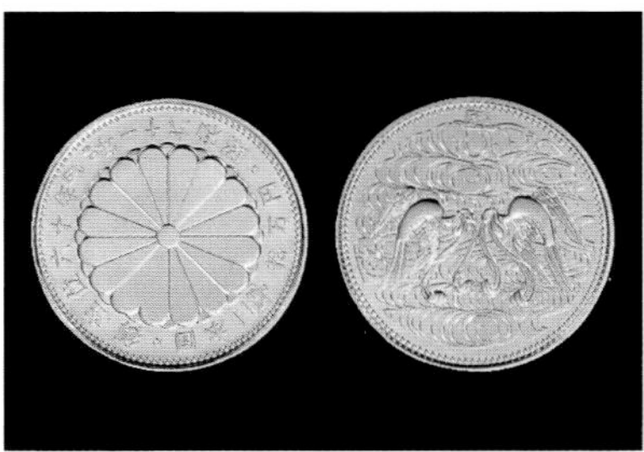

Hirohito. *Ten million of these coins were issued for Emperor Hirohito's 60th anniversary in 1986*

Just over nine million coins containing 182 tonnes of gold were issued initially in 1986, with a further issue of one million coins (including 300,000 proof quality) in 1987.

Cumulative bar hoarding outside Europe and North America

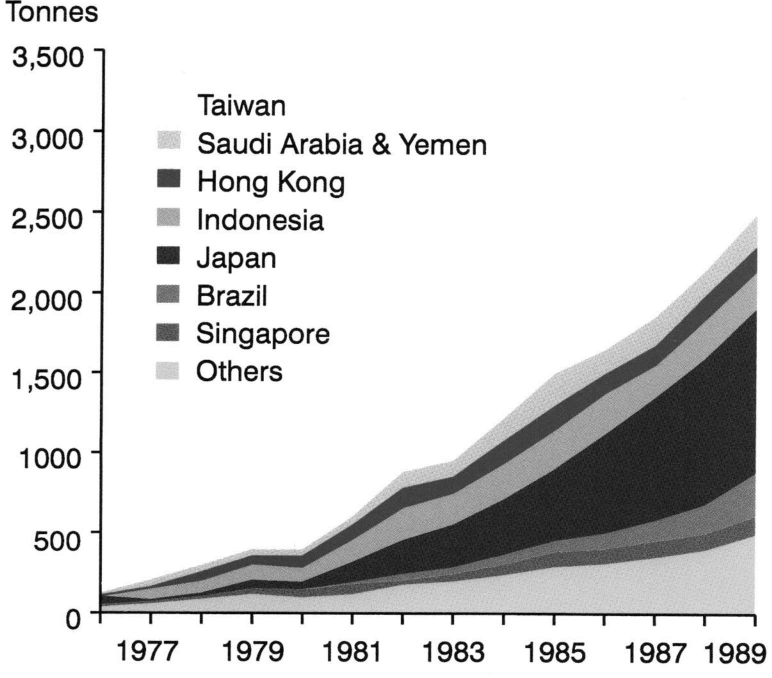

Hoarding. *Source: Gold Fields Mineral Services Ltd, Gold 1990*

Hoarding

The purchase of physical gold, either coins or bars, by private individuals, which is held, often hidden at home, as a safeguard against invasion, or political or economic upheaval. Such hoarding was particularly prevalent in France until the 1980s, especially of Napoleon coins and kilobars; stocks are estimated to exceed 8,000 tonnes. Coin hoarding was also common in Belgium, Greece (mainly Sovereigns), Italy and West Germany. But greater security and economic prosperity brought a sharp decline in European hoarding during the 1980s. Hoarding became focused more on Brazil, the Middle East (especially Saudi Arabia and Yemen), south-east Asia and Japan. Racial minorities in many Asian countries, such as Indonesia, hoard gold as a tangible and universally acceptable medium of exchange. Private bar hoarding usually accounts for between 300 and 500 tonnes of gold annually, but sudden price rises, as in 1980 and 1986, can lead to considerable profit-taking or dishoarding, especially in Asian countries. *See also* **Dishoarding; Souks**.

Hologram

The application of three-dimensional holograms to gold bars has been pioneered and patented by the Pamp refinery (q.v.) in Switzerland. They have successfully decorated their small ingots with coloured holograms. The technique also has important security implications if applied to larger bars, because it could guarantee that they are genuine and would make them tamper-proof.

Homestake Mining

Homestake is one of the oldest mining companies still in operation in the US, formed in 1877. Production of gold in 1989 was a record 1.014 million ounces (31.5 tonnes) and at the end of the year the company had attributable reserves of 14.7 million ounces. The original Homestake mine remains the company's largest gold producer, with an output of 381,788 ounces (11.9 tonnes) in 1989. In Australia the company has an 80 per cent interest in Homestake Gold of Australia, which has a 50 per cent share of the Kalgoorlie operations and contributed 170,187 ounces (5.3 tonnes) of gold in 1989.

Homestake Mining,
650 California Street,
San Francisco,
CA 94108-2788,
U S A.
Tel: (415) 981-8150
Fax: (415) 397-5025
Telex: 230340661

Hong Kong

The city of Hong Kong is a major regional gold market and jewellery manufacturing centre. Gold trading in Hong Kong dates from the foundation of the Gold and Silver Exchange Society (q.v.) in 1910, but it was strictly controlled from 1939 until 1974. Once liberalised it became a significant centre in round-the-clock gold trading because huge volumes on the exchange attracted other international bullion houses to establish essentially a parallel market in loco

Hologram. *Coloured three-dimensional hologram on a Fortuna bar from Pamp refinery in Switzerland*

The pattern of Hong Kong imports 1980–1989

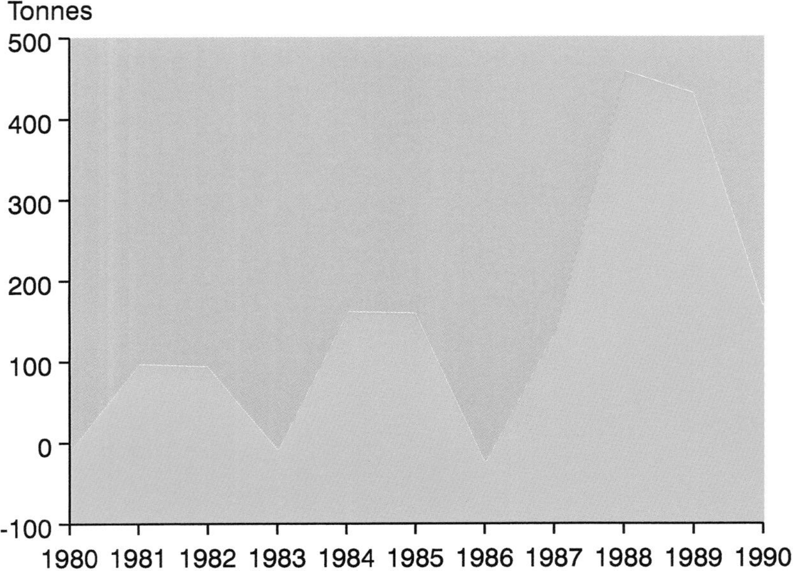

Hong Kong.

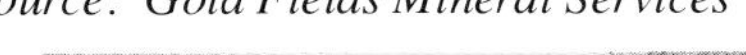
Source: Gold Fields Mineral Services

London during Hong Kong's trading hours. They took advantage of arbitrage between a Hong Kong price quoted in Hong Kong dollars per tael (1 tael = 2.1 ounces) and a London price in dollars per ounce. The international houses do not trade on the Exchange but operate more as wholesalers, dealing in lots of 2,000–4,000 ounces at a time. This alliance between local Chinese traders and the international bullion community made Hong Kong the pacesetter of the early morning price for gold.

Hong Kong is also a physical re-export centre for both tael bars and kilobars for China, South Korea, Thailand, Taiwan and Vietnam. Imports are usually 100 to 250 tonnes a year, but reached a record 460 tonnes in 1988 due to exceptional demand in mainland China and Taiwan. As a producer of jewellery, Hong Kong uses upwards of 50 tonnes annually for gem-set jewellery for Japan and the United States and *chuk kam* (q.v.) or pure gold jewellery for the local population. *See also* **Chuk Kam; Tael.**

Hong Kong Gold and Silver Exchange

(Chinese Gold and Silver Exchange Society Kam Ngan)

The Hong Kong Gold and Silver Exchange was founded in 1910. After free gold imports were permitted (1974) daily trading soared from 40,000 taels to over 1 million. The basic contract is a lot of 100 taels, made up of twenty 5-tael bars each 990 fine. The exchange has 195 members, of whom just over 100 are active, and 33 of the member firms make their own tael bars which are acceptable on the exchange. There is no price 'fix' — it is changing every moment of opening hours.

A unique feature of the exchange is that it imposes no time limit on settlement and thus the exchange is, in effect, an undated futures market. Pressure to settle depends on the

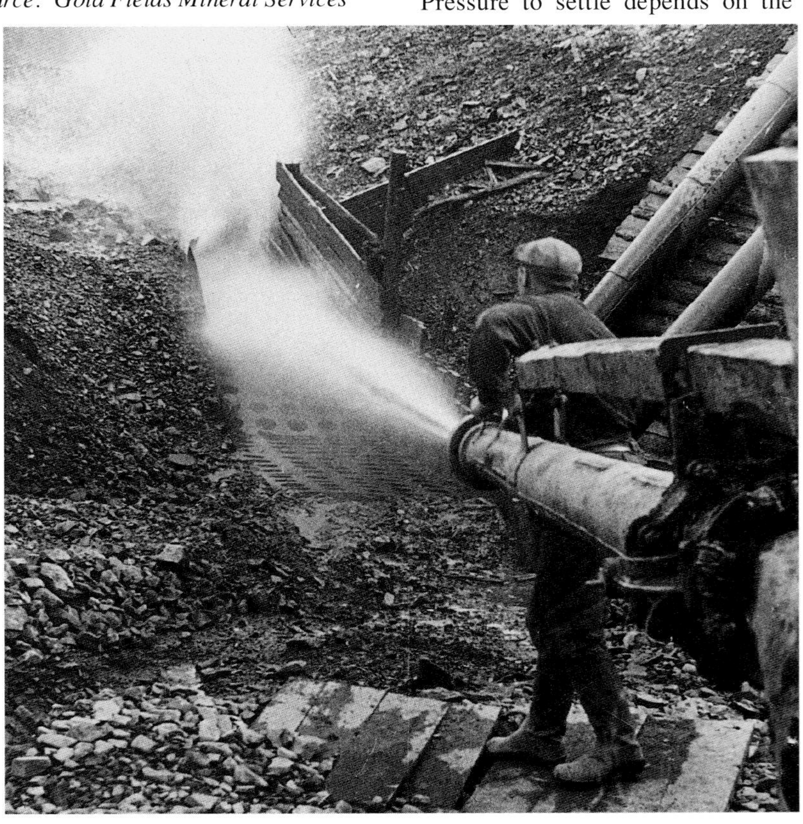

Hydraulic Mining. *High pressure hose breaks up alluvial deposit in the Soviet Union, where much gold is recovered from such sources*

Hong Kong Gold Exchange. *The action on the exchange floor reflects the Chinese love of kam — gold*

'interest factor', fixed daily at 11.30 a.m. (10.30 a.m. Saturdays), and which approximates to the spot price adjusted for physical availability and carrying costs.

Host Rock

The rock in which a deposit of gold or other metal or mineral occurs.

Hydraulic Mining

A surface mining method, often in alluvial (q.v.) deposits or on old dumps, using high-pressure water hoses to remove unconsolidated ore, consisting of sand, gravel and small boulders. Used in the later stages of the Californian gold rush and extensively employed in the 1980s in some South American gold fields, notably on the rivers in Colombia and Venezuela, causing considerable environmental damage.

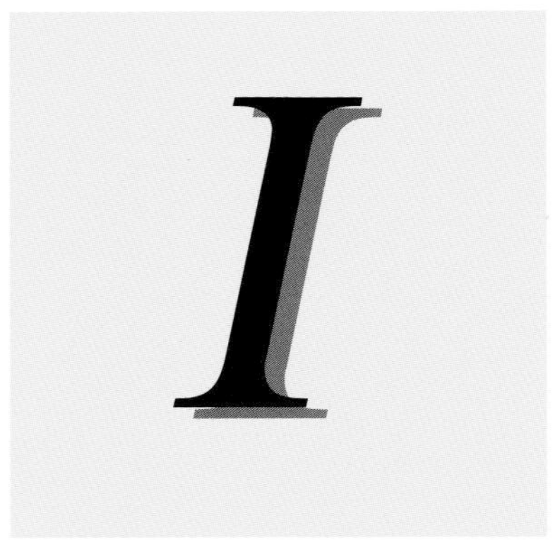

Incline

Also known as a **Raise**. An upward sloping, underground tunnel, providing access for exploration or mining, or connection between levels.

India

For centuries India has been a substantial market for gold and silver with both metals still woven closely into the social fabric of the subcontinent. At least 7,000 tonnes is estimated to be held privately. Gold remains the basic form of saving for the majority of Indian families, especially in the rural areas. Since the holding of bar (primary) gold was forbidden between 1962 and 1990 by the Gold Control Act (q.v.) this is usually in the form of jewellery.
Official gold imports into India have also been forbidden since 1947, except for limited amounts for jewellery made for export. With local production of less than 2 tonnes a year from two small mines, Bharat and Hutti, the main requirement has been met by smuggling. The gold is smuggled, usually in ten tola bars (q.v.), from such regional markets as Dubai, Singapore and Hong Kong. This is a highly organised business involving upwards of 150 tonnes in some years, encouraged by a premium of 30 per cent or more over the London price. Although the gold enters as ten tola bars, the Indian price is normally quoted in rupees per ten grammes.

Bombay is the main trading centre, where the Bombay Bullion Association, founded in 1948, is the trade forum that constantly campaigns for an easing of the regulations surrounding gold. The Bombay Mint is the largest refinery for recycling scrap, together with the Prem Sundari refinery in Calcutta but forty-two other refineries handle scrap informally. Ahmedhabad, Calcutta, Delhi and Madras all have local markets, whose prices often differ from Bombay. India has nearly 16,000 licensed gold dealers and over 400,000 goldsmiths. The annual demand is dictated both by the monsoon, with its effect upon the harvest, and the marriage season. In an auspicious year there may be upwards of ten million marriages, at many of which between 20 and 200 grammes of gold will be worn by the bride. The status of a family in its community is still judged by the gold that is exchanged as the Bride's dowry. The basic marriage 'set' is 2 earrings, 1 nosepin, 1 ring, 1 necklace and 2 bangles, all in 22 carat gold. These may often be made in part from remelting old ornaments already held by the family. Significant amounts of gold are thus recycled within India, but because of the price premium there, it does not

The price margin between Bombay and London

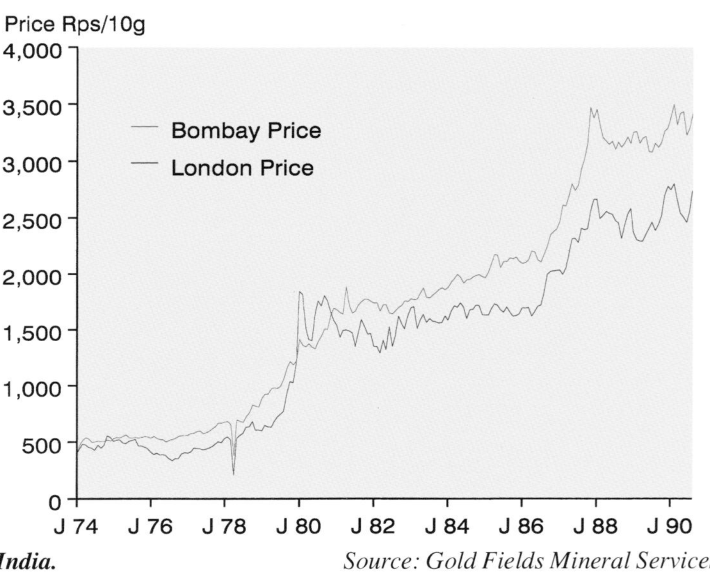

India. *Source: Gold Fields Mineral Services Ltd*

India. *An Indian bride adorned with the customary 22 carat gold ornaments*

circulate back on the international market. Virtually no gold has come out of India since the early 1930s, while from 1960 to 1990 about 2,400 tonnes were smuggled in.

Indonesia

Since the late 1960s, Indonesia, whose population is approaching 200 million people, has developed as a substantial market for physical gold, capable of absorbing upwards of 60 tonnes annually for jewellery and kilobar investment. Indeed, Indonesia has been the prime client of the Singapore gold market (q.v.) since it was launched in 1969. Not only is there considerable movement of gold from Singapore to Indonesia, largely through undeclared channels, but many Indonesian traders also maintain positions in Singapore so that often no actual shipment is necessary; they can buy Jakarta and sell Singapore or vice versa. Normally the price in Jakarta is about 2–3 per cent above the international level but a sudden price surge internationally is often not followed in Indonesia, so that the price there goes to a discount and gold is shipped out. In both 1980 and 1986 Indonesia dishoarded significant amounts of gold.

Within Indonesia there is considerable investment in both kilobars and 100 gramme bars made by the Jakarta refinery Logam Mulia. However, the investment is sporadic and is usually tied to fears of devaluation of the rupiah or political unease prior to elections. Jewellery manufacture, once a cottage industry, is becoming more mechanised, especially in Surabaya, at the east end of Java, where several factories, such as Itama Raya, are equipped with the latest chain making machinery. Given very low labour costs, Surabaya could emerge during the 1990s as a considerable jewellery manufacturing centre for export.

Gold production is also set to rise in Indonesia during the 1990s, from about ten tonnes annually towards twenty tonnes, through the expansion of Freeport's gold/copper mine in West Irian, and the development of epithermal (q.v.) deposits on the island of Kalimantan.

Industrial Scrap

Either scrap (q.v.) that is generated by a jewellery or watch case manufacturer as a natural part of his work — also known as process scrap (q.v.) — or from the scrapping of jewellery or obsolete electronics equipment.

Ingot

Originally from the old English meaning the pouring in or casting of metal in a mould, ingot came to mean the standard good delivery gold or silver bars. Now it is more widely used to describe any marketable bar.

Initial Margin

The initial or first deposit that a client places with his broker or dealer as evidence of good faith against a futures or forward contract (q.v.). This may vary between 5 and 20 per cent. *See also* **Margin.**

Intaglio

A technique for decorating the surface of metal using gold wire which is hammered into, etched or cut into channels in the metal.

International Monetary Fund (IMF)

The IMF was conceived at the Bretton Woods conference in 1944 to promote international monetary cooperation and stability. It opened in Washington DC in 1947. All members originally contributed to the Fund partly in gold or dollars and partly in their own currencies. But during the 1970s the IMF was in the forefront of the drive to demonetise gold. It created its own credit unit, the Special Drawing Rights (SDR), initially defining one SDR as equivalent to 0.888671 grammes of fine gold. This link was later snapped in the effort to end gold as the numeraire of the monetary system, and SDRs were linked instead to a basket of leading trade currencies. The IMF also reduced its own gold stocks from a peak of 4,772 tonnes to 3,217 tonnes partly by letting members buy back their gold and partly by a four year arrangement of monthly auctions started in July 1976. The aim was to reduce gold's role and create a trust fund to provide aid to developing countries. The IMF got an average price of $246 an ounce for 777.6 tonnes auctioned. Further proposals for the IMF to sell more of its gold, usually initiated by the US Treasury, were not approved by members. *See also* **Central Banks.**

International Monetary Market (IMM)

See **Chicago Mercantile Exchange.**

In the Money

An option (q.v.) which could be exercised immediately or cashed at a profit. A call option (q.v.) is in-the-money when the strike price (q.v.) is lower than the current price; a put option (q.v.) is in-the-money if the strike price is higher than the current price. Opposite of Out of the Money (q.v.). The amount by which an option is in-the-money is called its intrinsic value.

Intrinsic Value

In options (q.v.), the intrinsic value is the amount by which the option is in-the-money (q.v.). That is to say, on a call (q.v.) with a strike price (q.v.) of $400 and the current price at $425, the intrinsic value is $25 per ounce. *See also* **Extrinsic Value.**

Inventory

The working stock of a refiner, jewellery manufacturer, wholesaler or bullion dealer. The high cost of carrying gold in such inventories has led to such strategies as leasing (q.v.).

Investment

Investment in gold

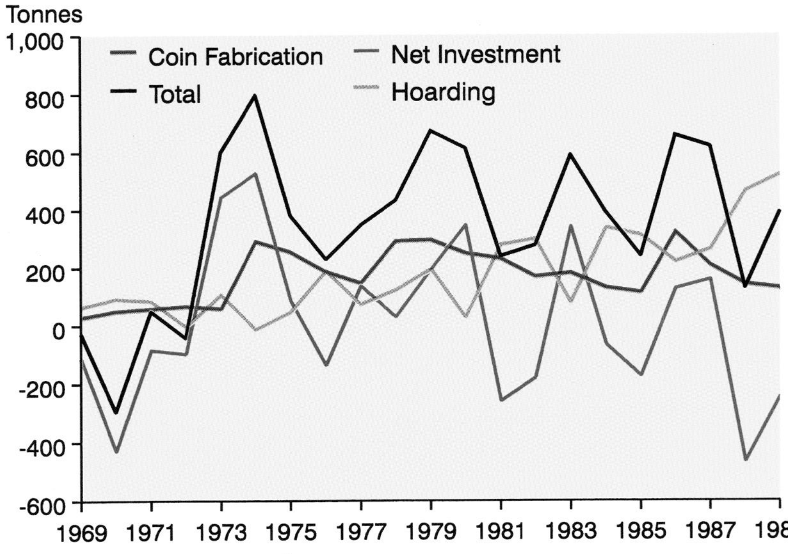

Investment.. *Source: Gold Fields Mineral Services Ltd*

Investment in gold covers a broad spectrum from the purchase of a single gold coin by an individual to portfolio holdings by a government investment institution which may amount to 100 tonnes or more. Investment attitudes to gold also vary considerably from region to region: in Asia it may be physically hoarded (q.v.), in Europe simply held on metal account or as part of a portfolio in a private bank. But of one thing there can be no doubt: since gold's last official link with the dollar and the concept of a fixed price was broken in 1971, it is investment demand which has provided the catalyst, the driving force to propel the gold price to new heights. The more conventional underlying physical demand for jewellery and industry provides at best a floor to the price; the appetite of investors propels it up. And its appeal to them has been enhanced because, for the first time in its history, the price of gold is mobile, no longer fixed. So one can, in theory, invest in gold as a way of making money, and not just, as was the traditional case, as a hedge or insurance against losing it.

The decade of the 1970s, beset by oil shocks, inflation and a weak dollar, seemed to show investors how gold could perform; the compound annual rate of return on gold in the ten years to 1980 was 31.6 per cent, compared with 7.5 per cent for stocks and 6.4 per cent for bonds. Only the performance of Saudi Arabian light oil matched gold.

The 1980s told a different story; gold was $850 an ounce in January 1980 and just less than half that a decade later.

Investment in gold in the last decade of the twentieth century is, consequently, different. First, the concept of physical gold coin or bars held or hoarded by an older generation of Europeans, notably in France and Germany, has disappeared. The political and economic uncertainty of two world wars that made them hold gold has gone. The collapse of the Berlin Wall in 1989 signalled that clearly. Second, the classic portfolio advice of private Swiss banks that up to 10 per cent of a portfolio should be invested in physical gold has given way to a more flexible policy of zero to 15 per cent depending on price expectations. Gold funds (q.v.) in Europe and North America also largely hold gold shares rather than the metal; indeed, the expansion of the gold mining industry in the 1980s gave investors a fresh opportunity for getting to 'gold' by simply buying the shares, diverting away much money that might have gone into the metal a decade earlier. Gold bonds and warrants (q.v.) were also variations of options on gold.

The shift in gold investment has been towards Asia, where a degree of uncertainty still prevails in many societies, coupled with new prosperity and, frequently, not many alternatives to gold for investment. For that reason, Asia has taken up gold investment where Europe left off. Hong Kong, Indonesia, Taiwan and Thailand have plenty of investors. So does Japan, where the concept of financial technology, '*zaiteku*', implied that the Japanese would be as diligent in managing their savings as they had been in making electronic equipment; '*zaiteku*' could include gold. The Japanese bought rather more than 1,000 tonnes of physical gold for investment during the 1980s, plus considerable undeclared holdings loco (q.v.) London. Japanese fire and marine insurance companies have also been permitted to put up to 3 per cent of their portfolios in gold since 1989, on the grounds that if Japan were struck by a major earthquake, it might so damage the local industries in which they were heavily invested that gold would be a useful insurance asset for such a crisis; the classic reason, of course, for buying gold.

The traditional investment attitudes to gold persist, therefore, in Asia, but much less in Europe and North America. There the investor who is interested in gold has become much more a short term speculator, trading in and out of the gold market on metal account (q.v.) or using futures (q.v.) and options (q.v.) which offer a foothold in gold without actually having to take delivery. That is the key to the investors' approach; they still like the idea of benefiting from a price rise, but they no longer need to have the metal at home under the bed. *See also* **Dishoarding; Hoarding; Gold Funds; Bonds; Futures; Options.**

Investment Casting

Also called precision casting or lost-wax process. *See* **Lost Wax Casting.**

Ishifuku Metal Industry Co. Ltd

Leading Japanese refiner and semi-fabricator, founded in 1929, whose bars have acceptable good delivery (q.v.) status in the London market. Ishifuku specialise in jewellery fabrication, wholesale and retail, and dental gold.

Ishifuku Metal Industry Co. Ltd
20-7 Uchikanda 3-chome,
Chiyoda-ku , Tokyo 101
Tel: (3) 252 3131
Fax: (3) 252 3143
Telex: 26175

Italy

Italian jewellery exports by region, 1989

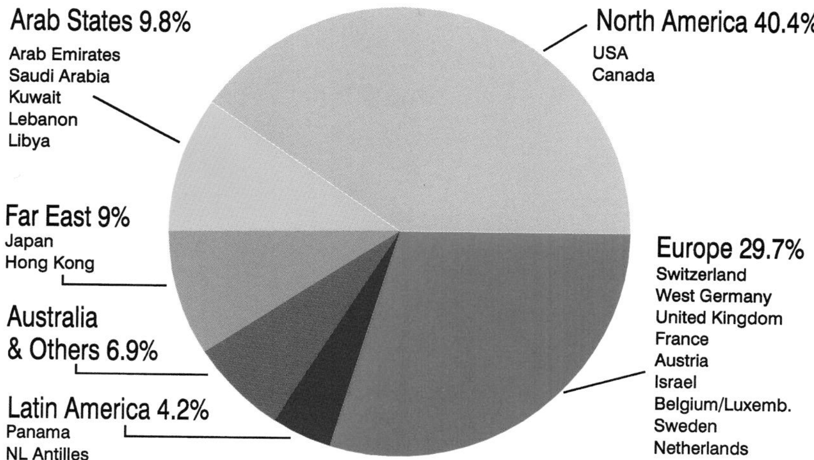

Italy. *Source: L'Orafo Italiano*

Italy is the foremost manufacturer and exporter of mass-produced carat gold jewellery. The fabrication is centred on four communities — Arezzo, Bassano del Grappa, Valenza and Vicenza — while the wholesalers are mainly located in Milan. In particular, Italy has pioneered machine-made chain through such companies as Uno-a-Erre, Arezzo, and Balestra in Bassano del Grappa. The industry regularly consumes between 200 and 300 tonnes of fine gold per year, with a record 345 tonnes in 1989. Up to 70 per cent of the jewellery is exported, with the United States as the biggest export destination. The scale of regular gold demand in Italy meant that it was one of the first markets in which the leasing (q.v.) or borrowing of gold by industry was developed, it being cheaper to borrow gold for a working inventory than to borrow money to buy gold. Much Italian production is also done *conto lavoro* (q.v.), or working account, in which gold is supplied to the manufacturer by a wholesaler, often abroad, and he is paid only the making charges. Major trade fairs are held at Vicenza in January and June. Details from:

Ente Fiera Vicenza
CP 805 , I-36100 Vicenza, Italy
Tel: (0444) 969 111;
Fax: (0444) 563954;
Telex: 481542 FIERVII

See also **Chain; *Conto Deposito*; Jewellery.**

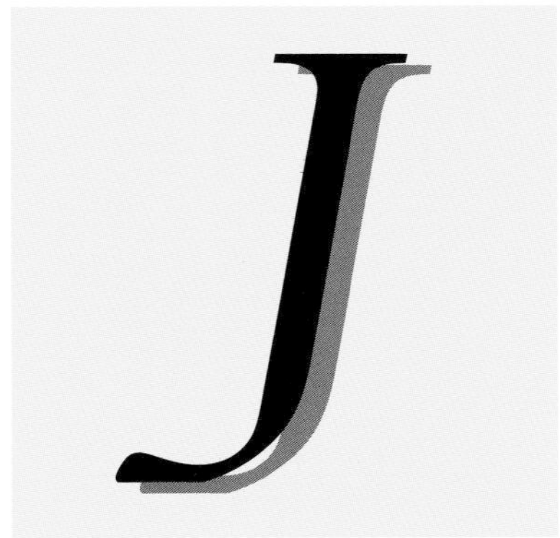

Japan

Japan has evolved as a major market for gold for fabrication and investment since trading was liberalised in 1974, but the gold business in Japan has much earlier origins. Tanaka Kikinzoku Kogyo, the leading precious metal trader and refiner, was established in 1885, and Tokuriki Honten, another important refiner and fabricator, traces its history back to 1727.

Actual mine production is limited. The only significant mine is Sumitomo Metal Mining's Hishikari on Kyushu island, opened in 1985. Hishikari is an exceptionally high-grade operation, with many areas grading over 100 grammes per tonne, though the average grade mined is around 50 grammes, to yield 5 to 6 tonnes annually.

The Japanese market, therefore, is supplied by imports of bullion. This is handled by the three traders/refiners, Tanaka K.K., Tokuriki Honten and Ishifuku Metal Industry, together with the trading companies Sumitomo, Mitsubishi, Mitsui, Marubeni and Nissho-Iwai. Japan ranks fourth in overall fabrication of gold for jewellery and industry, but first in gold use in electronics and in dentistry. The Japanese government also introduced special coin issues in 1986, with the Hirohito coin (q.v.) to commemorate the Emperor's sixtieth anniversary using 182 tonnes of gold. It is also the custom in Japan for companies to make gifts of 24 carat ornaments such as teapots, saki cups, vases and chopsticks. The golden tea ceremony room in the Moa Art Museum in Shizuoka province employed 50 kilos of gold for teapots and cups, plus gold leaf for the walls. Physical gold investment has also grown, often taking up between 100 and 200 tonnes annually. Gold has been subject to 3 per cent value added tax since April 1989, which has encouraged some investors to switch to loco London holdings. Investors and speculators have also made increasing use of the Tokyo Commodities Exchange (TOCOM)(q.v.) 1 kilo gold futures contract, first launched in 1982.

Gold fabrication in Japan, 1989

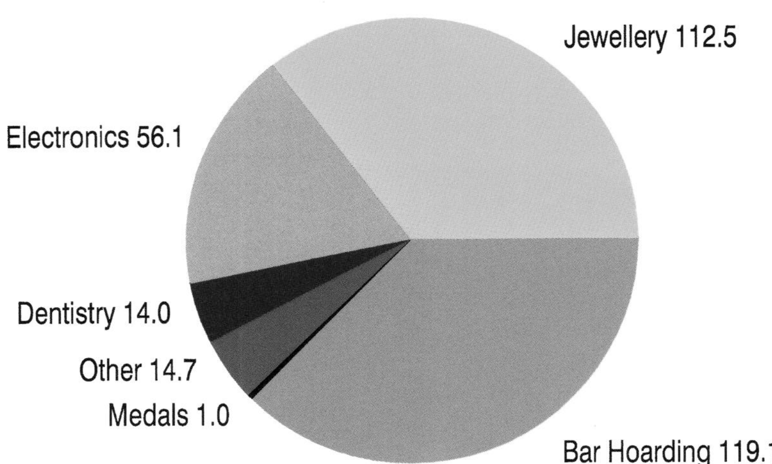

Japan. *Source: Gold Fields Mineral Services Ltd*

Jeweller's Rouge

Also called **plate powder**. Trade term for red ferric oxide, which is used in the polishing of gold and other precious metals.

Jewellery

From the very first discoveries of gold along the rivers of Africa and Asia the sheer ease with which the metal could be worked inspired craftsmen to shape it for adornment. Gold's versatility, besides its beauty, recommended it above all other metals. It was so malleable that it could

Japan. *Tea ceremony room at Moa Art Museum in Japan, decorated with 50 kilos of gold for utensils and gold leaf on the walls*

Japan. *Gifts in 24 carat gold at the Yamazaki store on Ginza in Tokyo*

be hammered cold into a thin translucent wafer, so ductile it could be drawn into thin wires making delicate chain (q.v.) and filigree (q.v.) work possible from earliest times. Its colour and sheen naturally equated it with the sun, while its incorruptibility (which makes the dating of early gold jewellery difficult) made it a symbol of permanence. Wearing it was also a symbol of wealth and power.

That is the major difference between jewellery ancient and modern. Today jewellery is a mass-market product and as such consumes most newly-mined gold. Between 1970 and 1990 about 65 per cent of all gold coming to the market went into jewellery fabrication; in peak years such as 1989, 96 per cent of all newly-mined gold was for jewellery.

That is nothing new; gold was made into jewellery long before it was used as money. The earliest gold jewellery, which dates from the Sumer civilisation flourishing between the Tigris and Euphrates rivers in southern Iraq around 3000 BC, was widely worn by both men and women.

The range has astonished archaeologists who discovered the treasure in the Royal Tombs at Ur. Besides a king's gold helmet of great elegance decorated in impeccable repoussé technique, and a queenly headress of golden beech leaves very naturalistically rendered, were earrings, bracelets and 'foxtail' chains (a style still widely used today). 'Sumerian jewellery fulfilled practically all the functions which were to occur during the course of history', observed the jewellery historian, Guido Gregorietti. 'In fact there were more different types of jewellery than there are today.' The goldsmith's repertoire of skills advanced rapidly. The Egyptians understood fire assaying (q.v.) to test the purity of gold, mastered the art of alloying (q.v.) with other metals for hardness or colour variations, and casting, including the lost-wax technique (q.v.), which remain at the heart of much

Jewellery. *Necklace from the Minoan civilisation in Crete, dates from 1700 BC; reveals exceptional gold work*

Jewellery. *Superbly chased gold funeral mask of Agamemnon found by Schliemann at Mycenae, dated from 1200 BC*

Jewellery. *Gold necklace from the catacombs of Tillia-Tépé in Afghanistan dating from the 6th century BC*

Jewellery. *Tenth century crown for the holy Roman emperor, from the workshop of the Abbey of Reichenau*

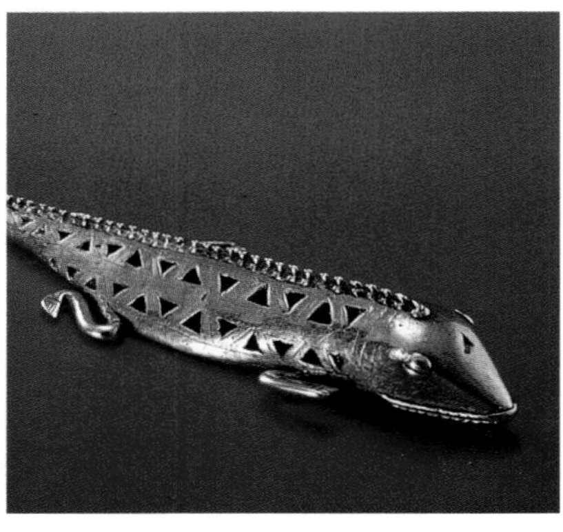

Jewellery. *An alligator shows the high quality craftsmanship achieved in Pre-Columbian Peru by the 12th century*

Jewellery. *Ashante goldwork from the 16th to the 19th centuries was primarily to indicate rank among the ruling class*

jewellery manufacture. Their achievements were preserved in the tomb of King Tutankhamun (q.v.), who died in 1352 BC. The treasure of that tomb with its necklaces, pectorals, earrings and the astonishing mask of solid gold, beaten and burnished over the head of Tutankhamun's mummy, was described by the archaeologist Howard Carter when he first glimpsed it as 'wonderful things'. Technical accomplishment proceeded with the Minoans on Crete producing the first known cable chain, another staple in modern catalogues, and the Etruscans in Italy perfecting granulation (q.v.) in which thousands of tiny grains of gold were used to outline and silhouette animal and human figures, giving a feeling of texture and light.

The Romans, however, ushered in a different phase: the love of gems and coloured stones. Until then gold itself had been the essence of jewellery. Roman goldsmiths applied it as a setting and framing for brilliant and valuable stones. Byzantine jewellery, too, which followed in the early Christian era was characterised largely by jewels embellished with coloured enamels, pearls and precious stones. Jewellery also became incorporated into the symbolism of the dominion of the Christian church and the growing power of kings. For much of the Dark and Middle Ages goldsmiths' talents served church and state.

Renewed joy in extravagant personal adornment came only with the Renaissance, with the rediscovery by wealthy Italian patrons of ancient art and jewellery just at the moment when Spain was finding fresh sources of gold in South America. Renaissance goldsmiths such as Caradosso and Cellini (q.v.) achieved a prestige equal to that acquired by the artists and sculptors of the age. The gold that Spain acquired, however, was at the expense of the great heritage of Pre-Columbian (q.v.) jewellery. As far back as 1200 BC the Chavin civilisation in Peru was making ornaments by hammering and embossing

Regional jewellery fabrication

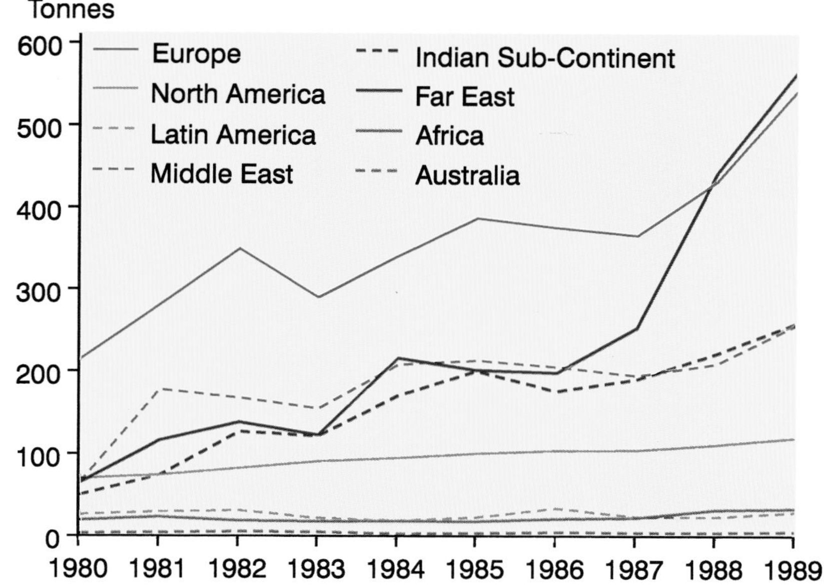

Jewellery. *Source: Gold Fields Mineral Services Ltd*

gold. The technique of casting was developed between 500 BC and AD 500 by the Nazca society in southern Peru. Technical skills reached their height during the Chimu Empire between AD 1150 and 1450. Chimu goldsmiths understood alloys, welding, plating, filigree and the lost wax process. Most of this incomparable work went into the melting pot for Spain, but the calibre of what was lost may be judged in the unique collection of Pre-Columbian objects in the Museo del Oro (q.v.) in Bogota.

Goldsmiths in South America and around the Mediterranean developed their craft completely unknown to each other in very different cultures, yet both the techniques and the concept of the richness of gold paralleled each other.

The Renaissance delight in gold jewellery was eclipsed in the seventeenth century by the improvement in the cutting and polishing of precious stones and a flow of diamonds from India brought back to Amsterdam and London by the Dutch and British East India companies. Gold again became the setting. The goldsmith's art was flourishing, however, on the Gold Coast of west Africa, in what is now Ghana. The Gold Coast was not just a prime source of gold but of goldwork by the Ashanti people from the sixteenth to the nineteenth centuries. Their 'jewellery', however, was not created for the adornment of women but to designate the rank of the ruling class.

In Europe it was not until the nineteenth century that the real transformation back to gold jewellery took place, through the combined influence of early mechanisation of such processes as chain-making and the huge increase in gold supplies brought about by the Californian, Australian and South African gold discoveries. What had previously been an exceptionally rare metal, largely the prerequisite of kings and princes, was suddenly in abundance. So was the technology to mass produce. The art of the goldsmith working for a wealthy patron, however, did have a final crescendo in the creations of Carl Fabergé (q.v.) for the Russian Czars. Moreover, the new industrial middle class of Europe and the United States provided a growing market for the jewellery. Gold wedding rings, for the first time, became commonplace.

Thus the story of gold jewellery in the twentieth century is primarily one of an ever-widening market for something that had previously been a restricted luxury. As gold was gradually phased out as a monetary metal (most still went into coin at the beginning of the century), so an alternative popular use was created, just as silver found salvation in its use in film for popular photography.

Technology has done the rest, especially in Italy (q.v.) where the creation of large factories with hundreds of chain machines has given a fresh impetus to gold consumption. Italy uses annually over 300 tonnes of gold for jewellery; world-wide annual fabrication is over 1,500 tonnes. Compare that with the 750 tonnes of gold mined in the entire one hundred years prior to 1850 and the new dimension of jewellery is apparent. The gold mining industry alone spends close to $50 million annually through the World Gold Council (q.v.) to promote jewellery in the competitive world of fashion, perfume and other consumer goods.

The rush to mass production, however, has not changed one historic feature of the goldsmiths' trade. Craftsmen still congregate in a few towns and villages like Arezzo, Bassano del Grappa, Valenza or Vicenza in Italy, Pforzheim in Germany, Birmingham in England, Attleboro, Massachusetts and Providence, Rhode Island in the United States and Valencia in Spain, where the craft tradition may go back centuries. In the Middle East most goldsmiths, although often dispersed now, were born in Aleppo in Syria, a centre of excellence since before the birth of Christ. Even in Indonesia, craftsmen may be tracked down to towns like Surabaya at the eastern end of Java.

Jewellery. *An 18 carat gold brooch decorated with small pearls, by the Finnish designer Björn Weckström*

Jewellery. *Braided necklace in 18 carat gold, weighing 100 grammes, by the American designer Henry Dunay*

Jewellery. *Necklace in 18 carat gold, weighing 68 grammes, by the British designer David Thomas*

Jewellery. *Necklace, bracelet, ring and earrings by the Italian design team Adriano Guandalini and Geetana Otto-Bruc*

Perceptions of jewellery, however, still vary widely. In most industrial nations gold jewellery is bought essentially as a fashion item for adornment and the customer usually pays a mark-up of between 200 and 400 per cent over the gold content for jewellery of 8, 9, 10, 14 or 18 carats (q.v.).

In the Middle East, the Indian subcontinent, and most of Asia, by contrast, the investment motive is equally important. The jewellery will be high carat, anything from 21 to 23 carat, bought on a low premium of no more than 10–20 per cent over the gold price of the day. This 'investment' jewellery is often part of a dowry at marriage. Where a western bride may have a four gramme gold ring in 14 or 18 carat gold, an eastern bride may be laden with at least 100 grammes and often a kilo or more of ornaments of almost pure gold. Good harvests anywhere from India to Thailand will be translated into a rising demand as farmers put their profits into gold jewellery. In Hong Kong the fashion is for *chuk kam* (q.v.), almost pure gold ornaments. Jewellery displays cascading down the windows of whole streets of shops in the 'souks', the markets of the Middle East, emphasise how much gold remains part of the social fabric of these countries; the gold souk becomes a social centre for whole families in the evenings. The measure of Asia's role in gold jewellery is that consumption more than tripled in the 1980s and over 60 per cent of all jewellery is made and bought there. Indeed, in a period when investment (q.v.) in gold declined, the expansion in jewellery shouldered the burden of rapidly increasing mine production. The future prosperity of the gold mining industry depends very much on it continuing so to do.

Johannesburg Consolidated Investments

JCI was founded over one hundred years ago and has developed into a leading South African mining house.

Although the company's interests are widely diversified, the company is dependent on a limited number of large holdings, including Rustenburg, Randfontein, H. J. Joel, the Premier Group and Consolidated Metallurgical Industries. Gold accounted for 3.2 per cent of net assets in 1990 and Randfontein, its largest producer, had an output of 27.88 tonnes in the year to June 1990.

Johannesburg Consolidated Investments
Cnr Fox & Harrison Streets
Johannesburg 2001
(P O Box 590, Johannesburg 2000)
South Africa
Tel: (011) 373-9111
Fax: (011) 836 6130
Telex: 483787

Johnson Matthey plc

Johnson Matthey began as refiners in Hatton Garden, London, in 1817, although the Johnson family were assayers of precious metals as early as the 1750s. They have evolved into a world-wide network of metallurgical companies engaged in the refining and semi-fabrication of precious metals; they control seven refineries, two in Australia and one in Belgium, Canada, Italy, the United Kingdom and the United States. Johnson Matthey Bankers was one of the original five members of the London bullion market, but in 1984 was taken over by the Bank of England and eventually bought by Mase-Westpac after difficulties with its loan book.

Johnson Matthey plc
78 Hatton Garden
London EC1
Tel: (071) 269 8000
Fax: (071) 269 8133
Telex: 267711

Joint Venture

A mineral exploration programme, or mine operation, funded by two or more parties.

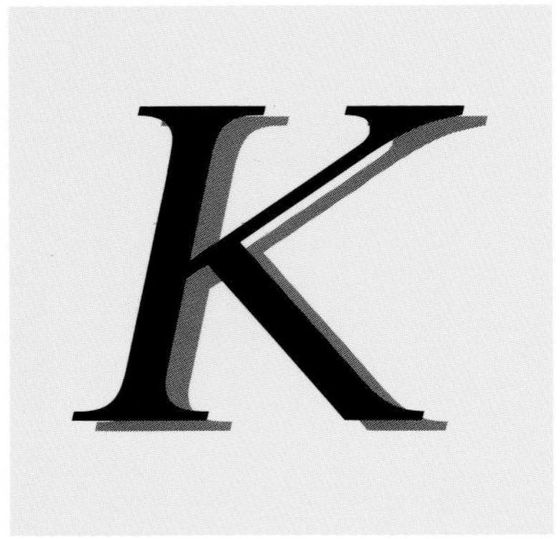

Kam

Chinese for gold. The Chinese have long revered gold for its durability and as a symbol of wealth and immortality. Proverbs abound. '*Jan kam butt par hung lo for*' means 'Real gold is not afraid of the fire of a real furnace.' '*Kam ngan moon oak*' means 'Gold and silver is everywhere in the house.' *See also* **Hong Kong Gold And Silver Exchange,***and* **Chuk Kam.**

Karat, Karat Gold

See **Carat.**

Kim Thanh. *These bars circulated widely in South-East Asia until the Vietnam war in the 1970s*

Key Reversal

In technical analysis (q.v.), a crucial change in price direction signalling, perhaps, the end of a bear market.

Kilobar

A 1.00 kg bar of fine gold, widely traded in the Middle East and South-East Asia. A 995 fine gold bar (Turkey) comprises 31.990 troy ounces, a 999 bar, 32.119 troy ounces and a 999.9 bar, 32.148 troy ounces.

Kim-Thanh

The wafer-like bars of Kim-Thanh, refiners and bullion dealers in Saigon, Hong Kong, Hanoi and Pnompenh, were widely known throughout South-East Asia before and during the Vietnam war and were used by many refugees and boat people from Vietnam and Kampuchia as the sole means of taking some of their savings with them. They are 990 fine and weigh 550 grammes.

Klondike

The site of the Canadian gold rush, 1896. *See* **Canada.**

Krugerrand

A 916.7 legal tender coin with no declared face value, minted in South Africa since 1967, containing exactly one troy ounce of fine gold (actual weight 1.09 ounces). The Krugerrand pioneered the concept of the bullion coin (q.v.); as it contained precisely one ounce of gold, its price could be related directly to the gold price. It was sold initially to distributors at a 3 per cent mark-up over the gold price. Aided by an active marketing campaign, the Krugerrand achieved wide circulation in the 1970s, particularly in West Germany and the United States. Smaller ½, ¼ and 1/10th troy ounce coins were also introduced. World-wide marketing of the coin ceased after 1984 because of economic sanctions against the marketing of South African goods but minting for the home (South African) market continued. Over 44 million Krugerrands have been minted and there is an active secondary market in which they trade at a little over the spot price of gold.

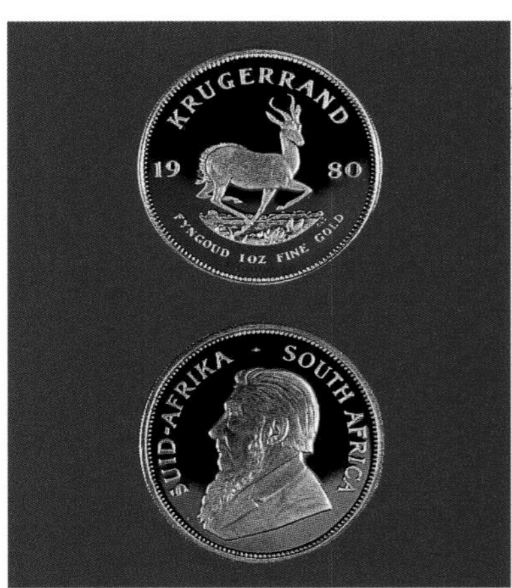

Krugerrand. *The pioneering bullion coin from South Africa, of which over 40 million were sold world wide*

LAC Minerals

LAC Minerals is a major North American gold producer and is also active in other metals in other parts of the world. The company's five current gold operations produced 370,875 ounces (11.5 tonnes) of gold in 1989, and are centred on the Cadillac belt of north-western Quebec and in the Kirkland Lake belt of north-eastern Ontario. The largest mine operated by LAC is the 50 per cent owned Doyon mine which produced 234,690 ounces (7.3 tonnes) in 1989. LAC also holds a 65 per cent interest in Bond International Gold, another significant gold producer. LAC is expected to yield an attributable 1.1 million ounces (34 tonnes) of gold per year by 1991.

LAC Minerals
Royal Bank Plaza
21st Floor, North Tower
P O Box 156
Toronto, Ontario
Canada M5J 2J4
Tel: (416) 865 0722
Fax: (416) 865 9597

Lakh

Indian term for one hundred thousand (100,000); frequently used to describe gold or silver orders of 100,000 ounces.

Last Trading Day

The last day on which an option of given maturity or a futures contract for delivery in a specific month may be traded. On COMEX (q.v.) this is four business days before the last calendar day. All open positions must be fulfilled by the close of trading on the last trading day.

Layback

Also known as **cutback**. The amount of waste which must be mined for the slope of a pit wall to be at a safe angle. *See also* **Stripping Ratio.**

Layered Metal

A layer of gold (or silver) as a finishing surface on a base metal; it may be applied by electroplating (q.v.) or gold fill (q.v.).

Leaching

A method used for the recovery of precious metals from certain types of ores and scraps, such as dissolving gold from an insoluble matrix using cyanide solution. *See also* **Heap Leaching.**

Lead

In alluvial mining (q.v.), a lead is a deep deposit of gold bearing gravel, often covered by rock or lava.

Leader

An auriferous quartz vein.

Leasing

This term is sometimes applied to central banks' gold deposits (q.v.) with the market, but more usually covers the leasing of gold by banks and bullion dealers to jewellery manufacturers and other professional users of gold to provide part of their working stock. A jewellery manufacturer, for example, needs a considerable inventory of gold while making and marketing new articles and it is cheaper for him to borrow gold rather than money. Gold leasing rates to the jewellery trade will usually be 4–5 per cent, perhaps half or less the cost of money. Many bullion dealers have developed special programmes for their jewellery customers, seeing it as part of the service they should provide to regular consumers; they may even lease a kilo or less.

Leasing also protects the borrower against market risk; e.g. a jeweller can borrow gold, make his product, then buy the gold on the same price basis as he sells the finished item.

Legal Tender

Officially minted coins which may be submitted as 'legal tender' as a medium of exchange for any payment for their face value. Under the gold standard (q.v.), a coin such as the Sovereign (q.v.) was legal tender payment for £1, its face value, or a US Double Eagle (q.v.) for $20.

On modern legal tender coins the declared face value is normally less than their gold content; the US Eagle one ounce bullion coin has a face value of $50, but it contains more than six times that value in gold, so it is not likely to be used in payment for a $50 charge. By contrast the Japanese Hirohito coin (q.v.) has 100,000 yen face value (which it costs to buy) but contains only 40,000 yen in gold. It may be used for 100,000 yen payment.

Level

The workings or tunnels of an underground mine which are on the same, (almost) horizontal plane.

Leverage

In both futures (q.v.) and options (q.v.) markets, the buyer has enormous 'financial muscle' or leverage because he has only to pay a small initial margin (q.v.) to secure the contract. In futures, initial margin may be less than 10 per cent; in options, the premium (q.v.) is only a fraction of the total value of the underlying gold. Thus buyers of futures and options can build up large positions without having to commit substantial amounts of capital to cover the total exposure.

LIFO

An accounting term, used in the valuing of precious metals, meaning 'last in, first out'. Opposite of **FIFO** (q.v.).

Limit Move

The maximum fluctuation in price in a day's trading session permitted on some futures exchanges, leading to the phrase 'limit up' (on a rise) or 'limit down' (on a fall). COMEX (q.v.) had a limit of $25 but this has been removed. On TOCOM, the daily limit move is 80 yen per gramme.

Limit Order

An order which specifies a price at which a broker (q.v.) or dealer should buy or sell gold; this compares with a market order (q.v.) to buy or sell at the price the moment the order is received. *See also* **Stop-Loss.**

Liquidation

Closing out or getting out of a futures market or options position.

Liquid Gold

Liquid gold, or liquid bright gold, is widely used in the decoration of ceramics and glass, particularly perfume bottles, and also has special applications in aerospace and electronics.

Liquid Gold. *A bright film of 22 carat gold adorns a Limoges plate*

Liquid gold was first manufactured by the technical manager of the Royal Porcelain Factory at Meissen in Saxony in the early 1830s, but the formula for mixing gold powder in suspension with natural oils and chemicals was kept secret until 1851 when a patent was taken out. Degussa (q.v.), the German precious metals group, started liquid gold production in 1879, and shortly afterwards shared its knowledge with Johnson Matthey (q.v.) in Britain. From 1905 Engelhard Industries (q.v.), Hanovia Liquid Gold division, became the main supplier for the American market. These three companies have always dominated production, which requires about ten tonnes of fine gold annually.

A typical liquid gold solution may contain between 4 and 12 per cent gold dissolved from granules with as many as forty ingredients including natural oils from lavender and balsams, natural resins and organic acids. Hundreds of formulae exist, depending on the precise needs of the decorator. The liquid gold may be applied to ceramics and glass by manually brushing, screen printing or spraying. The object is then heated in air to burn off the organic components, leaving behind a thin 'bright' film of 22 carat gold. While used primarily in the ceramics and glass industries, liquid gold is also applied to glazing tiles or bricks for the outside of buildings. The most notable was the Richfield building in Los Angeles, which had a ceramic veneer finished with liquid gold.

Gold's efficiency as a reflector of heat and infra-red radiation has led to liquid gold being used to reduce heat transmissions from aircraft engines and in the US Apollo space programme, in which reflective gold-coated plastic film was wrapped around parts of the lunar landing module and the moon buggy to protect sensitive parts from solar radiation.

Liquid Market

A market in which selling and buying can be easily accomplished because of many participants willing and able to trade substantial quantities of gold at small price differences. COMEX (q.v.) is a prime example of a futures market whose gold contract has thrived precisely because of a world-wide clientele trading there and providing huge turn-over and thus liquidity. By contrast attempts to launch gold futures contracts in London and Singapore never took off because of a lack of interest and hence liquidity. But in spot gold the fixing (q.v.) in London is an example of a liquid market in which large volumes can normally be done at a single price.

Loans, Gold

See **Gold Loans.**

Local

An independent trader on a futures market who is trading on his own account.

Lock-up

A phrase in refining to indicate the precious metals which form part of the permanent inventory, being tied up in electrolytic circuits and other processes.

Loco

The place at which gold is physically held and to which a particular price applies. The prime example is loco London gold, which means not only that the gold is held in London, but that the price quoted is for delivery there. Many banks and bullion dealers quote a loco London price automatically, and many institutions keep part at least of their position loco London (Japanese investors have done this to avoid local sales tax since April 1989). International bullion houses located in Hong Kong (q.v.) make a parallel market in loco London gold to the Hong Kong Gold and Silver Exchange during trading hours there.

The description does not apply exclusively to London. Gold may be quoted loco Zurich, New York, Tokyo (and considerable effort has been made to start a distinct market in loco Tokyo gold) or any other centre.

Lode/Lode Deposit

A large mineral deposit in which the metal is either disseminated throughout the orebody, or is in a widespread network of narrow veins.

London Bullion Market Association (LBMA)

The London Bullion Market Association was established in late 1987 to represent the interests of the participants in the wholesale bullion market. The Association monitors its members' adherence to a Code of Conduct covering such matters as confidentiality, market ethics, inducements and conflicts of interest. It has also assumed the functions previously performed by the London Gold Market (and the London Silver Market) in connection with the technical aspects of deliverable material, the rules governing application for inclusion in the list of acceptable Melters and Assayers and the codification of market practices as far as clearing and settlement are concerned. Membership is open to those companies and other organisations which are actively engaged in trading, refining, melting, assaying, transporting and/or vaulting gold (and/or silver) within or with or for persons in the UK and is made up of two classes: Market Making Member and Ordinary Member. There are 11 Market Making Members, who quote prices for buying and selling gold (and silver) throughout each working day, and 53 Ordinary Members. *See also* **Good Delivery Bar; London Good Delivery List; Fixing; Mocatta & Goldsmid; Mase-Westpac; N. M. Rothschild; Samuel Montagu; Sharps Pixley.**

London Bullion Market Association
6 Frederick's Place
London EC2R 8BT
Tel: (071) 796 3067
Fax:(071) 796 4345

London Good Delivery List

A list of acceptable smelters and assayers of gold whose bars meet the required standard (of fineness, weight, marks and appearance) of the London Bullion Market Association. There are forty-nine organisations on the current list, from twenty-one countries.

London Price

See **Fixing.**

Long

A long position or 'going long' means the purchase of gold, whether on metal account (q.v.) or in terms of futures (q.v.) and options (q.v.), normally in the expectation that the price will rise. It can also mean anyone, such as a refiner or jewellery manufacturer, with unhedged inventory. The opposite of **short**(q.v.).

Longwall Mining

A mining method used in large thin tabular orebodies, usually of shallow dip, particularly in South African gold mines (q.v.) at great depth. The face is advanced forward by drilling and blasting, with the ore then removed by scrapers; the 'hanging-wall' (q.v.) is supported by timber or hydraulic props. The longwall mining technique is applied most successfully where ore occurs in zones of consistent payability (q.v.)

Lost Wax Casting

Lost Wax Casting, also known as *cire perdue* and investment casting, is the traditional method for the faithful reproduction of intricate designs in carat gold jewellery (q.v.). One of the most ancient of goldsmiths' techniques, it has been used at least since the Egyptians in 1500 BC.

To begin with, a master pattern is made by hand, usually in high carat gold, to which a metal flow channel, known as a sprue, is brazed as a feed for molten gold later. The master pattern is imbedded in rubber, which is then vulcanised. The rubber mould thus formed is cut in half, the master pattern removed, and wax is injected into the space. When set, the wax model is taken out of the mould, the

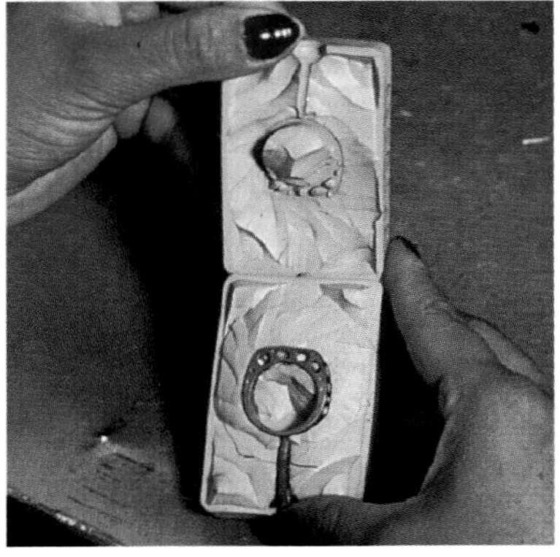

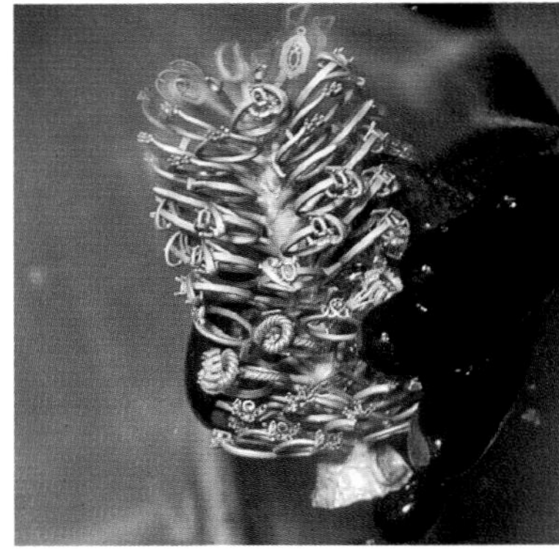

Lost Wax Casting. *Left-hand column, top to bottom: master pattern set in a rubber mould; liquid wax ready for injection; assembling the wax tree; heating the tree in the investment can.*

Right-hand column, top to bottom: the tree of gold ornaments; stripping ornaments off the tree; the tree with ornaments removed; final cleaning and polishing

process is repeated many times and the resulting wax models are assembled on a central wax spine to form a 'tree'. This tree is placed inside another mould, known as the 'investment can', which is heated until the wax runs out, hence the name 'lost wax', leaving an empty tree pattern within. Molten gold is poured into this space and the investment can spun centrifugally to ensure the metal fills every indent. Once it is cooled and the gold solidified, the can is opened to reveal a tree of golden articles, which can be cut off, cleaned and prepared for final polishing.

Lot

Commonly used word for a standard futures contract on COMEX (q.v.). 'Buy three December lots at market' means buy three contracts of 100 ounces each for December delivery.

Low Grade

Ore within a mine which has a much lower gold content than the average run of the mine. Low grade ore may be mined as part of an orebody, when it is not below the economic cut-off grade, and is usually blended with higher grade ore to produce an average grade. Low grade mineralisation may also be mined, if practical, if it becomes economic, such as in periods when the gold price is high or when new technology is introduced. Orebodies, notably in the United States and Western Australia, which have a very low gold content of 1 gramme per tonne or less, can now be mined by heap leaching (q.v.) and carbon-in-pulp recovery (q.v.). Such new technology has made payable many deposits that were previously considered uneconomic.

Luxembourg Gold Market

Luxembourg became an important regional gold market during the 1980s, particularly after the imposition of value added tax on gold coins in Germany, the abolition of anonymous gold buying in France, and, for a few years, a sales tax levied on gold delivered within Switzerland. Luxembourg, which levies no tax, is a convenient 'off-shore' centre for investors to buy gold bars and coins. German banks were able to switch much of their gold investment business to their Luxembourg branches, offering certificates for gold held there. Kredietbank and Banque Internationale have also become significant gold dealers. In all Golddealers Luxembourg (q.v.) has ninety members. A daily price fixing for one kilo and good delivery bars (q.v.) is held.

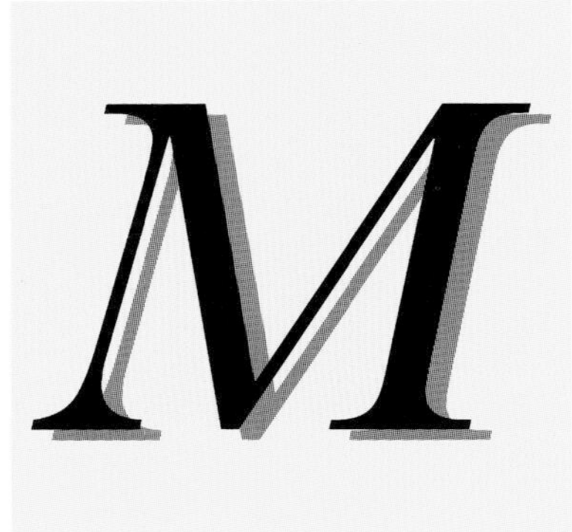

MacArthur Forrest Process

Developed in 1887 by two Glasgow doctors, Robert and William Forrest, and a chemist John S. MacArthur, this cyanide process became the basis of most gold extraction, especially in South Africa whose gold mining industry might not have expanded so soon without it. In the MacArthur Forrest process the ore is crushed to a fine powder and circulated through tanks containing a weak solution of cyanide, which has an affinity for gold. The solution dissolves the gold and the remaining rock pulp is filtered off. Zinc dust added to the cyanide solution to replace the gold causes the fine specks of gold to be precipitated out and the precipitate is then refined.

Maintenance Margin

See **Margin.**

Malaysia

Malaysia became an important jewellery manufacturing centre during the 1980s, working increasingly for export to the Middle East and Germany. The main fabrication was centred in the duty-free zone on the island of Penang, where overseas wholesalers set up joint ventures with local entrepreneurs. Total jewellery fabrication exceeded 20 tonnes by 1989, more than half for export.

Malleable

Originally from the Latin *malleus*, a hammer, it applies to metals that can be hammered (or nowadays rolled) into thin sheets without breaking. Gold is the most malleable of all metals; it can be hammered into a translucent wafer five-millionths of an inch thick.

Maple Leaf

The first 'four nines' legal tender bullion coin (q.v.), the Maple Leaf was launched by the Royal Canadian Mint (q.v.) in 1979. It weighs one troy ounce, is 999.9 fine and has Can$50 face value; smaller coins of ½, ¼ and 1⁄10 of an ounce are also available. The Maple Leaf has become the best selling bullion coin since the Krugerrand (q.v.) was hit by economic sanctions against the purchase of South African goods.

Maple Leaf. *This Canadian 999.9 bullion coin has become the best seller during the 1980s*

Margin

The money deposited by a client on forward or futures contracts to guarantee performance of the contract. He will deposit 'initial' (q.v.) or original margin of 5–20 per cent when a futures or forward contract is purchased, but thereafter on every business day he will be liable for additional 'variation margin' (q.v.) if the price of gold moves against him. The client may also be liable for 'maintenance margin', which is the cash balance that must be maintained at all times in forward or futures arrangements.

Margin Call

The request by a broker or bullion dealer for additional funds to cover forward or futures contracts if the price moves against the client. Margin calls can be crucial to holders of large positions if there is a big price swing against them, because they may suddenly be required to post substantial additional amounts of cash, within a matter of hours, which may not be available to them. The failure to meet such margin calls can lead to the immediate liquidation of the position. Margin calls can also prove difficult for central banks who may have entered into large forward positions with bullion dealers, against foreign exchange, and may also suddenly be liable to put up more margin in gold itself if the price falls to maintain the foreign exchange facility.

Mark

The stamp of an accepted melter or assayer (q.v.) and the stamp of the fineness on bars of gold or silver. *See also* **Chop.**

Mark to Market

The revaluation of a client's position at current market levels which may result in margin calls.

Mark-up

The premium or 'agio' over the spot gold price paid by a retail customer for a gold bar, coin or ornament.

Market Maker

A dealer or trader who is ready to quote clients and counterparties both a bid and offer price, usually at a narrow spread, in spot gold and options (there are no market makers in gold futures). The London Bullion Market Association (q.v.) distinguishes between market maker members, of whom there are 11, and ordinary members, who may also be international dealers but do not wish to make a market at all times to all comers.

Market Order

An order to buy or sell a stated amount of bullion or futures contracts immediately at the best price obtainable in the market. Opposite of **'limit order'** (q.v.).

Marubeni Corporation

Market maker in gold and silver in Tokyo and member of TOCOM (q.v.).

Marubeni Corporation
4-2 Ohtemachi 1 chome
Chiyoda-ku, Tokyo 100
Japan
Tel: (3) 282 3141
Fax: (3) 282 7169
Telex: J23453
Reuters: MBCQ

Mase Westpac

The bullion banking/dealing subsidiary of Westpac Banking Corporation, which took over Johnson Matthey Bankers in 1986 after their rescue by the Bank of England, securing a place at the fixing (q.v.), and as market-making members of the London Bullion Market Association (q.v.). The Mase Westpac group are also market-makers in Hong Kong, Sydney and New York.

Mase Westpac Ltd
Westpac House, 75 King William St
London EC4N 7HA
Tel: (071) 283 7801
Fax: (071) 283 4659
Telex: 884491
Reuters: MASL

Master Alloy

An alloy that is added to gold to achieve a particular caratage, colour or hardness, for instance, palladium and silver used in making 'white' gold (q.v.).

Medals/Medallions

Commemorative coins struck both by government and private mints to honour historic events, anniversaries or other special occasions. Many 'gold medals' awarded are actually gold plated and actual fine gold use is very limited as compared with coins (q.v.).

Medical Uses

The exceptional properties of gold and the mystique surrounding it naturally led from the earliest times to possible medical applications, not least as an elixir sought by alchemists (q.v.). Pliny, in the first century BC, suggested gold 'is laid upon wounded men and little children to protect them against magic potions'. From the Middle Ages until the eighteenth century alchemists devised a multitude of recipes for potable gold for most ailments, though one sceptical sixteenth-century metallurgist rightly noted that gold gave warmth to the heart, 'particularly to those who have great sacks and chests full of it'. Advances in scientific knowledge by the eighteenth century ended gold's prescription as a cure-all cordial, but no genuine uses were quickly found. A French physician, J. A. Chrestian, however, developed a double gold chloride by mixing sodium chloride with gold chloride, a prescription which was quite widely used in the treatment of syphilis in Europe and the United States during the early nineteenth century. An American doctor, Leslie Keeley, also achieved considerable notoriety in the 1890s by using multiple injections of double gold chloride as a cure for alcoholism.

The most significant genuine medical use of gold, developed in clinical trials in the 1920s, is in the treatment of rheumatoid arthritis. A very mild solution of gold cyanide, at a concentration of only 0.5ppm is injected into the patient's muscles in cautiously increased doses to a level of 25 milligrams per week. The gold solution inhibits the growth of the tubercle bacillus which causes the disease and considerable relief is achieved after about six months. Gold also has a limited application in the treatment of cancer, in which 'seeds' of radioactive gold-198 are used.

The most widespread belief in the medicinal benefits of gold persists in India, where it is used in Ayurvedic medicine for many ailments such as sclerosis, cirrhosis of the liver and hardening of the arteries. An official allocation of about 75 kilos a year has long been made to India's pharmaceutical manufacturers for these remedies.

Melt

Coins which are in surplus or for which there is little demand so that they are trading at or even just below the spot price of gold may be bought in by dealers at 'melt' or for 'melt' (i.e. to be melted down) at about half a per cent under the gold price.

Melt and Assay

Refiners will normally melt and assay scrap gold before confirming the purchase price.

Melters and Assayers

The usual description of organisations whose gold and silver bars are 'acceptable' (q.v.) on a particular market or exchange. The London Bullion Market Association's (q.v.) good delivery list (q.v.) for gold recognises 49 melters and assayers currently operating and a further 20 melters and/or assayers no longer operating, or whose name has changed but whose bars are still accepted as good delivery.

Melting

Melting and casting (q.v.) are the primary stages in the production of semi-fabricated gold alloys. In melting, solid metal is reduced to liquid to which the correct weight of the different elements to make up the right assay in the alloy can be added. Melting may be undertaken in air using gas or electricity (induction) as the heat source, or under vacuum in a sealed vessel to exclude the possible formation of metal oxides.

Mercex

An abbreviation for New York Mercantile Exchange (q.v.).

Merrill-Crowe Process

Merrill-Crowe is one of the two main processes for recovering gold from pregnant cyanide solution. The other is carbon adsorption (q.v.).

The Merrill-Crowe process involves precipitation with zinc dust, and is applicable particularly to gold ores with high silver content due to better silver recovery than by carbon adsorption.

Before gold can be precipitated with zinc dust, all solids must be removed from the pregnant solution. The Merrill-Crowe process then comprises three stages:

1. de-aeration, to prevent gold from redissolving;
2. zinc dust precipitation;
3. precipitate filtration: the zinc dust and gold are mixed with sulphuric acid to dissolve the zinc, filtered, and the remaining solids smelted to a gold bullion bar.

Metal Account

Many banks and bullion dealers offer metal account facilities to their customers, who may be substantial traders or small jewellers. The advantage of metal accounts is that gold is not normally delivered, thus occasionally avoiding sales tax. Metal account business in Switzerland increased enormously in the early 1980s when gold deliveries were taxed for a time. Metal account gold is normally 'unallocated' (q.v.) so the client is an unsecured creditor. The metal account is offset by the dollar account in Account/Account or Deferred Settlement Trading (q.v.).

Metallurgy

The science of extracting, smelting and refining metals; the word comes originally from the Greek for metal work or working.

Métaux Précieux S.A Metalor

This precious metals refinery at Neuchatel, Switzerland, had its origins in a firm of gold smelters and watch-case manufacturers, Martin de Pury & Cie, at Le Locle in 1852, which was taken over by Swiss Bank Corporation (q.v.) in 1918. It became a separate subsidiary company of Swiss Bank Corporation in 1936. The historic link with the watch industry remains through the fabrication of semi-finished products, but embraces jewellery alloys, dental golds, electrical, electronic and chemical products, together with the recovery, smelting and recycling of precious metals and production of the complete range of gold bars marketed by Swiss Bank Corporation. The Metalor group has representation in Germany, Denmark, Spain, France, United Kingdom, Hong Kong and the USA.

Métaux Précieux S.A. Metalor
Av. du Vignoble
CH2009 Neuchatel
Switzerland
Tel: (38) 206 111
Fax: (38) 206 606
Telex: 952 504

Mexico

See **Centenario** .

Mid-America Commodity Exchange (MACE)

This Chicago exchange originally launched a 33.2 ounce gold futures contract in 1984. Trading months are: spot, February, April, June, August, October and December. Trading hours are 7.20 to 1.40 CST. Volume has been small compared with COMEX (q.v.) in New York. A gold options contract for 33.2 ounces was launched in 1984. Since 1986, the Exchange has been affiliated to the Chicago Board of Trade (q.v.) and shares the same building.

Mid-America Commodity Exchange
141 West Jackson Blvd
Chicago IL 60604
USA
Tel: (312) 341 3000
Fax: (312) 341 7302
Telex: 253223

Mill/Milling

(i) In mining, the term mill has come to cover the broad range of machinery inside the mineral treatment plant where the gold is separated from the ore. The type of mill will vary from mine to mine depending on the type of ore and processing method. Each mill, in short, is tailor made. But it often represents the largest single capital cost in the development of a new mine, and the milling may account for up to half the working costs if a complex ore is involved. The scale of the milling operation can be immense: in South Africa upwards of 100 million tonnes of ore is milled each year to produce about 600 tonnes of gold. However, to meet the need of small-scale open-pit mines in Australia, mobile milling plants have been developed that can be readily moved from one site to another.

Before it reaches the mill itself, the ore will often have been through primary and secondary crushers to break it down into more manageable pieces. The initial stage of milling is to grind this broken ore into a fine powder by passing it through rotating cylinders filled with steel balls, known as ball mills, or with short steel rods, known as rod mills. In the emerging rock dust most of the tiny particles of gold contained in the ore will have been exposed. The gold dust then goes into the cyanidation mill, where it is dissolved out into a solution; a technique originally pioneered with the MacArthur Forrest process (q.v.). The gold is recovered from this solution either by the more traditional method of adding zinc dust, which has the effect of taking gold's place, allowing it to be precipitated out, or, increasingly, by the modern technique of carbon-in-pulp (q.v.). The next stage is smelting (q.v.). The gold is heated in a furnace with silica, borax and soda ash which soaks up most of the impurities, forming black molten slag which rises to the top of the furnace while the heavier gold settles to the bottom. This gold is poured into doré bars, usually with a minimum fineness of 850 fine that are shipped from the mine to be refined.

Mill. Ore being crushed and milled in tube mills until it resembles talcum powder

(ii) In the semi-fabrication (q.v.) of gold products, the term mill is applied to a variety of processes in rolling (q.v.). A breakdown mill is used for the fast reduction of cross-sectional dimensions of sheet or strip by hot or cold work (q.v.). In a finishing mill, rolls of sheet or strip gold alloys are carefully prepared to impart good surface qualities. A tape mill is used for continuous rolling of narrow tapes of thin material which may be used for chainmaking (q.v.).

Miller Process

The basic process of refining gold by the use of chlorine, which was first developed at the Sydney Mint in Australia by Dr F. B. Miller. It is based upon the fact that chlorine readily combines with silver and any base metals to form chlorides, while gold is unaffected. Doré (q.v.) is placed in clay pots in a furnace; once it is molten, chlorine is pumped into each pot and is absorbed by the base metals, forming volatile chlorides. After two to three hours, the pot is removed from the furnace and the molten chlorides skimmed off, leaving gold of 996–997 fineness which can be poured into moulds. Once perfected, the Miller Process largely replaced the Wohlwill Process (q.v.) for refining most of the world's gold production.

Mine/Mining

Gold is found in primary and secondary deposits. Primary deposits formed when silica-rich liquids carrying gold (and other valuable minerals) were forced up into fissures in the earth's surface and solidified into quartz veins or lodes (q.v.). The orebodies (q.v.) in which these veins or lodes occur are located anywhere from a few metres below the surface to several thousand metres down. Secondary deposits are alluvial (or placer (q.v.)). These deposits are much younger and comprise gold dust, particles and nuggets produced

Mine. Setting blasting charges into holes drilled into the rock

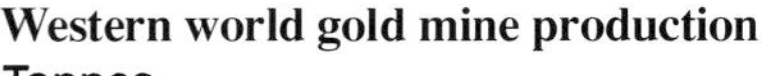

Western world gold mine production

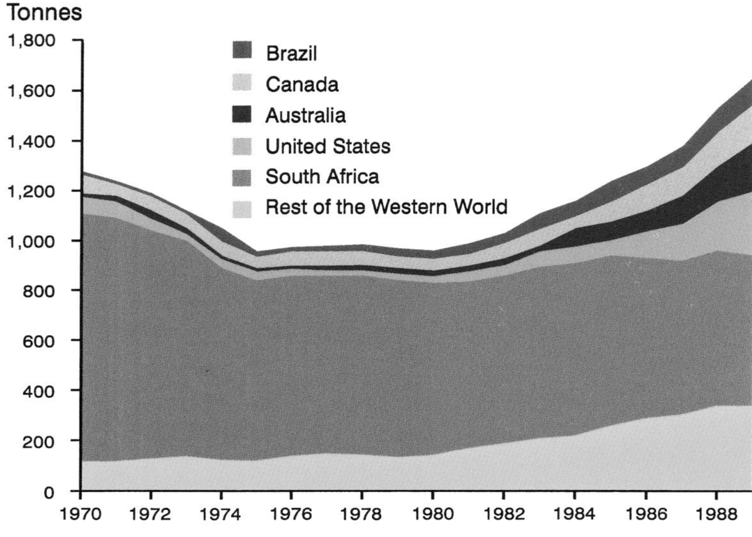

Mine. *Source: Gold Fields Mineral Services Ltd*

by the erosion of primary deposits and found in gravel beds along the sides or bottom of rivers, as in Brazil (q.v.) or the Soviet Union (q.v.). Ancient river and lake beds often become buried over millions of years and sometimes contain conglomerate, a cemented rock comprising fragments of pre-existing rocks. They are often metamorphosed (altered by heat, pressure and chemically active fluids).The classic example of a gold-bearing conglomerate is the 'banket' of the Witwatersrand basin (q.v.) in South Africa (q.v.) where the individual beds are referred to as 'reefs'.

The earliest discoveries of gold were undoubtedly placer deposits in the rivers of Asia Minor and Africa, but underground mining of lode deposits was undertaken at least by 2000 BC by the Egyptians between the Nile and the Red Sea. Early gold mines were also located in what are now Ethiopia, Sudan and Saudi Arabia, in the greenstone belts of the greater Arabian shield which match geologically the greenstone belts where many of Australia's, Brazil's and Canada's gold deposits are found. Rough calculations suggest the Egyptians may have mined 850 tonnes of gold in one thousand years. Many of these historic deposits are now being mined again, at Gebeit in Sudan and Mahd ad-Dhahab in Saudi Arabia.

The Romans also developed gold mines in Africa and Spain to finance their empire. Once it collapsed, little gold mining took place for well over a thousand years, except in the mountains of central Europe in what is now Austria and southern Germany.

Although the Spanish and Portuguese empires brought back gold from South America, much of it was plundered and fresh output was largely from placer deposits. The early gold rushes in the Soviet Union in the eighteenth century, thence to California (q.v.) and Australia in the mid-nineteenth century, were also essentially for placer gold, although some lode deposits were mined. Even so, they quadrupled production levels to nearly 300 tonnes annually.

Gold mining in the modern sense really developed only with the discovery of the gold reefs in South Africa in the 1880s. Their exploitation called for a combination of skills in deep level mining, new technology (in the form of cyanidation in the MacArthur Forrest process (q.v.)) and major capital investment. Even in the early days, £500,000 was needed to develop a new South African mine and as time went on it took between five and seven years to bring a new mine into production. This led to the establishment of large mining finance houses, such as Gold Fields of South Africa (q.v.) and Anglo American (q.v.), to oversee the financing and development of mines down to 4,000 metres in depth, that might then often produce 40 tonnes and even 100 tonnes annually. South Africa ousted the United States as the foremost producer in 1898 and has held that position ever since; for much of this century South Africa has

Mine. *Tunnel development a thousand feet below the Arctic tundra at the Lupin mine in Canada's North West Territories*

been in a league of its own, reaching a peak output of 1,000 tonnes in 1970. In its first century the South African mining industry produced just over 40,000 tonnes of gold, about 40 per cent of all the gold ever mined.

South Africa's pre-eminence in gold mining waned, however, in the 1980s from accounting for over 70 per cent of western (i.e. non-communist) production to just over 30 per cent. Gold mining experienced as big a revolution in that decade as occurred when the South African reefs were first discovered a hundred years earlier.

Large-scale mining methods and new technology in the form of heap-leaching (q.v.) and carbon-in-pulp recovery (q.v.) has made possible open-pit (q.v.) mining of very low grade deposits of gold, with as little as one gramme of gold per tonne, compared with 6 to 10 grammes in conventional mines. The decade also saw the growth of significant new gold-mining groups, such as Newmont Mining (q.v.), Placer-Dome (q.v.) and American Barrick (q.v.), using new techniques such as gold loans (q.v.) for financing. Mining groups also made use of forward sales (q.v.) and options (q.v.) to hedge their output in a volatile gold market. As a result the alliance between the gold mining industry and major bullion dealers became much closer. Indeed, gold mine finance was as important a profit centre as gold trading for many gold departments. In Australia banks evolved complete 'packages' for prospective mines, offering gold loans, technical advice, mobile milling plants (q.v.) and, not least, the marketing of the gold then produced.

Gold mine output responded, virtually doubling between 1980 (962 tonnes) and 1990 (about 1,700 tonnes). Output in Australia, Brazil, Canada and the United States showed astonishing increases. The potential for developing further mines, especially huge low-grade epithermal (q.v.) deposits in Papua New Guinea (q.v.) and other countries of the Pacific 'rim of fire' (q.v.) means that a high level of production will be maintained for the rest of the twentieth century. The gold mining industry faces tests, however, from rising costs and greater environmental controls.

See also gold mining discussed under individual countries (e.g. Australia, South Africa), main mining groups, geological terminology (e.g. orebodies), mining terminology (e.g. stopes, longwall) and recovery techniques (e.g. heap-leaching).

Mineral Lease

See **Mining And Exploration Rights**.

Mineralised Zone

Any mass of host rock in which minerals of potential commercial value occur.

Minimum Charge

Refiners handling very small amounts of low-grade scrap (q.v.) or sweeps (q.v.) may qualify their charges with a minimum charge regardless of how much metal is contained, or a minimum lot size, or a minimum return under which they return or account for no metal to the customer if it is below a certain amount.

Mining and Exploration Rights

The process of acquisition of land for exploration or mining varies throughout the world. The process can involve the negotiation of agreements with existing private owners, the outright purchase of lands, the staking of lands, or acquisition from the government of these rights under a licence or other form of permit.

In the United States, mineral rights pass with the surface estate and consequently many mineral deposits are privately owned. Lease areas or claims can also be staked and maintained by working the project, and subsequently title to the deposit and surface estate can be acquired.

In Canada, the right to explore or mine is granted according to each provincial mining act, but in general the mineral estate is severed from the surface estate. In British Columbia, for example, rights to mine gold from a claim area are acquired in the form of either a placer lease or a mineral lease.

In Australia, all gold mineral rights are vested in the Crown, with the individual state governments granting mining rights. A miner's right is usually sufficient to explore Crown lands, although further approval is required for private lands. A mining lease may be required from the state for large scale mining operations.

In South Africa, mineral rights and prospecting rights in respect of precious metals are granted by the government. The government may grant a prospecting or mining lease for consideration of a lease payment.

Mint

While most governments have their own mint for making legal tender coins, few specialists make gold coins, except those producing bullion coins (q.v.). The principal mints striking gold coins are:

Australia: Perth Mint (q.v.), now renamed The Western Australian Mint, making Nugget bullion coin (q.v.);

Austria: Austrian Mint making Philharmoniker (q.v.) coin and, formerly, 100 Corona restrike (q.v.);

Canada: Royal Canadian Mint (q.v.) making Maple Leaf bullion coin (q.v.) and special issues;

China: China Mint, Beijing making Panda coin (q.v.);

Mexico: Casa de Moneda, making Centenario coin (q.v.);

Singapore: Singapore Mint, part of Chartered Industries, making some special gold coin issues

South Africa: The South African Mint, making Krugerrand (q.v.) and some special issues of one and two rand coins

United Kingdom: Royal Mint (q.v.), making Britannia bullion coin (q.v.), Sovereigns and some special issue proof coins for other clients;

United States: United States Mint, making Eagle bullion coin (q.v.).

Mint Mark

Small mark on a coin, often invisible to the naked eye, in letters or symbols to identify the mint from which it originates.

Mint State

An uncirculated coin showing no trace of wear.

Mitsubishi Corporation

Market maker in gold in Tokyo and member of TOCOM (q.v.).

Mitsubishi Corporation
6-3 Marunouchi 2 chome
Chiyoda-ku, Tokyo 100-86
Tel: (3) 210 3693
Fax: (3) 210 3994
Telex: MITSUBISHI J 22793
Reuters: MCGQ

Mitsubishi Metal Corporation

Market maker in gold and silver in Tokyo and member of TOCOM (q.v.).

Mitsubishi Metal Corporation
Ohtemachi Building
6-1 Ohtemachi 1 chome
Chiyoda-ku, Tokyo 100
Tel: (3) 287 2985
Fax: (3) 213 2185
Telex: 2226227 MMGOLDJ

Mitsui & Co. Ltd

Market maker in gold, silver and platinum in Tokyo and member of TOCOM (q.v.).

Mitsui & Co. Ltd
2-1 Ohtemachi 1 chome
Chiyoda-ku, Tokyo 100
Tel: (3) 285 3407
Fax: (3) 285 9915
Telex: J28137 MBKTKHTR
Reuters: MBKR

MKS Finance SA

A Geneva based company, founded in 1979, dealing in physical gold, over-the-counter and listed options and other gold instruments, with particular speciality in the Middle East. They are also specialists in location swaps of precious metals between different physical locations and in different types of gold. MKS is a member of COMEX (q.v.) and owner of Pamp S.A. (q.v.) the precious metals refiners. It is also in commodity futures trading through Falcon Brokers and Investments S.A., and interbank foreign exchange dealing through Management Investment and Trade (London) Ltd.

MKS Finance S.A.
10 Promenade St Antoine
P.O Box 738
1211 Geneva
Tel: (22) 21 79 91
Fax: (22) 21 18 00
Telex: 427 999 MAR CH

Mocatta & Goldsmid

The oldest members of the London gold market, who were founded in 1671 by Moses Mocatta and from 1720–1841 were exclusive brokers in gold and silver to the Bank of England. Market making members of the London Bullion Market Association (q.v.) and one of the five houses at the 'fixing' (q.v.), Mocatta are owned by Standard Chartered Bank and have associate companies in New York (Mocatta Metals Corporation), Hong Kong and Singapore.

Mocatta & Goldsmid
Mocatta House
4 Crosby Square
London EC3A 6AQ
Tel: (071) 638 3636
Fax: (071) 256 7750
Telex: 889231
Reuters: MNGL

Modern Collector Coins

For some mints the production of proof issues of bullion coins (q.v.) or other well known coins, such as the Sovereign (q.v.), or of special limited issues, is an important part of their gold coin output. At the Royal Mint (q.v.) in Britain, for example, the minting of what are called 'modern collector coins' is the biggest part of the mint's gold business. These coins, quite distinct from historical numismatic coins (q.v.), are often sold by direct mail or advertising in coin magazines to collectors' clubs. The Royal Mint's regular modern collector coin output covers proof issues of the Britannia bullion coin (q.v.), the Sovereign, and special issues. Other mints with regular output of modern collector coins include the Royal Canadian Mint (q.v.), the Singapore Mint, the South African Mint and the United States Mint (q.v.).

Montagu

See **Samuel Montagu**

Morgan Guaranty

The bullion department of Morgan Guaranty Trust Company, a subsidiary of J. P. Morgan & Co. Inc., is a market-maker in New York, London and Hong Kong, and is also active in over-the-counter options (q.v.) in New York and London.

Morgan Guaranty Trust Co.
60 Wall Street
New York, N.Y. 10260
USA
Tel: (212) 648 2300
Fax: (212) 837 5930
Telex: 232993 MGTGT
Reuters: MGTNGL (New York) or MGTLGL (London)

Mother Lode

Originally the term used by prospectors in the Californian gold rush (q.v.) to describe the main belt of quartz-bearing rock in the High Sierras from which the alluvial gold found in the Sacramento river had been washed down. Now it may refer to any major ore vein running through a region.

Moving Average

In technical analysis (q.v.) the moving average is one of the key trend lines that is plotted on a bar chart reflecting the progress of the gold price over weeks, months or one year compared with the day-to-day price. Many analysts plot both a three month and a one year moving average. When the moving average moves above or below the daily chart it may generate a buy or sell signal

Museo del Oro

This museum in Bogota, Columbia, was started by the central bank, Banco de la Republica, in 1939 to preserve the best remaining Pre-Columbian (q.v.) jewellery and ornaments. Museo del Oro houses a unique collection of more than 10,000 items.

Museo del Oro. *Tairona figure pendant from the Sierra Nevada de Santa Maria region of Columbia*

Naked Option

The sale of a put (q.v.) or call (q.v.) option (q.v.) on gold or gold futures by someone who is not holding either gold or gold futures to back it up.

Napoleon

Among the French 20 franc gold coins produced were those bearing the image of Napoleon I or III, but many 20 franc coins were produced with varying designs.

Napoleon. *An early example, minted in 1815, of France's most popular gold coin*

Like the Sovereign in Britain, the Napoleon became the generic term for a generation of French gold coins, and the favourite of French investors. First minted in 1803, the coin, weighing 6.4516 grammes, contained 0.1867 troy ounces of 900 fine gold.

Nearby/Nearby Delivery

The closest active trading month on a futures exchange. In January, for example, on COMEX (q.v.) the nearby month is February.

Newmont Australia

Newmont Australia is one of Australia's leading gold mining and exploration companies. The company is 25 per cent owned by Newmont Mining of the United States. The principle assets of Newmont Australia are a 70 per cent stake in the Telfer mine and an 80 per cent interest in the New Celebration mine. Production at Telfer commenced in 1977, and in the last decade it has been the largest single gold producer in Australia. In 1989 the mine produced 225,794 ounces (7 tonnes). Newmont Australia's production totalled 250,868 (7.8 tonnes) of gold and output is expected to be about 300,000 ounces (9.3 tonnes) in 1990. A merger with BHP Gold was proposed at the end of 1990.

Newmont Australia
9th Floor, 600 Kilda Road
Melbourne, Victoria 6004
Australia
Tel: (03) 522-5333
Fax: (03) 522-2996 Telex: 32026

Newmont Gold Company

Newmont Gold is the largest gold producer in North America and also has the largest gold reserves. The company is 90.1 per cent owned by Newmont Mining.

Newmont Gold operates along a thirty-eight mile stretch of the Carlin Trend in Nevada and has fifteen deposits with measured gold resources and five mills as well as heap leaching facilities. Ten of these resources have mineable reserves of 20.7 million ounces (644 tonnes). Total gold output from these facilities in 1989 was 1.468 million ounces (45.7 tonnes). Output in 1990 is expected to be about 1.7 million ounces (52.9 tonnes) of gold.

Newmont Gold Company
One United Bank Centre
1700 Lincoln Street
Denver. Colorado 80203
USA
Tel: (303) 863-7414
Fax: (303) 837 5837
Telex: 910 9970913

New Scrap

Scrap (q.v.) which is produced naturally during jewellery, watchcase and bracelet or coin manufacture which will be processed back into alloys as part of the working inventory; also known as process scrap (q.v.).

New York Commodity Exchange

See **COMEX/Commodity Exchange Inc.**

New Zealand. Alluvial mining operation by L & M Mining on the Shotover river

New York Mercantile Exchange

The New York Mercantile Exchange (NYMEX) launched 1 kilo and 400 ounce futures contracts in 1975, but withdrew in 1980 due to lack of volume. In precious metals this exchange is best known for its platinum contract. Plans to merge with COMEX are advanced.

New York Mercantile Exchange
4 World Trade Center
New York NY 10048
USA
Tel: (212) 938 2222
Fax: (212) 938 2985

New Zealand

Gold was first discovered near Dunedin on the south island of New Zealand in 1861. A steady output of 15 tonnes from alluvial deposits was maintained annually until 1870, but has not been equalled since. Production is being revived, however, in the 1990s. Alluvial mining continues throughout the south island, much of it with dredges. The largest alluvial mining company, L & M Mining, operates on the Shotover river and at Rimu Flat. A new mine is being developed at Macraes Flat on the south-east tip of the island.

The real potential is at huge epithermal deposits on the north island, which some geologists regard as the richest in the southern Pacific. The Martha Hill underground quartz mine (Amax Gold 28.35%, ACM Gold 28.35%, Mineral Resources (NZ) Ltd. 27%, Goodman Fielder 16.2%) at Waihi opened in 1988 and Golden Cross (Cyprus Minerals 80%, Todd Corp 20%), on the nearby Coromandel peninsula, due in the early 1990s, will lift output. But a strong environment lobby has delayed many projects and is likely to curtail major expansion. Output was about 7 tonnes in 1990 and will rise towards 15 tonnes by 1995.

Nissho-Iwai Corporation

Market maker in gold and platinum in Tokyo and member of TOCOM (q.v.).

Nissho Iwai Corporation,
4-5 Akasaka 2 chome,
Minato-ku, Tokyo 107.
Japan.
Tel: (3) 588 3497
Fax: (3) 588 4827
Telex: J34228 NICPMTL
Reuters: NISQ

Nominal Price

On futures markets if, for some reason, no contracts have been traded in a commodity on a particular trading day, an exchange committee will determine a 'nominal price' for clearing house (q.v.) purposes. *See also* **Settlement Price.**

Nugget. *Private collection of nuggets found by a Western Australian prospector*

North Korea,

North Korea produces between 12 and 15 tonnes of gold annually, together with over 50 tonnes of silver, which it normally sells on the international market through its central bank. The bars marked with Central Bank Pyongyang Refiners or Central Bank DPR of Korea are acceptable delivery (q.v.) on the London market.

Nugget. Australia's Nugget bullion coin originally featured famous nuggets, but from 1990 the red kangaroo has been substituted

Nugget

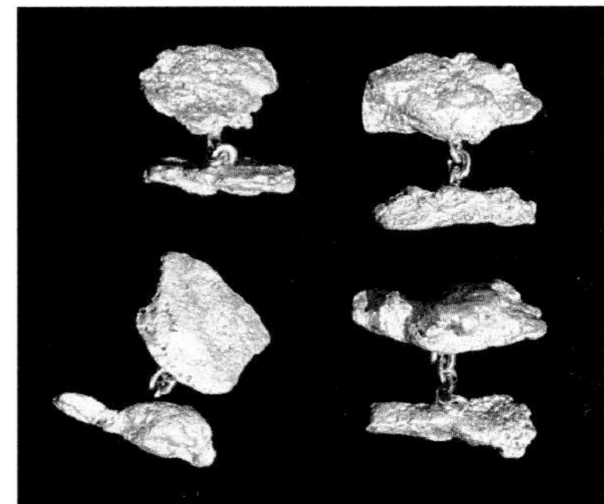

Nugget. Cuff links made from nuggets found in the Australian outback

(i) Chunks or pieces of gold, mainly found in alluvial deposits (q.v.) are known as nuggets. Many are of beautiful crystalline design; some are large: the biggest nugget is the Welcome Stranger, found in Australia in 1858, which weighed 2,284 ounces (71.04 kilos) and is featured on the original Australian Nugget one ounce bullion coin (q.v.). Prospectors in Brazil's gold rush (q.v.) to Serra Pelada in 1980 also found sizeable nuggets, including one of 215 ounces (6.7 kilos). Nuggets usually have a gold content over 900 fine and may even be close to 995. They are usually sold at a premium over their gold content and are bought by collectors or used as jewellery. Auctions of nuggets are organised by Union Bank of Switzerland and Christie's.

(ii) The first legal tender gold bullion coin minted by Australia, first issued in 1986. There are four sizes of coin, weighing one troy ounce, ½ ounce, ¼ ounce and 1⁄10 ounce and each containing gold of 999.9 fineness. The name 'Nugget' reflects the design of a famous nugget discovery featured on the reverse of the coin; each size shows a different nugget, and each year of issue features four different nuggets discoveries.

In 1990 a major design change introduced the Kangaroo to replace the nuggets, tying in with the koala on the reverse of the Australian platinum bullion coin and the kookaburra on the silver coin.

Numismatics

Numismatics is the specialised sector of the coin (q.v.) business for the study and collection of rare coins and other media of exchange, particularly those with archaeological or historic interest. Numismatic dealers are usually quite distinct from banks, trading in more conventional gold coins, although a few, like Bank Leu in Zurich, do have separate numismatic departments. Generally, however, it is the province of firms like Baldwin's, Seaby's or Spink's in

Numismatics. Coins, early bank notes and other collectors' items at Spink & Son in London. Many rare coins command high premiums

London or Stack's in New York. They belong to the International Association of Professional Numismatists (IAPN), which has 110 members from numismatics firms in 22 countries. Numismatics is not limited to gold and silver coins, but covers everything from cowrie shells to early bank notes that have been used for exchange in some way.

In respect of gold, however, the numismatist's interest ranges from the first coins of electrum (q.v.), the natural alloy of gold and silver, issued in Lydia around 550 BC, through Greek, Roman and Byzantine gold coins to the earliest British Sovereigns (struck in 1489 as a symbol of Henry VII's new Tudor dynasty), Guineas (first struck in 1662 just after the Restoration) and early American Eagles and Double Eagles (first launched in 1837). The rarest coins fetch high prices. A Victoria Gothic gold Crown, dated 1847, sold in 1988 for £113,000; only two examples of this coin were known.

International Association of Professional Numismatists
Loewenstrasse 65
CH 8001 Zurich
Switzerland
Tel: (1) 221 1885

Nymex

See **New York Mercantile Exchange.**

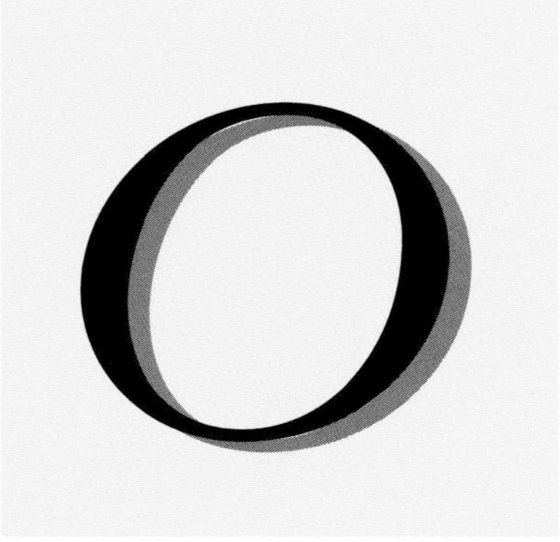

Offer

The price at which a market maker will sell gold. Opposite of **bid** (q.v.). Also often known as **'asked'**.

Olympic Coins

Special commemorative gold coins are usually issued for the Olympic Games every four years and sold at a substantial premium. *See also* **Commemorative Coins.**

On Stream

Expression in mining to indicate that a new mine has actually come into production.

Onza

One ounce 900 fine bullion coin (q.v.) launched by Mexico in 1981 to compete with other bullion coins. The coin made little impact because, due to its debt crisis, Mexico had no funds for an adequate launch.

Opencast/Opencut/Open-pit Mining

Surface mining, in which the ore is excavated from a pit, has been used extensively in Australia, Canada, Papua New Guinea and the United States in recent years for the recovery of low-grade finely disseminated oxide ores. Depending on the geometry and depth of the orebody, the advantage of open-pit, as opposed to underground, mining is that it is usually easier, cheaper and quicker to bring into production. Open-pit mines in Nevada and in Western Australia have often been brought on-stream (q.v.) within a year at a cost far below the development of underground mines, and in both regions account for virtually all gold production. Although open-pit deposits often have a relatively short life-span (on average, four to five years), after which it may become necessary to move to underground mining techniques to access deeper ores (if they are available and economic), the continued identification of new surface deposits, such as along the Carlin Trend (q.v.) in Nevada, often provides replacement ore reserves. Heap-leaching (q.v.) and carbon-in-pulp recovery (q.v.) have also resulted in the mining of large tonnage, low grade, near-surface gold deposits. Over half of all gold production in Australia, Canada and the United States came from open-pit mining by 1990.

Opencast. *Newmont Gold's opencast Gold Quarry on the Carlin Trend in Nevada*

Open-pit versus underground mining

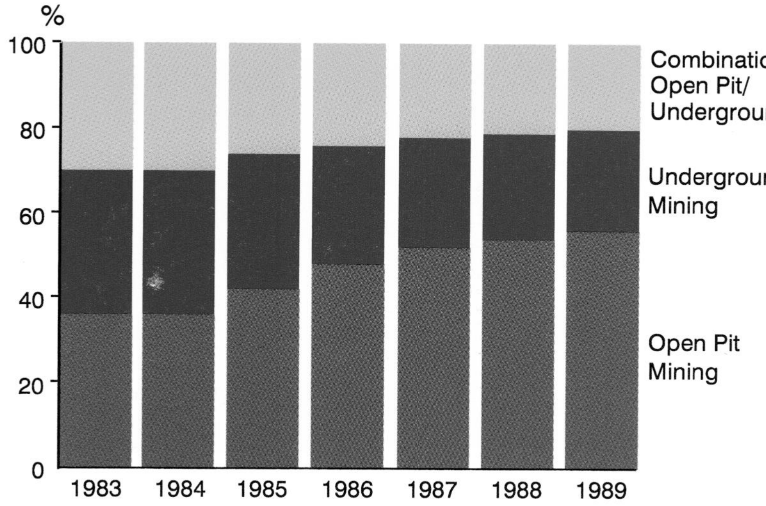

Opencast. *Source: Gold Fields Mineral Services Ltd, Gold 1990*

Open Interest

On a futures exchange such as COMEX (q.v.) or TOCOM (q.v.) the open interest is the daily statistic that indicates the number of gold futures contracts which have not been fulfilled, either by making or taking delivery or by liquidation; they are those still in play.

The level of open interest is an important signpost to how liquid the exchange is and how lively action in a given trading month (q.v.) will be before the last trading day by which time all contracts must be offset or liquidated.

Analysts also monitor changes in the level of open interest to detect trends. Rising open interest in a rising market signals new buyers joining in a bullish trend; conversely rising open interest with falling prices signals new sellers going short, reflecting a bearish mood. Again, declining open interest coupled with a declining price suggests profit-taking or stop-loss selling from long positions, while declining open interest when prices are rising indicates short positions being bought back or covered. In sum, the level of open interest is a barometer of a futures exchange's fortunes.

Open Outcry

Trading conducted on an exchange such as COMEX (q.v.) or Kam Ngan (q.v.) in a ring or pit by calling out the price, contract month, and number of contracts or lots. This contrasts with, for example, the London market, where there is no market place as such, and deals are concluded privately by telephone, telex or through the Reuters Dealing System (q.v.).

Open Position

A market position, long or short, which has not been closed out.

Open Stoping

An underground mining method leaving large unsupported open stope areas during initial mining.

Opening Range

Futures market price during the first five minutes of trading, while the mood of the day is set. Specific orders may be given to buy or sell 'market on open' and can be executed during this period.

Options

Options have become the third dimension of the gold market, after physical gold and futures; in the 1980s they were the fastest expanding sector. Options are surrounded by terminology and trading and hedging strategies of some complexity; at the outset an understanding of the language is necessary.

An option gives the holder the right, but not the obligation, to buy or sell gold at a pre-determined price by an agreed date, for which privilege he pays a premium. This premium, or cost of the option, is the compensation the writer or grantor receives from the buyer. The right to buy is known as a call option (q.v.); the right to sell is a put option (q.v.); normally abbreviated to 'call' and 'put'. The predetermined price is known as the strike or exercise price (q.v.).

The premium or cost of the option is calculated on a combination of the current gold price, the strike price, current interest rates, the time before expiry and the anticipated volatility of the gold price. This is worked out using a mathematical formula called the Black-Scholes model (q.v.), or a derivative of it. In fact, only the anticipated volatility of the price is not known, so that most option market makers quote premiums based on similar calculations; only their expectations of volatility and the position in their book will vary. Although premiums naturally fluctuate considerably, a working generalisation is that they are in the range of \$15 to \$25 an ounce but on occasion will be much more. That is both the attraction and subsequent importance of options; they offer immense leverage (q.v.) because the buyer only has to pay the premium and can build up large positions with small capital outlay.

Options contract volume on COMEX

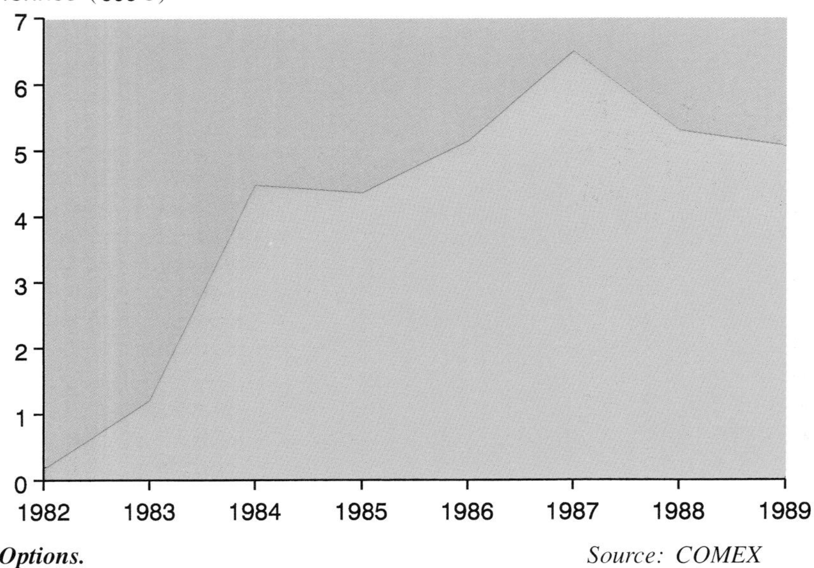

Options. *Source: COMEX*

The premium is also all that is at risk for the buyer of an option, whether call or put; if it is $20 that is all he stands to lose. For the grantor on the other side of the option transaction, the attraction is the premium income but he stands exposed if the price moves against him and must normally hedge.

All options strategies, no matter how complicated, are made up of a combination of those two basic transactions — calls and puts. For example, gold is $375 and a call option is bought at a $400 strike price; if the price now rises to $400 during the life of the option, it is described as 'at market' (q.v.) and could be exercised to buy gold at that price, or held: if gold then went to $410 it would be described as 'in-the-money' (q.v.) and could also be exercised to buy gold at $400 resulting in an immediate profit. Similarly, a put option may be purchased when gold is $400 at a strike price of $375; if gold falls below $375 before the expiry date, the holder can exercise the right to sell at $375. Mining companies, in particular, can buy this kind of price protection. Of course, with either the call or the put, if the strike price is not reached, the option expires worthless or 'out-of-the-money' (q.v.) with only the premium lost. The mining company, to continue that example, will not mind if a $375 put expires, with gold actually up at $450; they had insurance. That is the simplest case. Complex option strategies have been devised according to the needs of the buyer, the protection or generation of income desired, and expectations of what the market will do.

Normally a grantor of options seeks insurance using what is known as delta hedging (q.v.), a formula measuring the amount of gold to be bought or sold to cover the exposure; the formula is a by-product of the Black and Scholes model used in initial option pricing. The variable factor in delta hedging is the measure of probability of an option being exercised against a grantor; if, for instance, the strike price is $400, the closer gold gets to that the more the grantor must buy or sell to become 'delta neutral'. Delta hedging can have considerable impact on the market price if large options positions of 100,000 ounces or more have to be covered by the equivalent purchase or sale of part or all of this gold.

Options trading has attracted many participants, including many Australian and North American mining companies, the South African Reserve Bank (q.v.) which markets South Africa's gold, the Bank for Foreign Economic Affairs (q.v.), which markets Soviet gold, other central banks and, of course, speculators who like the leverage options offer. It has also evolved into a two-tier market with over-the-counter (OTC) options (q.v.) being offered by many banks and bullion dealers, and exchange options (q.v.) offered by futures markets, notably COMEX, where the option is actually on a gold futures contract.

While options on commodities and securities are not new, gold options were pioneered only in the late 1970s by Mocatta Metals Corporation (q.v.) in New York and Valeurs White Weld (later renamed Crédit Suisse First Boston Futures Trading) in Geneva. They were the forerunners of the OTC options which are now offered by most international bullion houses in London, New York and Zurich.

OTC options are significantly more flexible than exchange options, being a private agreement between the grantor (usually the bullion house) and the buyer. The buyer indicates his exact requirements on strike price, date of expiry and quantity (which in the case of mining companies or central banks may be 100,000 ounces or more); the grantor then quotes a premium for this order. Such OTC options are not tradeable instruments: they constitute an agreement between two principals. In effect they are tailor made by the bullion house for each client. Moreover, unlike exchange options, no details of volume are revealed; everything is confidential so that there are no statistics on the size of the OTC market, although it certainly exceeds the exchange options volume.

Exchange options were first launched on COMEX in New York in October 1982 and subsequently on the American Stock Exchange and the Mid-America Exchange, but only COMEX achieved significant volume. The Bolsa Mercantil et de Futuros (q.v.) in Sao Paulo, Brazil, however, has achieved considerable volume with a 250 gramme gold option. Exchange options offer a standard contract to all comers. Thus a COMEX option on gold futures provides the holder with the right either to buy (call) or sell (put) a COMEX gold futures contract of 100 ounces at the exercise price on or before the expiration date. Contract months are the nearest four of the following contract months: February, April, June, August, October and December. A $400 February gold call option, for example, gives the holder the right to buy a February gold futures contract at a price of $400. This exchange option has a value and can be traded on the exchange many times before it expires. Although COMEX options are used by the mining industry and other professionals, they also attract many speculators, especially if prices are rising when as many as 80 per cent of participants may be speculators.

Since gold options are relatively new, considerable debate attaches to how much, or little, they influence the spot price. The exchange option, being a standard contract with a specific expiry date, will tend to influence the spot price on or near expiration day, particularly when options are only just out-of-the-money and a small movement in the current price could bring them in-the-money. Options trading can then almost pull the spot price towards the strike price.

The influence of OTC options is harder to gauge because they have no standard expiry dates and no details are published, though it is common practice for expiry dates to coincide with COMEX (q.v.). Certainly the volume of both OTC and exchange options has reached proportions where not only are they an integral part of all daily gold market activity, but the potential for them to have considerable short-term influence on the price must be noted.

See also: **Delta Hedging; Exchange Options; Over-the-Counter Options.**

Ore

Originally from the Old English for crude or unwrought metal, ore refers to any economic mineral deposit of precious or other metals. Many combinations of the word are used in mining, such as orebody (q.v.), ore dressing (q.v.), ore grade (q.v.), ore pass (q.v.) and ore reserve (q.v.).

Ore. *Very high grade ore, grading over 100 grammes per tonne, with gold easily visible*

Orebody

A sufficiently large amount of ore that can be mined economically.

Ore Dressing

The preparation or concentration of ore by treatment or cleaning to remove waste material.

Ore Grade

The amount of mineral or metal contained in an ore, usually expressed as troy ounces per ton or grammes per tonne for precious metal orebodies. *See also* **Grade**.

Ore Pass

A steeply dipping tunnel in which ore (or waste) travels under the force of gravity.

Ore Reserve

The prime measured assets of a mine as to tonnage and grade that can be extracted at a profit at current prices and current technology, or in the near future. Ore reserves may be classified as proven, probable or possible. Other reserve terms, which do not necessarily constitute the definition of ore, include geological, in-situ, measured and mineable.

Proven reserves: ore in place for which the tonnage grade and shape have been computed from dimensions revealed in outcrops or trenches or underground workings or drill holes for which the grade is calculated from results of adequate sampling to a high degree of confidence.

Probable reserves: ore in place for which tonnage and grade are calculated partly from specific measurements, samples or production data and partly from projection for a reasonable distance on geological evidence and for which the sites available for inspection, measurement and sampling are too widely or otherwise inappropriately spaced to outline the orebody completely or establish its grade throughout.

Possible reserves: ore in place for which quantitative estimates are based largely on broad knowledge of the geological character of the area and for which there are few, if any, samples or measurements.

Geological reserves: reserves of all categories; proven, probable and possible.

In-situ reserves: mineralisation that is still in the ground. It may or may not be economically recoverable.

Measured reserves: usually proven and possible reserves.

Mineable reserves:, usually proven and probable reserves that may be extracted by mining, taking into account the mining method and the amount of waste dilution.

Ormolu

An imitation gold, made up of a yellow alloy of copper and tin, occasionally also with zinc, used to decorate furniture and art objects. In France, especially in the eighteenth century, very fine quality ormolu was cast and chiselled for furniture mounts, clock cases, candlesticks and chandeliers.

Original Margin

See **Initial Margin; Margin.**

Ounce (Troy)

See **Troy Ounce**.

Outcrop

A vein or orebody (q.v.) which breaks the surface. An outcropper is a miner who works an outcrop.

Outlier

A distant or outlying part of the main orebody (q.v.) where the intervening part is of different material, either country rock or low grade mineralisation. *See also* **Satellite Deposit.**

Out-of-the-Money

An option (q.v.) which has no intrinsic value (q.v.). A call (q.v.) is out-of-the-money if its strike price (q.v.) is higher than the current price; a put (q.v.) is out-of-the-money if the strike price is lower than the current price.

Outturn

The fine gold and other metal proceeds of a refining operation.

Overbought

A market in which the gold price has risen too high and too fast without genuine fundamental support to maintain the new price. Opposite of **oversold** (q.v.).

Overburden

In open-pit mining (q.v.) the waste rock that has to be removed on the surface to access the orebody.

Overmining

This occurs when the grade of ore taken from the mine is substantially and persistently higher than the average grade of the ore reserves. *See also* **High Grading.**

Oversold

A market in which the gold price has fallen too far, too fast, perhaps due to exceptional stop-loss selling, and which is expected to stabilise and move back to a more realistic level. Opposite of **overbought** (q.v.).

Over-the-Counter (OTC) Options

These options (q.v.) differ from exchange options (q.v.) in that they are significantly more flexible, being a private agreement between the grantor, or writer, and the buyer, each acting as a principal. The buyer indicates his exact requirements on strike price, date of expiry and quantity; the grantor then quotes a premium. In effect it is a tailor-made option agreement and, unlike an exchange option, it is not a tradeable instrument, though the holder may trade against his options position. Since everything is confidential, no details of volume are given and the true size and scope of the OTC market is not known, though it is estimated to exceed exchange options. Between fifteen and twenty international banks and bullion dealers offer OTC options, which will reflect the client base of each institution. Some will handle more business with mining companies hedging their production, others will work with central banks who have found that options can provide a useful way of making some return on gold reserves. All the main dealers in London, New York and Zurich offer OTC options.

Oxide Ore

Mineralised rock which has been subjected to weathering and oxidation of primary minerals. Oxidation tends to make an ore more porous. This permits a more complete permeation of cyanide solutions so that minute particles of gold within the minerals can be readily dissolved. Oxide ores are a particular feature of the open-pit mining in Australia and the United States, which expanded so rapidly in the 1980s. These ores, especially in Nevada, could be treated by heap leaching (q.v.). The contrast is with the sulphide ores (q.v.) underlying them, which can usually be reached only by much more costly underground mining and which require more complex mineral processing technology to unlock the gold from the ore.

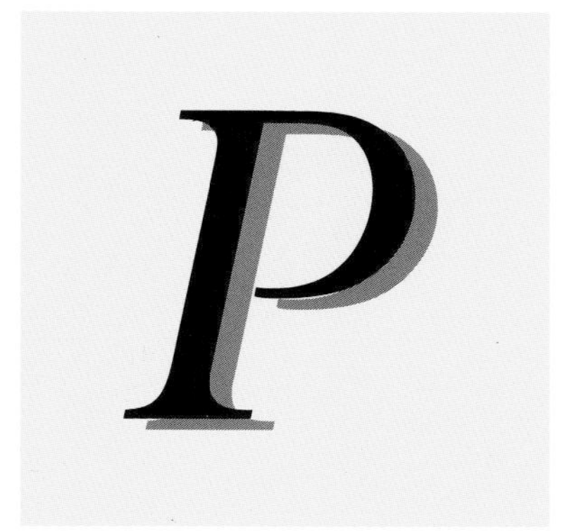

Pad

A large, impermeable foundation used as a base for ore during heap leaching (q.v.). The pad prevents the loss of leach solution from the circuit.

PAMP S.A.

Originally opened in Chiasso, Switzerland in 1977, PAMP S.A. (Produits Artistiques de Métaux Précieux) moved to a new refinery at Castel San Pietro, near Chiasso in 1984. The facilities can refine doré from mines and scrap gold up to 995 or 999.9. Pamp produces a wide range of bars but is noted for small bars of less than 50 grammes, including the distinctive Fortuna (q.v.) brand which did much to widen the vogue for small ingots. PAMP bars are acceptable as good delivery (q.v.) on the London market, and at COMEX (q.v.) in New York and TOCOM (q.v.) in Tokyo. PAMP is affiliated to MKS Finançe S.A. (q.v.).

PAMP S.A.
Castel San Pietro
Switzerland, CH 6874
Tel: 91 - 438041
Fax: 91 - 436979
Telex: 842079

Pan/Panning

The classic and simplest method of mining alluvial gold (q.v.). Gravels from a stream bed are washed in a pan, rotated by hand with a circular motion, causing the lighter sand and gravel to spill out while the heavier particles of gold settle to the bottom. Although professional prospectors would use panning more as an exploration technique nowadays to determine if an area warranted further exploration, many amateur prospectors in the United States spend their weekends panning in the Sacramento and American rivers of California, the scene of the original gold rush.

Pan. *Garimpeiro panning for gold in a tributary of the Amazon in Brazil*

Panda

Chinese one ounce gold coin (not strictly speaking a bullion coin (q.v.)) of 999.9 quality made by the China Mint Company in Beijing, sold on a low premium and first launched in 1982. The design of the Panda is changed annually and all are made to half proof quality.

About 300,000 are produced each year of which two-thirds are sold in the United States where a collectors' market for the coin has been established. Early years trade at a significant premium. The coin is also available in ½, ¼ and ⅒ ounce sizes.

Paper Gold

A general term to describe gold contracts, such as loco London, futures certificates (q.v.) and options (q.v.), which do not necessarily involve the delivery of physical gold. Such 'paper gold' is preferred by many investors and speculators who do not wish to be bothered with the delivery and storage of gold. In fact on the exchanges very little gold is actually delivered; on COMEX (q.v.) usually less than 1 per cent of contract turnover.

Panda. *China's one-ounce coin, launched in 1982, sells about 300,000 annually*

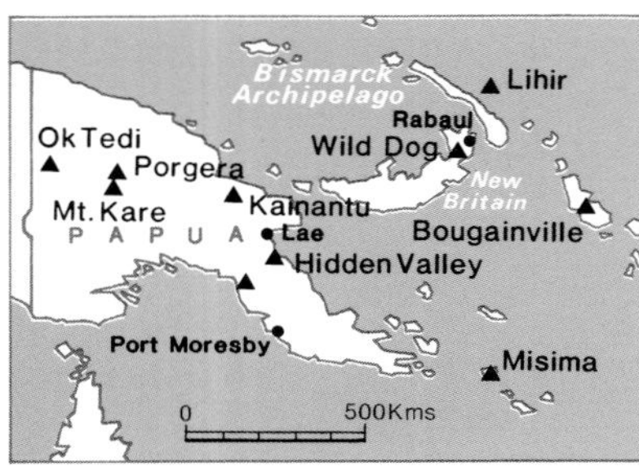

Papua New Guinea. *Existing and prospective mines are scattered through many of the islands*

Papua New Guinea (PNG)

Papua New Guinea, strategically placed on the Pacific basin's 'Rim of Fire' (q.v.) with its many epithermal (q.v.) gold deposits, is emerging as a major gold producing nation. The size of epithermal deposits being explored suggests that Papua New Guinea will be a significant producer into the twenty-first century.

In fact, gold was first reported near Port Moresby in 1873 and thereafter alluvial mining, including several large dredge operations, produced at least four million ounces (about 125 tonnes) during the next hundred years. Alluvial mining, especially around Mount Kare, still accounts for about 3–5 tonnes annually.

The first important mining operation came with CRA's discovery of the Panguna copper/gold deposit on the island of Bougainville, where production started in 1972, reaching annual output of around 20 tonnes of gold (the Bougainville operation was shut down in 1989 due to action by local tribal separatists). The Ok Tedi mine, operated by Australia's BHP, came on stream in western Papua New Guinea in 1984; again, it is a copper mine with a gold 'cap' which yields about 12 tonnes annually. Placer Pacific (q.v.) opened another mine on Misima Island in 1989 with annual production scheduled for 10 tonnes over a ten-year life. Placer also has a much bigger project at Porgera on the mainland, in association with Highlands Gold and Renison Goldfields Consolidated, scheduled to produce up to 28 tonnes annually in the mid-1990s.

Gold mine development in Papua New Guinea has been beset by a hostile climatic environment, considerable local landowner and tribal resentment, and technological problems with difficult ores. However, overall output should rise from the 30–35 tonnes annually of the late 1980s to towards 100 tonnes annually before the year 2000, making Papua New Guinea the sixth or seventh largest producer.

Papua New Guinea. *The Porgera gold mine, set to produce 28 tonnes annually from 1991*

Paris Gold Market

The Paris gold market has been essentially a domestic one, with exchange controls limiting the free import and export of gold by individuals. In 1987, the freedom of trading physical gold was extended beyond France's frontiers. The traditional anonymity of gold trading was removed in 1981 but restored in 1986. An individual fiscally domiciled in France is, however, liable to a 7 per cent resale tax. Turnover is much less than in the 1950s and 1960s when the French were regarded as the greatest hoarders (q.v.) of gold in Europe. There are three daily sessions, two for 12.5 kg (good delivery) bars and a third for the kilo bar and the most common gold coins such as the 20 franc Napoleon (q.v.), the US Double Eagle (q.v.) and the Mexican Centenario (q.v.). There is no quotation in France for the Krugerrand or Maple Leaf. There are ten participants: BNP (Banque National de Paris), Banque de Paris et des Pays Bas, CMP (Compagnie des Métaux Précieux) (q.v.), Compagnie Parisienne de Rescompte, CLAL (Comptoir Lyon-Alemand Louyot) (q.v.), Crédit de la Bourse, Crédit Lyonnais, Crédit du Nord, Neuflize Schlumberger Mallet and Société Générale. Bidding at the fixing is by open-outcry (q.v.) with a broker who is selling shouting *'Je l'ai'*, while buyers call *'Je le prends'*.

Parting

The separation of silver from gold in the refining process.

Paste Golds

Heavy compositions of powdered gold suspended in a solution of flux and binder applied by brush or screen printing, followed by firing to produce a tarnish-resistant gold colour and texture for a number of decorative and electronic/electrical uses.

Pay Dirt/Payable/Payability

Economic gold ore extracted from mining operations.

Pay Limit

See **Cut-off Grade.**

Pegging

Australian term for staking a mining claim.

Pennyweight

Originally the weight of a silver penny in Britain in the Middle Ages, it is still widely used in North America as the unit of weight in the jewellery trade. There are 20 pennyweights in one troy ounce (q.v.).

Perth Mint

Australia's oldest government mint was established in Perth, Western Australia in 1899 as a branch of the Royal Mint to refine the gold from the Kalgoorlie gold rush. It made its own Sovereigns and Half Sovereigns with its own mint mark (q.v.), issuing over 106 million of the coins. It remained a branch of the Royal Mint until 1970, when it was taken over by the Western Australian government. The Mint is now the centre of the Australian International Precious Metals Coin Programme, issuing the nugget bullion coin (q.v.), the platinum Koala coin, and the Kookaburra silver coin marketed through GoldCorp (q.v.) Australia. It also refined much of the gold from the new mining boom of the 1980s. Its bars are acceptable as good delivery (q.v.) on the London market. The Mint has also been renamed the Western Australian Mint.

Perth Mint
310 Hay Street
East Perth, WA 6004
Australia
Tel: (9) 421 7277

Philharmoniker. *The Austrian bullion coin before the home of the Vienna Philharmonic Orchestra, which it honours*

Fax: (9) 221 4713
Telex: GOLDAA 197171

Peru

Gold was being recovered from the rivers of the Andes at least by 1000 BC and in a succession of ancient civilisations over the next 2,500 years the goldsmiths' art was raised to an exceptional level in Pre-Columbian (q.v.) jewellery and other ornaments. Some gold has always been produced as a by-product of Peru's silver mines, and alluvial mining continues at a level of about 10 tonnes annually.

Pesos

The 50 pesos restrike coin dated 1947, 900 fine, fine gold content 1.2057 troy ounces, based on the original Centenario coin launched in 1920 in Mexico. Also available in 20 pesos, 10 pesos, 5 pesos, 2½ pesos and 2 pesos coins. *See* **Centenario.**

Pforzheim

The town of Pforzheim, just west of Stuttgart, is the centre of Germany's jewellery manufacturing industry. Over four hundred of the nation's nine hundred jewellery manufacturers are located there (the other main centres being Ida Oberstain and Swabisch Gmund), accounting for over 70 per cent of Germany's carat gold jewellery manufacture of between 40 and 50 tonnes annually. All the major German semi-fabricators (halbzeug) are located there, including Degussa (q.v.), Heraeus (q.v.), Allgemeine Gold under Silber Scheideanstelt, Hafner, and Weiland, along with specialist manufacturers for rolled gold (q.v.). A permanent exhibition is maintained at the Industriehaus (Industrierveband Schmuck und Silberwaren, Industriehaus, 7530 Pforzheim).

Philharmoniker

One ounce legal tender 999.9 bullion coin, with face value of 2,000 schillings, struck by the Austrian Mint and launched in 1989. The coin is named in honour of the Wiener Philharmoniker, the Vienna Philharmonic Orchestra, and bears the design of their instruments. Also available as a ¼ ounce coin.

Philipp Brothers

See **Salomon Brothers Inc.**

Philippines

The Philippines ranks as the sixth largest gold producer in the western world, with output around 40 tonnes annually. Regular production has been maintained since 1907. Up to the late 1960s most gold came from primary gold deposits, but since then, more than 50 per cent of output has come from porphyry (q.v.) copper deposits. The Philippines is on the Pacific basin 'Rim of Fire' (q.v.) and, like its southern neighbour Papua

New Guinea, has both porphyry copper and epithermal (q.v.) gold deposits. Primary gold mining, however, revived in the 1980s with the new technology of heap leaching (q.v.) and carbon-in-pulp (q.v.) making exploitation of low grade deposits viable.There are 13 primary gold and seven copper/gold mines operating. The biggest primary producer is Benguet Corporation, which operates seven deposits, of which three are open-pit mines (Antamok, Tuding and Cal Horr) and the rest are lode veins being mined underground. Benguet also has a gold/silver/copper mine at Dizon, with good gold grades of 0.6–0.8 grammes per tonne. Atlas Consolidated's Masbate is the biggest single deposit being mined, grading 1.5 to 3.0 grammes per tonne and using both heap-leaching and carbon-in-pulp. Surigao Consolidated has the Siana mine, the only Carlin-type (q.v.) disseminated gold deposit yet discovered. Other mines include Manila Mining's Placer gold project which is both underground and open-pit, and the Masara mine on Davao, working an underground gold-quartz vein. Atlas Consolidated also has a porphyry copper deposit with low grade gold, while the Philex porphyry mine grades much better at over 0.6 grammes per tonne. The only non-porphyry copper producer is Lepanto's Mankayan mine, the oldest in the Philippines, which has copper vein ores with a good gold grade; additionally a gold-rich porphyry copper deposit has been found beneath the present workings, which may be developed.

Small scale alluvial mining is also prevalent in the Philippines, especially around Davao on Mindanao and around Baguio, involving several hundred thousand prospectors. They have been helped by the government putting in small cyanidation plants to improve recovery. Output from these mines is between 10 and 15 tonnes per year. Most of this output is bought by local buying stations of the central bank.

The central bank has its own refinery at Quezon City, near Manila, where the gold is refined. All primary producers must sell their output to the central bank. The Central Bank of the Philippines refinery has acceptable good delivery status in London.

See also **Chamber of Mines of the Philippines.**

Philosopher's Stone

The principal aim of alchemists throughout the Middle Ages was to find the Philosopher's Stone, a mysterious agent which possessed the properties of producing gold and prolonging life.

See also **Alchemy.**

Physical Metal

Gold bought and delivered in bullion form is called physical metal, or actual metal, in contrast with paper transactions such as futures (q.v.), options (q.v.) or loco London (q.v.).

Pillars

Blocks of ore left intact to act as supports for shafts or other underground workings after primary extraction. Pillars are often the last sections of ore removed during the mine break-up stage.

Pit

On North American futures exchanges each commodity, such as gold, is traded in its own pit by open-outcry (q.v.) on the floor of the exchange. Each pit is like a small amphitheatre with a range of steps; each step is assigned a specific delivery month (q.v.), so that a floor broker doing February business will stand on the February step and so forth.

Pitting

The exploration of an alluvial (q.v.) deposit by the sinking of a number of small shafts to gather samples.

Placer

A gravel-type deposit formed by the erosion of rocks and veins and accumulated alluvially (q.v.) or glacially, that contains particles of gold or other minerals. It may be found at the surface or underground. Historically, most gold rushes have been placer discoveries where the gold is easily accessible to thousands of diggers. The original Australian and Californian rushes of 1848 and 1852 were to placer deposits. In 1980, similar discoveries drew thousands of prospectors in Brazil and Venezuela.

Placer Dome

Placer Dome is the second largest gold producer in North America. The company has interests in 17 operating gold mines in Canada, the United States, Australia and Papua New Guinea, which in 1989 produced 1.183 million ounces (36.8 tonnes). Four mines were brought on-stream in 1989 and two others in 1990. Production from Australia and PNG is derived from a 75.8 per cent interest in Placer Pacific. Placer Dome's largest producer, at present, is the wholly-owned Campbell mine which produced 267,876 ounces (8.3 tonnes) of gold in 1989.

Placer Dome,
P.O Box 49330,
Bentall Postal Station,
1600-1055 Dunsmuir Street,
Vancouver, B.C. V7X 1P1,
Canada.
Tel: (604) 682-7082
Fax: (604) 682-7092
Telex: 04-55181

Placer Pacific

Placer Pacific is a significant Australian-based gold producer. It is 75.8 per cent owned by parent Placer Dome of Canada. The company achieved dramatic growth in 1989, progressing from one major mine, Kidston, to four, with the commissioning of Big Bell, Misima and Granny Smith. In addition, the company has a 30 per cent interest in the huge Porgera project in PNG which began commercial production in August 1990. Placer Pacific's production in 1989 totalled 322,784 ounces (10 tonnes) of gold; however, the company is poised to become an 800,000 ounces (nearly 25 tonnes) per year producer in the early 1990s.
Placer Pacific
Gold Fields House
1 Alfred Street,
Sydney, NSW 2000, Australia
Tel: (02) 241-1873
Fax: (02) 233-6326
Telex: AA121356

Planchet

Usual term in the United States for a coin blank (q.v.) with milled edges before it is struck.

Plate/Plating

See **Electroplating; Gold Potassium Cyanide.**

Plumb Gold

A carat gold alloy which assays (q.v.) exactly (plumb) as the title stamped on it — 14 carat, 18 carat — with no tolerance.

Porphyry Gold

An homogenous igneous deposit in which the crystals of several minerals are finely disseminated. They are found in regions of volcanic activity, such as the Pacific basin 'rim of fire' (q.v.) often as copper-gold ore bodies, like that at Bougainville in Papua New Guinea or Benquet Corporation's Dizon (which is copper, gold, silver), in the Philippines.

Position

The exposure of a trader to the market, either long or short.

Position Trading

A trader who remains long or short for an extended period.

Precinox SA

Swiss fabricator of special tubes and sections in precious metals and a wide range of carat gold alloys.
Precinox SA,
Boulevard des Eplatures 42,
2304 La Chaux-de-Fonds,
Switzerland.
Tel: (39) 26 63 64
Fax: (39) 26 89 25
Telex: 952206

Precious Metal

Originally referring to gold and silver, as metals of great value, but extended in modern times to include platinum and other platinum group metals. Similarly diamonds, emeralds and rubies have always been precious stones.

Pre-Columbian

The general term for jewellery (q.v.) and ornaments in gold made in South America, chiefly in what are now Colombia and Peru, before Columbus discovered the Americas. Until the nineteenth century the gold objects that pre-dated the Spanish conquest were usually attributed to the Incas themselves, but it is now known that the goldsmith's art reached a high level much earlier. The first great Peruvian civilisation of Chavin around 1200 BC was already making gold ornaments by hammering fine sheets of metal and decorating them by embossing. The technique of casting (q.v.) gold was developed by the Nazca people in the deserts of southern Peru before AD 500. The apogee of technical skills came during the Chimu Empire between AD 1150 and 1450, when goldsmiths perfected lost wax casting (q.v.), alloys (q.v.), welding, and plating.

They learned how to do filigree (q.v.) by rolling gold under tension into fine wires. Plating was done with an alloy of 30 per cent gold, 70 per cent copper; after being poured onto an ornament, this alloy was treated with acids extracted from plant juices producing a copper oxide which

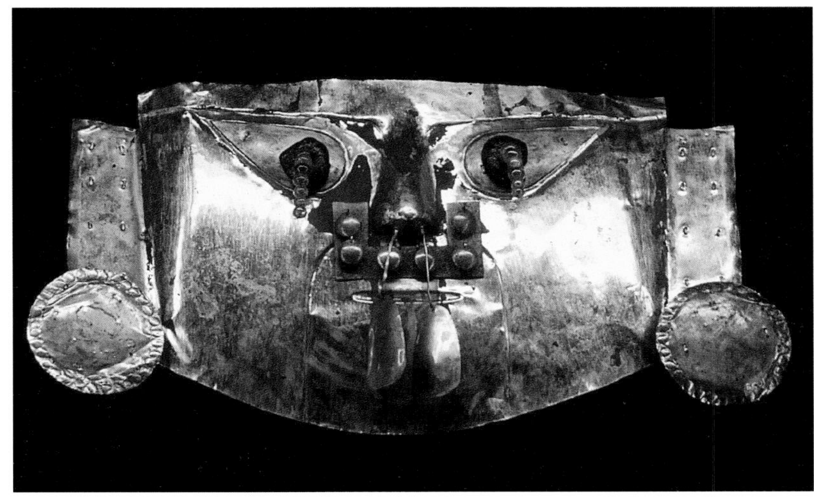

Pre-Columbian. *Gold burial mask of the Chimu Empire, when magnificent work was created by craftsmen of high technical accomplishment*

could be cleaned off, leaving the surface covered with a thin film of pure gold. Wonderful replicas of animals, birds, plants (golden corn in a sheaf of silver leaves) were made. When the Incas conquered the Chimu, they still employed their best goldsmiths, for the craft was highly esteemed; gold was 'the sweat of the sun' (and silver 'the tears of the moon'!). This tradition, however, was shattered by the Spanish invasion of South America and Pizarro's capture and ransom of the Inca. An estimated eight tonnes of Pre-Columbian ornaments were melted down to pay it, and a tradition of craftsmanship built up over 2,500 years destroyed. The best collection of surviving Pre-Columbian gold is in the Museo del Oro (q.v.) in Bogota, Colombia.

Premex AG

Zurich broker, owned by Crédit Suisse, Swiss Bank Corporation and Union Bank of Switzerland, which caters to the professional market in spot, options and forwards.

Premex AG
Munsterhof 17, 8001
Zurich , Switzerland
Tel: (1) 211 92 11
Fax: (1) 211 78 96
Telex: 813 697 pre ch
Reuters: PREZ

Premium

(i) In options (q.v.) the premium is the cost of the option, and that is the specific amount at risk to the buyer. The premium is usually calculated on the Black-Scholes model (q.v.). For the grantor, or writer, of options the attraction is the premium income.

(ii) A premium is normally charged for extra quality on bars over 995 fine.

(iii) A premium is also normally charged on the manufacturing costs of bars smaller than the 400 ounce (12.5 kg) good delivery bars, i.e. on such bars as kilobars and ten tola bars (q.v.).

(iv) A premium over loco London may also be charged for bars c.i.f. certain locations, such as regional markets like Dubai or Singapore.

(v) The percentage mark-up over the actual gold content of a coin or small bar. Bullion coins (q.v.) were conceived to keep this premium as low as possible.

Pressure Burst

Also known as a seismic event. A sudden release of energy in a mine, often causing damage to the operations.

Common in deep South African gold mines caused by the release of stress built up during mining.

Pressure Oxidation

See **Autoclave.**

Prestito d'Uso

Common terminology in the Italian market for leasing. Differs from *Conto Lavorazione* (q.v.) where the precise quantity of metal delivered to a manufacturer retains its identity and must be returned or exported in manufactured form. By contrast, under *Prestito d'Uso*, a dealer lends gold to a manufacturer and delivers it in Italy, usually under a bank guarantee. The metal will then lose its identity, and the borrower's only responsibility is to repay the gold on maturity of the loan.

Pre-stripping

The initial removal of overburden (q.v.) prior to the commencement of normal open pit mining operations.

Price of Gold,

Gold's reputation as a store or standard of value is based upon the historic stability of its price; it was fixed and thus a bench-mark against which other commodities could be judged. 'Its purchasing power in the middle of the twentieth century was very nearly the same as in the midst of the seventeenth century,' noted Professor Roy Jastram, the statistician who analysed the price for his seminal work *The Golden Constant* (q.v.). The classic example of gold's fixed price was the sterling price set in 1717 at £3.17.10½d per standard troy ounce (this was for 916 gold, equal to a fine gold price of £4.4.11½d per troy ounce) which survived until Britain went off the

Gold price in US$ 1969–1990

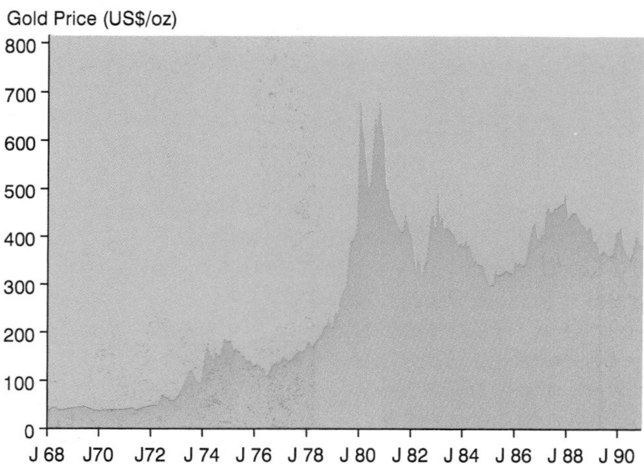

Price of Gold. *Source: Gold Fields Mineral Services Ltd*

gold standard (q.v.) in 1931; within that period of over 200 years, there was little variation in the price except during the Napoleonic Wars when the gold standard was briefly suspended, and the price reached £5.7.0½d per standard ounce.

Throughout that long period the sterling price was also the international price. But after World War I, the US dollar price (then $20.67 an ounce) increasingly became the bench-mark for gold. This was confirmed from 1934 when President Roosevelt raised the price to $35 an ounce, at which level the US Treasury stood ready to buy gold from all comers (and sell to approved central banks). The $35 price was defended until 1968, including massive interventions by the gold pool (q.v.) of central banks. After 1968, gold was left to float free in private market trading, though $35 was preserved for central banks in a short-lived two-tier market.

The London gold market's fixing (q.v.) also switched in 1968 from a sterling to a dollar price, marking the final acceptance of the dollar as the world-wide quote for gold. But the price itself entered a new era; no longer fixed, no longer stable, fluctuating often in a day more than it had in a century. From $35 in 1968 it was $850 by 1980, by which time no one was sure where it ought to be. It took the 1980s to settle down to a more realistic range. But the performance of the dollar price became, in many ways, merely a reflection of the dollar's own strength or weakness. Any modern analysis of the gold price must look at its performance in a range of currencies, particularly Deutschmarks, Swiss francs and yen.

Prill

In assaying (q.v.), the bead or globule of metal left after cupellation (q.v.). It may also refer to a small nugget of gold.

Primary/Primary Gold

Newly mined gold that has been extracted from ore but not yet refined. It also refers to mines where gold is the primary product, as opposed to mines, such as porphyry copper deposits, from which gold is also recovered as a by-product (q.v.). Contrast also with secondary metal (q.v.) and scrap (q.v.).

Principals

In trading, dealers or others who operate on their own account, as opposed to brokers or agents. In forward trading (q.v.) or over-the-counter options (q.v.), for example, the agreement is directly between principals, such as a bullion house and a mining company.

Process Scrap

Scrap (q.v.) which occurs as a normal part of a jewellery or watch manufacturer's operations and is reprocessed back into fresh alloys as part of his working inventory.

Production

Historically the production of gold may be divided into two eras: before and after the California gold rush of 1848. Prior to the Californian discoveries, gold was, indeed, a rather rare metal. Exactly how much was mined from ancient times is not precisely known, but rough annual estimates are shown in the table below.

From 1848 the California gold rush, swiftly followed by that in Australia, lifted production into another dimension. Output by 1852 was up to 280 tonnes, and an estimated 10,000 tonnes was mined in the second half of the nineteenth century. By the end of the century it was averaging 400 tonnes annually. In the twentieth century production increases have mirrored price increases; first from 1935 to 1940 following gold's rise to $35,

Annual Production of Gold Pre-1848

Egyptians from 2000 BC	1 tonne	Egypt/Sudan/Saudi Arabia
Roman Empire	6-9 tonnes	Mainly from Spain/Portugal
500-1400	0.5 tonnes	Germany/Austria
1450 onwards	5-8 tonnes	Gold Coast of West Africa
1500-1600	5-10 tonnes	Gold Coast/South America
1600-1700	10-12 tonnes	Gold Coast/South America
1700-1800	15-25 tonnes	Gold Coast/Brazil and other South American countries/Russia
1800-1840	25-50 tonnes	Gold Coast/Brazil and other South American countries/Russia
1847	77 tonnes	Russia over 30 tonnes, plus Africa/South America

Worldwide Annual Gold Production (1840-1989)

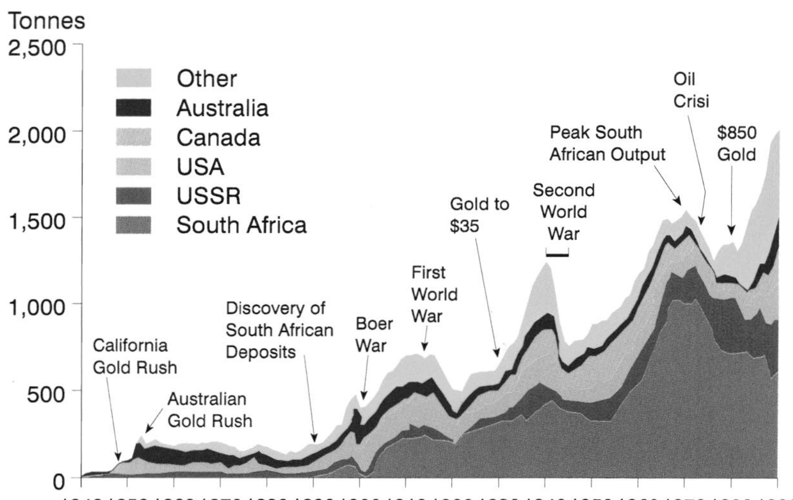

Source: Gold Fields Mineral Services Ltd

and again in the 1980s, as the chart shows.

Production Cost

See **Cash Production Cost**.

Proof Coins

The finest quality of coin struck with specially cleaned and prepared dies and usually marketed for collectors or presentation purposes at a premium. A small number of proof coins are usually made each year, even of bullion coins (q.v.) and other popular coins such as Sovereigns.

Prospect/Prospector

The search for gold carried out by individual prospectors looking for surface indications. Both words took on this special meaning after the California gold rush (q.v.) of 1848. It was this gold rush which ushered in the age of the gold prospector, who for the next 50 years explored for gold throughout the western United States, Canada, Australia and New Zealand. The concept of the prospector has a rather romantic image, though the life was intolerably hard, and persists today among the fifty thousand members of the Gold Prospectors Association of America who go out in the hills in an unending search for gold. The true modern successor to the American image, are the *garimpeiros* (q.v.) of Brazil or small miners in the Philippines and Indonesia. *See also* **Gold Rushes.**

Pure Gold

Gold that is of 999.9 fineness or 24 carat, with no alloy, is the highest or purest standard accepted by the market.

Purple of Cassius

A mixture of colloidal gold and stannic acid.

Put Option

A contract between buyer and seller, which gives the buyer the right, but not the obligation, to sell a specified amount of gold (or other commodity) at a predetermined price on or before a specified date. The seller, or grantor, of the put option is obliged to take delivery if the buyer wishes to exercise the option and for that charges a premium.

Usually abbreviated to 'put' and is the opposite of **call option** (q.v.). *See also* **Options.**

Pyx

The special box at the Royal Mint in Britain into which specimen coins are placed to be assayed by the Goldsmiths' Company (q.v.) at their annual Trial of the Pyx, which dates back to 1282.

Quartation

The process in which silver is separated from gold by dissolving it out with nitric acid.

Quartz/Quartz Mining

Quartz is a common silica mineral found in all kinds of rocks and mineral veins, and in many primary gold deposits. Such deposits were formed when siliceous liquids bearing gold were forced up through fissures in the earth's crust, where they cooled to form lodes or veins. Auriferous quartz deposits account for a significant number of mining operations, particularly in Canada.

In South Africa, gold is extracted in a quartz-pebble conglomerate of the Witwatersrand Basin (q.v.).

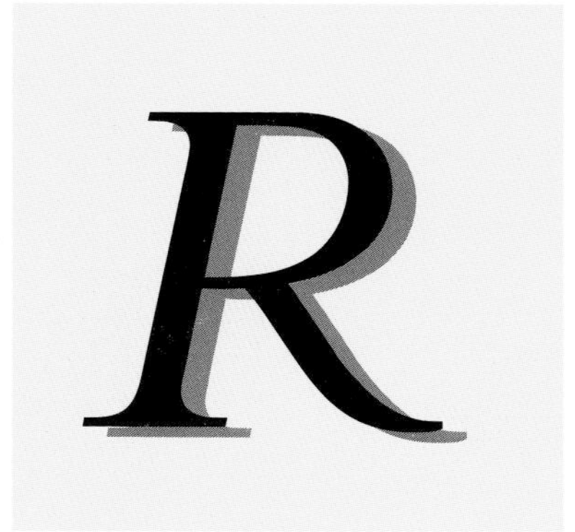

Ramp

Also known as a **Decline**, or **Winze.** A downward sloping underground tunnel which provides access for exploration or mining, or a connection between levels of a mine.

Rand Refinery

The Rand Refinery first opened in 1921 to refine South Africa's gold, which had previously been refined in London. The refinery, which handles all of South Africa's gold output of around 600 tonnes annually, was largely re-built in the late 1980s and is the world's largest. It has three sections:

(i) The refinery section, which upgrades bullion from the mines — which on average contains 85 per cent gold, 10 per cent silver and 5 per cent base and platinum group metals — into 995 good delivery (q.v.) bars, and further refines some gold to 999.9.

(ii)The smelter section which recovers silver/gold bullion from by-product low-grade materials which are not amenable to the cyanide process on the mines.

(iii) The coin section, where gold blanks are produced for the minting of Krugerrands (q.v.) or other coins, which after striking by the South African Mint are returned to the refinery for warehousing and selling. This section also produces small bars, mainly of one kilogramme.

Rand Refinery
P O Box 565,
Germiston
South Africa 1400
Tel: (011) 873 2222
Fax: (011) 825 1806
Telex: (011) 744 445

Ratio

The number of ounces of silver that can be bought with one ounce of gold. *See also* **Gold/Silver Ratio.**

RDS

See **Reuter Monitor Dealing Service**

Recovery

The amount of gold or silver extracted in the initial milling or concentrating process, usually expressed as a percentage of the total contained metal. *See also* **Grade.**

Recycled Gold

Scrap generated from jewellery, electronics, and dentistry, either during the manufacturing process or when items are redundant, or by members of the public selling items when the gold price is high. *See also* **Dishoarding; Scrap.**

Red Gold

Alloys consisting of gold, silver and sometimes zinc, but with copper in high percentages to give a red colour.

Reduction Plant

The ore treatment plant on a mine, also known as the mill, where the ore is crushed and gold is first extracted or concentrated before being sent for actual refining. *See also* **Mill/Milling.**

Reef

A stratified deposit commonly found in sedimentary rock, which may contain gold-bearing conglomerate. The classic example is the reefs of the Witwatersrand Basin (q.v.) of South Africa (q.v.).

Refining/Refineries

The separating and purifying of gold from other metals is called refining, as distinct from smelting (q.v.) which is the separation of gold from impurities. Gold going through refineries may either be recycled scrap (q.v.) being purified and upgraded or on the final stage of its transformation from ore in the mine to bullion bars. Two basic processes are used: the chemical Miller Process (q.v.), employing chlorine as the purifying agent; or electrolysis (q.v.), a technique originally developed in the 1870s by Dr Emil Wohlwill (q.v.)

Refining. *Pouring a 999.9 good delivery bar at the PAMP Refinery*

and since much modernised. Using chlorine, gold can be refined up to a fineness of 995 parts per thousand but for fineness up to 999.9, electrolysis is essential. Markets do not recognise bars stamped with a fineness higher than 999.9, although a 999.99 (five nines) gold wire is refined for the electronics industry (q.v.).

Refineries traditionally produced most of their bars by the chemical chlorine process simply because it was quicker and the gold was not tied up for several days as it is if electrolysis is used. But the shift in the demand for gold from monetary applications (for which central banks will take 995 gold) to jewellery, industry or coin has meant that since the 1960s electrolytic facilities are installed increasingly in refineries.

The consistent technical ability required for a refinery to maintain the quality of its bars means that achieving international acceptability is relatively difficult. About fifty refineries world-wide have their bars accepted as good delivery (q.v.) by the London Bullion Market Association (q.v.). The largest refinery is the Rand Refinery (q.v.) in South Africa.

See also: **Argor-Heraeus; Degussa; Engelhard Industries; Heraeus; Johnson Matthey; Ishifuku; Métaux Précieux; PAMP; Tanaka K. K.; Tokuriki; Valcambi.**

Refractory Ore

Mineralised rock in which much of the gold is encapsulated in sulphides or other minerals and is not readily amenable to dissolution by cyanide solutions (unlike oxidised ore) even with fine grinding. Mines with this problem include McLaughlin, California (Homestake) and Goldstrike in Nevada (American Barrick).

See also **Autoclave; Roaster.**

Registered Commodity Representative (RCR)

On US futures markets (q.v.) a broker or account executive registered with the Commodity Futures Trade Commission and legally permitted to solicit or accept customer orders is known as a Registered Commodity Representative.

Republic National Bank of New York

New York bank, owned by Edmond Safra, that is a dealer in precious metals, coin, futures and options; also one of the main suppliers to the US jewellery industry. The bank is also active in London, as a member of the London Bullion Market Association (q.v.), in Singapore and Hong Kong.

Republic National Bank of New York
452 Fifth Avenue
New York, NY 10018
USA
Tel: (212) 525 6000
Fax: (212) 525 6148
Telex: 236927
Reuters: RNBN

Reserve Bank of Zimbabwe

The central bank of Zimbabwe, to which all local gold production must be sold and which then markets the gold.

Reserves

Ore assessed by a mining company for future development and extraction. *See* **Ore Reserves**.

Resin-in-Pulp

Technology by which gold is recovered from crushed ore by making it adhere to a special resin solution. The process was initially fully tested at the Soviet gold mine Muruntau in the 1970s, as an alternative to the carbon-in-pulp (q.v.) process which was more widely adopted elsewhere. (Resins are small water-insoluble beads of plastic-like material used in ion-exchange columns for the collection of precious metals from solutions.)

Resistance

In technical analysis, resistance is a temporary barrier or ceiling along a rising trend line at a price level from which there has previously been a substantial collapse.

If gold was trading, for example, for some weeks or months above $400, and then collapsed back to $360, considerable 'resistance' would be met before that $400 barrier could again be breached, with sellers becoming more aggressive than buyers.

Resource

A mineral deposit that may eventually become recoverable economically but at present insufficient data is available on the mineralisation to classify it as an ore reserve.

Restrikes

Low-premium gold coins (q.v.) such as the Austrian Corona (q.v.) and the Mexican Centenario (q.v.) which are minted officially according to demand, always with the same design and date. The Centenario, for example, bears the date 1947.

Reuter Monitor Dealing Service (RDS)

Communications system established by Reuters and available to users on subscription. RDS is used increasingly by professional traders in gold, especially by banks who also trade foreign exchange through this medium.

RDS
85 Fleet Street, London EC4
Tel: (071) 250 1122
Fax: (071) 324 5607

Reuters Codes for Gold and Precious Metals Information

Reuter Gold/Silver News Index	RCOH-J
Bullion Pages	
Hong Kong Gold Reports	GDHB-C
London Gold Reports - Bullion/Futures	GDLS-V
Tokyo Gold Report	GDJB-C
Hong Kong On-Line Gold Price Conversion	HONK
U.S. Gold Report	MMGU-V
Zurich Gold Report	GDLW-X
Exchanges	
Chinese Gold and Silver Exchange Society, Hong Kong	HKGG
International Monetary Market, Chicago	IMMY-Z
Gold Dealing - New Subscribers	GNSA-C
Multicontributor/Composite Page Information	
World Gold Prices	GLDA
Multicentre Gold Price	GLDB
24 Hour Bullion Market	GLDC
European Multicontributor Gold Prices	GLDE
US Composite Gold Prices	GLDP
Asian Gold and Silver Prices - Hourly	GLDQ
London Gold Price - Hong Kong Market	LDR
Singapore Loco London Gold Price	GLDT
Australian Gold and Silver Prices	GLDU
Loco London Gold Price - Hong Kong Market	GLDV
Swiss Multicontributor Gold	GLDW
London Gold Price	GLDX
Gulf Gold and Silver Prices	GLSK
London Interbank Bullion Forward Rate	GOFO
North American/International Bullion Rates	NYMG/RMFB

Rho

In options (q.v.) this is the factor in pricing indicating the sensitivity of an option's theoretical value to a change in interest rates.

Rhodite

A naturally occurring alloy of gold and rhodium.

Ring

See **Pit.**

Roaster/Roasting

A furnace in which refractory gold ores with a very high sulphide content are heated in air, or 'roasted' to burn off the sulphur leaving an oxide ore which is more easily treated. Because the sulphur poses environmental problems and because of improved gold recovery, roasting is being replaced by pressure oxidation in an autoclave (q.v.).

Rolled Gold/Rolled Gold Plate

The process in which a layer of carat gold alloy is mechanically bonded to another metal. In the United States

Royal Mint. *Making Sovereigns at the Royal Mint soon after their launch in 1817*

the designation 'rolled gold' or 'rolled gold plate' means that the proportion of gold alloy to the weight of the entire article is less than 1/20th; if it is over 1/20th it will be designated gold filled (q.v.). Elsewhere the term tends to be interchangeable with 'gold fill'. *See also* **Gold Filled.**

Rolling

The process of producing gold alloys (q.v.) in the form of sheet or strip by rolling it through one or more mills (q.v.). This is usually done without heat and is known as cold working (q.v.).

Rollover

The renewal of a forward (q.v.) or futures (q.v.) position that is nearing the delivery date, or the renewal of a gold loan (q.v.) reaching maturity.

Rothschild, N. M. & Sons Ltd

Nathan Mayer Rothschild established this merchant banking house in London in 1804 and at once became active in the bullion trade. Rothschild bought the Royal Mint Refinery in the 1850s and operated it until it closed in 1968. A representative of Rothschilds has been chairman of the daily gold fixing (q.v.) since its inception on their premises in 1919. Rothschilds are also active in gold trading in Hong Kong, New York and Singapore.

N. M. Rothschild & Sons Ltd
New Court, St Swithin's Lane
London EC4P 4DU
Tel: (071) 280 5000
Fax: (071) 929 1646
Telex: 888031
Reuters: NMRB

Royal Canadian Mint

The Royal Canadian Mint in Ottawa works both as a refinery, treating gold mine production and scrap, and as a producer of gold coin. As a refinery, its bars have good delivery status on the London market. As a Mint, it manufactures and markets the Maple Leaf (q.v.) bullion coin and other special proof gold coin issues for collectors.

Royal Canadian Mint
320 Sussex Drive
Ottawa K1A 0G9. Canada
Tel: (613) 993 2248
Fax: (613) 952 8342
Telex: 1053 4493

Royal Mint

The minting of coins began in Britain in the first century BC. The Royal Mint itself was established in the Tower of London at least by 1279 and remained there for over 500 years until 1811, when it moved to new facilities on Tower Hill nearby. In 1968 the Royal Mint moved to an entirely new plant at Llantrisant in Wales, where it makes the coinage for Britain and many other countries. Historically, it minted the gold Sovereign (q.v.) and the golden Guinea (q.v.). Sovereigns are still minted, together with the Britannia bullion coin (q.v.) and other collector coins (q.v.) in proof and uncirculated quality, and commemorative medals, in gold and silver. The Royal Mint has its own coin clubs for Britain and North America, with combined membership of over 225,000.

Royal Mint
Llantrisant, Pontyclun
Mid-Glamorgan CF7 8YT, Wales
Tel: (0443) 222 1111
Fax: (0443) 228 7999

Royalty

Any fee paid to another party by a producing mine relating to the use of the property.

RTZ Corp.

RTZ, perhaps the largest mining company in the world, is a diversified metals and minerals producer and has a significant interest in gold. The majority of the company's present gold interests were acquired in June 1989 following the purchase of BP Minerals.

In the first six months of 1990, RTZ produced 408,000 ounces of gold, with gold and copper accounting for 66% of the company's net attributable profits. By far the most important operation is the Bingham

Canyon gold–copper mine which produces 450,000 ounces per year of gold.

The other significant project is the Lihir Island prospect in Papua New Guinea. The project is perhaps the largest undeveloped known gold orebody in the world. The mine is expected to start production in the first half of the 1990s, at an average output of around 810,000 ounces per year of gold.

RTZ Corp.
6 St James's Square
London SW1Y 4LD
Tel: (071) 930 2399
Fax: (071) 930 3249
Telex: 24639

R & I Gold Bank

Located in Perth, this bank is an autonomous division of the Rural and Industries Bank of Western Australia, concentrating on gold mine finance and marketing.

R & I Gold Bank
101 St George's Terrace
Perth, Western Australia 6000
Tel: (09) 483 5555
Fax: (09) 321 3609
Telex: GOLDAA 197297

Run-of-Mine Ore

Typical, average grade ore that has been mined but not crushed or processed.

Salomon Brothers Inc.

The precious metal trading arm of Philipp Brothers in New York was transferred to Salomon Brothers in October 1990 as Salomon Brothers Precious Metals Inc. They operate as market makers in spot, options and forwards to customers of the firm and offer hedging and trading strategies to producers and consumers. Salomon Brothers International Ltd in London is also a member of the London Bullion Market Association.

Salomon Brothers Precious Metals Inc.
1 New York Plaza
New York, NY 10004
USA
Tel: (212) 747 9510
Fax: (212) 747 5320
Telex: 6790730
Reuters: SBBL

Sample

A small specimen from a mineralised outcrop or from a refining consignment taken for assay (q.v.).

Sampling

Taking small pieces of rock at intervals along exposed mineralisation for assay to determine the mineral content.

Samuel Montagu & Co. Ltd

Montagu began as a bullion broking partnership in London in 1853, as part of the expanding market there to cope with gold from the Australian gold rush (q.v.). It is now part of Midland Montagu, the international banking and investment arm of Midland Bank. Montagu has been a member of the fixing (q.v.) since it began in 1919 and is a market making member of the London Bullion Market Association (q.v.). Its *Annual Bullion Review*, which has been published since 1911, is an important record of gold and silver trading in London.

Samuel Montagu & Co. Ltd
10 Lower Thames Street
London EC3R 6AE
Tel: (071) 260 9000
Fax: (071) 488 1630
Telex: 88713
Reuters: SMBLGL

Satellite Deposit

Also known as **Outlier**. A mineral deposit located sufficiently close to an existing mining and milling operation to enable the ore to be handled at these facilities. This proximity often allows for profitable extraction of an orebody which might otherwise be uneconomic.

Saudi Arabia

Since the mid-1970s, Saudi Arabia has become a major market for physical gold and the source of much speculative gold trading on international markets.

On the physical level, Saudi Arabia has the capacity of importing upwards of one hundred tonnes a year in bar gold, mainly 999.9 kilobars, small ingots or ten tola bars, and jewellery. Saudi Arabia became, in fact, a significant client both of Italian and south-east Asian jewellery manufacturers; indeed, Saudi orders helped to develop the manufacturing of export jewellery in both Singapore and Malaysia.

The imposition of import duties on finished jewellery in the late 1980s, however, encouraged the establishment of jewellery factories in the kingdom itself. Large factories, often employing several hundred migrant workers, were established in Jeddah, Riyadh and Taif, making both jewellery and coins.

Gold bars are also widely held for investment and the small bars are distributed throughout Asia by migrant workers on their return home. Much of the gold for India, the Philippines or other Asian countries is first bought in the souks (q.v.) of Saudi Arabia.

Saudi banks and exchange dealers also became substantial traders in international markets, often operating large positions which have considerable impact on the price. Sales by one Saudi bank, for example, were largely credited with triggering precipitous falls in the gold price in the first half of 1990.

Scoria/Scorification/ Scorifier

Scoria, from the Greek for 'dung', is the slag (q.v.) or waste remaining after gold (or other metal) has been smelted from an ore by the process of scorification. Scorification often refers to the processing of molten lead to extract any precious metal content. A scorifier is a cup of fire-clay used in assaying precious metals.

Scrap

Scrap is the broad term for any gold which is sent back to a refiner or processor for recycling; it is also known as secondary metal. Scrap can be a significant element in gold supply, especially in times of sudden price rises.

Refiners normally divide scrap into seven categories:

Industrial scrap: residues from industrial plating processes: electroforming, printed circuit boards and electrical contacts are all sources for metallic scrap;

Hallmarked scrap: gold jewellery which bears the quality mark of an approved assay office;

Clean scrap: cuttings from gold alloys which are not mixed with other metals, that can be immediately remelted and rolled or drawn into semi-fabricated products;

Lemel: mixtures of unclean gold scrap including solders, filings and other metal from a jewellery factory;

Sweeps: originally the material swept up from the floor of a jewellery factory, but basically any very tiny bits of scrap;

Polishings: gold particles mixed with polishing compounds, mops, buffs and cleaning cloths.

Much of this scrap may be more generally classed as 'process' (q.v.) scrap, being part of the regular material circulating as part of a jewellery manufacturer's working stock. This is a fairly constant amount. What is more important to the gold market is the scrap which becomes a sudden source of extra supply either through distress sales from a particular country (as has been seen from Argentina for many years) due to economic difficulties, or simply because the price rises. Sharp increases in the gold price in 1974, 1980 and 1986 brought a considerable amount of scrap back onto the international market, mainly through dishoarding (q.v.) in the Middle East and Asia; in 1980 and 1986 nearly 500 tonnes of scrap was forthcoming, close to 25 per cent of total supply (see Table). Even though much of this scrap is not actually shipped back to international refineries, it can have a significant impact upon gold demand, because it will simply be remelted locally and re-used in jewellery, thus eliminating the need for fresh gold imports from the international market place.

Saudi Arabia and Indonesia are but two examples of countries in which locally recycled scrap will account for up to half of all fabrication at times; in special economic circumstances nations such as Egypt and most of Latin America may rely for many years entirely upon local scrap for jewellery fabrication. Scrap from the melting down of bullion coins (q.v.) has also been an increasing source of supply in Europe.

Scrap can be generated within a matter of days if the price increases fast and can prevent a further rise. The only limiting factor is often refinery capacity, which simply cannot handle all the material that may be offered. If the scrap cannot swiftly be assayed, and thus paid for, the process of buying it slows down through lack of cash flow. In 1980, in particular, much more scrap might have come back had the refineries been able to assay and pay quickly enough.

Scrap supply as a percentage of total supply

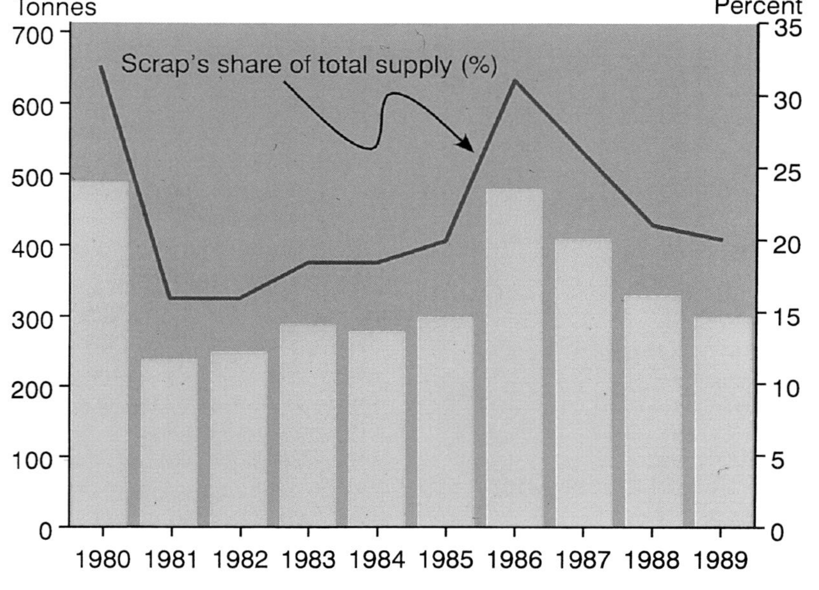

Scrap. *Source: Gold Fields Mineral Services Ltd*

SDRs

See **Special Drawing Rights.**

Secondary Metal

See **Scrap.**

Selective Plating

This technique is used in the electroplating (q.v.) of contacts and connectors in electronics (q.v.), where only parts of surfaces are plated to conserve gold use.

Sell Signal

In technical analysis (q.v.) a pattern, such as a double top (q.v.) or head and shoulders (q.v.), which indicates a key reversal downwards in price and, therefore, the moment to sell. Opposite of **Buy Signal**.

Semi-Fabrication

Semi-fabrication, sometimes shortened to 'semis', is the production by rolling (q.v.) or drawing (q.v.) of gold into alloys (q.v.) of sheet, tube, wire and other specialist articles for the jewellery or watch-making trade. This is undertaken by many of the large refiners (q.v.), whose bars are acceptable good delivery (q.v.), but in most countries there are also firms which specialise in semi-fabrication. In Germany, for example, they include Hafner and Weiland; in Switzerland Cendres et Métaux and Précinox; in Britain, Knight and Day Ltd; in the United States, Stern Leach.

Settlement Date

The date on which a contract for gold must be fully paid. In the spot market, for example, it is international practice for payment to be made two working days after the contract is agreed.

Settlement Price

On futures markets (q.v.), the settlement price is set by the exchange committee at the end of each trading day, for each delivery month (q.v.). On the basis of the settlement price the clearing house (q.v.) then determines what margin calls (q.v.) may be necessary.

Shaft

A vertical or steeply inclined opening providing access to a mine for men and materials and to hoist out ore and waste. It is also used for ventilation. At Western Deep Levels in South Africa the No. 2 and No. 3 shafts are identical tertiary systems (three stages) sunk to a depth of 3.78 kilometres. *See also* **Sub-Vertical Shaft.**

Sharps Pixley Ltd

Sharps Pixley is the second oldest member of the London gold market. Originally there were two brokers: Sharps & Wilkins which began in furs and pearls in the eighteenth century and started brokerage in gold and silver in 1811; and Pixley & Abell founded in 1852 by Stewart Pixley, a senior clerk in the cashier's office at the Bank of England at the time of the Australian gold rush which brought much new gold business to London. The two brokers merged in 1957 as Sharps Pixley, which is a wholly owned subsidiary of Kleinwort Benson, the merchant bankers. Sharps Pixley is a member of the gold fixing (q.v.) and is a market-making member of the London Bullion Market Association (q.v.).

Sharps Pixley Ltd
10 Rood Lane
London EC3M 8BB
Tel: (071)) 623 8000
Fax: (071) 626 9509
Telex:887017
Reuters: SPGLGL

Shekel

Ancient Hebrew unit of weight. Gold shekels were about 235 grains troy or just over half a troy ounce.

Short/Short Cover/Short Position/Short Sales

An open position resulting from a sale is known as a short position. It is created because the trader or speculator believes the price will fall and he can cover later at a lower price at a profit. So he may sell gold at $400, hoping the price will fall to $380 at which level he can buy to cover the position.

The establishing of short positions can depress the price, because it implies steady selling. But 'going short' can also cause problems both for the individual and the market if, instead, the price rises. If substantial short positions have been built up (and there are examples of speculators on COMEX (q.v.) being short between 1 and 1½ million ounces) a sudden increase in price may force them to cover. Such a run for cover, known as a 'short squeeze' or 'short covering', only accelerates the rise.

In options (q.v.) the grantor or writer of a call is also potentially short, because he may be called upon to deliver gold and he will normally delta hedge (q.v.) his position.

Shot

Also known as **Grain**. Small globules of pure gold obtained by pouring molten metal into cold water. Used in fabrication, particularly jewellery.

Shrinkage Stoping

An underground mining method used in steeply dipping orebodies with potentially difficult wall rock conditions.

The ore is drilled and blasted in slices advancing upwards. As broken rock requires a larger volume than solid, some ore must be drawn off as the stope advances. Only enough ore is drawn off after each blast to provide adequate working space for the next cycle. Once a complete lift of ore has been broken the ore is completely loaded out from the bottom of the stope.

Used at Bell Creek, Ontario, Canada, operated by Canamax Resources.

SIMEX (Singapore International Monetary Exchange)

The Singapore International Monetary Exchange Ltd was established in late 1983 from an alliance between the Gold Exchange of Singapore and the International Monetary Market (IMM) in Chicago. It is an open outcry market with a 100 fine troy ounce futures contract quoted in US dollars, deliverable on even months on a one-year cycle. The last trading day is the second last business day of the month preceding the contract month. Under a revised contract initiated in 1990 it is cash settled. On the delivery date the contract is settled in cash against the loco London a.m. fix on the last trading day of the contract. The minimum price fluctuation is US$0.05 per fine troy ounce; the value of one tick is US$5.00.

The trading hours are 9.00 a.m. to 5.15 p.m. Singapore time.

Singapore International Monetary Exchange Ltd
1 Raffles Place , OUB Centre
Singapore 0104
Tel: 5357382
Fax: 5357282
Telex: RS38000 SINMEX
Reuters code: GDSE
Telerate 6178 Quick 275 MKT

Singapore

Singapore's gold market opened on 1 April 1969, as part of the strategy to make this city-state an important financial centre. It has become the main distribution centre for physical gold to such south-east Asian countries as Indonesia, Malaysia, Thailand and Vietnam and to the Indian sub-continent. Imports, mainly in kilobars, but also some ten tola bars, are normally 100–250 tonnes annually, but reached close to 300 tonnes in 1990. Up to 20 tonnes of this gold is used in the local jewellery manufacturing industry, which exports primarily 22 carat ornaments to Dubai and Saudi Arabia. Many Singapore wholesalers also work closely with the jewellery manufacturing centre of Penang in Malaysia. The Singapore Assay Office hallmarks some of this jewellery, but it is not compulsory. The local refinery, Degussa (Private) Ltd, a daughter company of the West German precious metals firm, has London good delivery status.

Singapore, unlike Hong Kong, is essentially a physical market; it has not become a major trading centre. The Gold Exchange of Singapore, opened in 1978 with two futures contracts of 100 ounces and 1 kilo, achieved little turnover. The exchange allied with Chicago's International Monetary Market (IMM) in 1983 to form SIMEX (q.v.).

Skillet

A shallow mould for casting precious metals.

Slag

Also known as scoria (q.v.). The dross or waste comprising impurities left over after smelting and refining.

Slimes

The fine fraction of tailings (q.v.) discharged from a mill after the valuable minerals have been recovered. Sometimes re-treated as technology improves for further gold recovery. The East Rand Gold and Uranium Co. (Ergo) in South Africa recovers gold, uranium and sulphuric acid from slimes dams and sand dumps on the East Rand. The Ergo and Daggafontein divisions treat a total of 2.7 million tonnes per month of old gold slimes.

Sluice Box/Sluicing

In alluvial (q.v.) or placer (q.v.) mining, the separation of gold in a flowing stream of water is known as sluicing. This is often done in a rectangular sluice box, with riffles or slats placed across the bottom to check the current of water and allow the gravity separation.

Smelt/Smelting

The process of melting ores or concentrates to separate out the gold, or other metal, from impurities. A flux or fluxes, such as silica, borax or soda ash, are used to dissolve out impurities which form into slag, leaving the gold free to be poured off. On most gold mines smelting is the final stage of recovering gold from an ore, thus obtaining a doré (q.v.) bar that is upwards of 850 fine, which can be sent to a refinery for purifying up to 995 or 999.9 fineness. Copper smelters also produce by-product gold, which then goes for refining.

The terms smelting and refining sometimes overlap but essentially the former implies separation, the latter is purification or up-grading.

Smelting. *Doré bullion cools at the smelter at Zortman-Landusky mine in Montana*

Solders/Soldering

Solders, also known as **Brazing Alloys**, are fusible alloys used in the form of sheet, wire and pastes for

Souks. *Gold ornaments and coins cram windows in a Middle East souk*

joining and assembling jewellery. They are made to melt at a lower temperature than the jewellery itself so that they can be applied to join two parts without damaging them. Solders are used in conjunction with hand-held brazing torches, or for mass-produced jewellery, in a brazing furnace, which is heated to just the right temperature for the solder to join together the various pieces without melting them. Complex jewellery assemblies will be put together by stage or step soldering, using solders that melt at different temperatures, so as not to disturb the joints already soldered.

Pastes (often known as brazing pastes) are simply alloys in the form of fine powder, mixed with flux and binders to form a mixture which can be dispensed in repeatable doses through fine needles. Pieces can then be heated by torch or furnace.

Solid Gold

In the United States, the Federal Trade Commission permits any article of 10 carat gold or more that is not hollow to be called solid gold.

Souk

The *souk*, also sometimes written *suk*, is the local name for 'market' throughout the Arab world. Within the *souk* a whole alleyway or street is often devoted just to shops selling gold jewellery, coins and small gold bars with a mark-up of 10–20 per cent over the gold price of the day. The *souk* is both a social centre and a trading place, particularly for women, who will spend many hours in gold shops choosing new ornaments and paying for them partly by trading in old ones. Thus the turnover in gold shops, each of which may well carry a stock of 100–200 kilos of ornaments, is substantial in comparison to a jewellery store in Europe or the United States. Customers are also very price sensitive, trading in ornaments if the price rises, essentially taking a profit on their investments. This response to price changes means that *souks* are a signpost to medium term gold market trends. Heavy buying in the *souks* indicates that the gold price is nearing the bottom of a bear cycle; selling back in the *souks* signals that the price is getting too high. The swings in the 'mood of the *souks*' can be significant in the hoarding (q.v.) and dishoarding (q.v.) pattern of gold and scrap (q.v.) supplies.

South Africa

South Africa is the world's leading producer of gold, a position first

'Mood of the Souks': Dubai, Hong Kong, Singapore

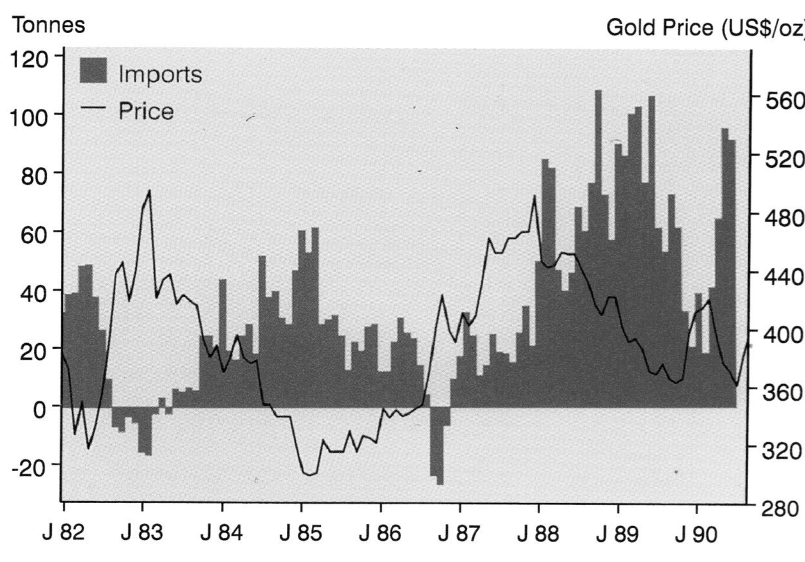

Souks. *Source: Gold Fields Mineral Services Ltd*

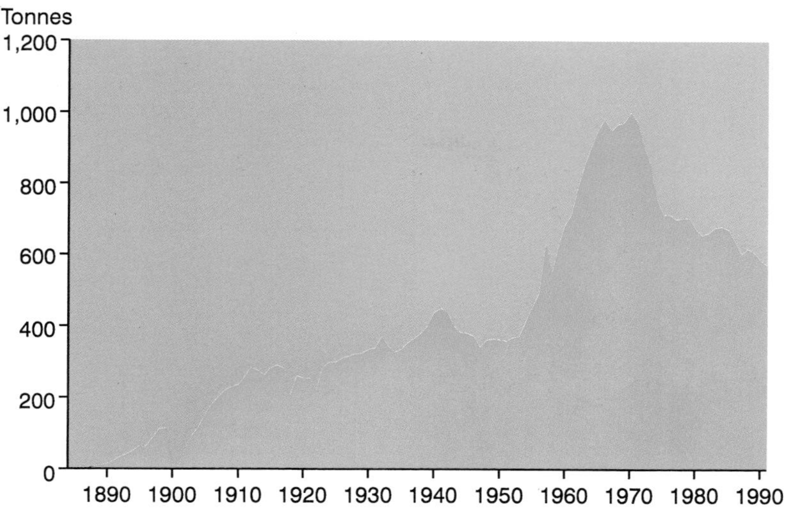

South Africa. *The pattern of South African production since the first discoveries in the 1880s, which reached a peak in 1970*

gained in 1898 and lost only momentarily since then during the Boer War in the first four years of this century. From 1884, the first year of recorded output, through 1990, just over 42,600 tonnes of gold had been mined in South Africa, about 40 per cent of all gold ever mined. In the best year, 1970, just over 1,000 tonnes were mined, which represented 78.5 per cent of all gold produced in the non-communist world that year.

For over a century gold has been South Africa's major foreign exchange earner and the driving force in her economy. For many years it accounted for 50 per cent or more of foreign exchange earnings, but the contribution is now under 40 per cent. The geology of the gold deposits also created from the outset a unique structure in the South African gold mining industry.

Although there were isolated reports of alluvial gold (q.v.) and some quartz (q.v.) deposits as early as 1853, the real discovery eventually came on the back of the diamond rush to Kimberley, which began in 1871. The diamond boom provided two essential ingredients: an army of prospectors (many of whom had dug gold in Australia and elsewhere) and substantial capital from British and European banks to finance the emerging diamond mining houses created by such men as Cecil Rhodes, Alfred Beit and Barney Barnato, who eventually came together in De Beers Consolidated Mines Ltd. Thus powerful entrepreneurs were on hand when George Harrison found the main reef of gold-bearing conglomerate (q.v.) outcropping on Langlaagte farm near Johannesburg in February 1886. The difference between this find and earlier discoveries in California (q.v.) and Australia (q.v.) was that it was not an alluvial deposit to which thousands of individual diggers could flock but the tip of low grade reefs which could be mined only at depth and at great initial capital cost.

What outcropped briefly on Langlaagte farm was one of a crescent of gold reefs around the whole Witwatersrand Basin (q.v.). These reefs, some of which outcrop to surface, plunge at an angle of 25 degrees or more, sloping inwards towards the centre, to depths of at least 5,000 metres. Indeed they have not yet 'bottomed out'. This gold-bearing conglomerate, usually grading no more than 15 grammes per tonne and often less, stretches from 40 miles east of Johannesburg to 90 miles west, then swings down south-west to the Orange Free State 200 miles away. Another field, Evander, was found much later 80 miles to the south-east of Johannesburg outside the main Witwatersrand system. The Witwatersrand reefs were deposited between 3,000 and 2,700 million years ago. The reefs vary widely but the majority are conglomerate (q.v.), with pebbles of quartz and chert in a matrix of quartz grains, silicates and various sulphides, mainly pyrite. They range from thin, small-pebble reefs, often with great lateral extent, to thick conglomerate. Many reefs are clearly the product of reworking of fluvial agencies, while others have features compatible with formation on a beach-like surface in the environment of lakes and seas. They were all formed under shallow water.

A large number of different reefs are mined and include the Main reef, Ventersdorp Contact reef, Kimberley reef, Carbon Leader reef and Basal reef. The reefs, averaging 20–30 centimetres in thickness, are extracted from stopes (q.v.) of around 1 metre high at planned depths of up to 4,000 metres below the surface. The narrow stoping widths, mining hard rock reefs at extreme depths, has given the South African industry its particular character.

From the first moment, capital was required to develop deep underground mines. That was swiftly forthcoming; Cecil Rhodes founded Gold Fields of South Africa (q.v.) in 1887. The other main houses, Rand Mines (q.v.), Johannesburg Consolidated Investments (q.v.) and General Mining Union Corp. (now Gencor (q.v.)) were quickly in place, all backed by men who had started in diamonds. Only Sir Ernest

Oppenheimer's Anglo American (q.v.) came much later in 1917.

New technology, fortuitously, was also forthcoming. Previously mercury had been the principal agent for dissolving out gold from crushed ore, but mercury was only effective enough to recover 65 per cent of this gold. With high mining costs that was not a good enough return. What made South African mining viable was a new technique using cyanidation (q.v.) called the MacArthur Forrest process (q.v.) patented in 1887.

With finance and technology in place, South Africa overtook the United States as the leading gold producer in 1898. Thereafter the story is very much the discovery every few decades of major new extensions to the gold reefs of the Witwatersrand Basin; the 'West Wits Line' west of Johannesburg was located by Gold Fields in the 1930s, the Orange Free State field was pioneered by Anglo American from 1946, and Evander developed by General Mining Union Corporation from the late 1950s. In all of them the development of new mines was costly and slow. It takes from four to seven years to bring a new mine into production at costs, in modern terms, of between a half and one billion US dollars. The mining house structure was essential to raise the necessary capital. However, although there has always been intense competition between the houses in the geological detective work to find and prove a new mine, once the decision is taken the other houses will usually buy a share of it, while the originating house operates it. The mining houses also work together in the recruitment of labour, the settlement of wage negotiations, research, and in lobbying the government on tax and other matters through the Chamber of Mines of South Africa (q.v.).

While South African mines have always been in a class of their own, with virtually all mines having an output of 10–20 tonnes a year or more

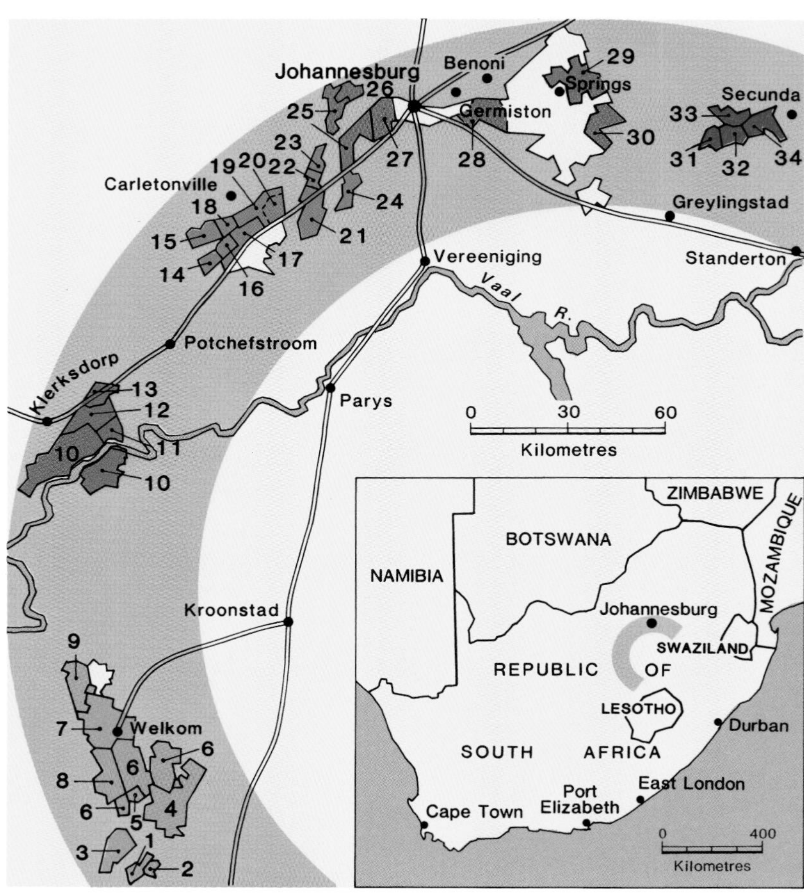

South Africa. *The major gold mines on this map are identified in detail on the table on the opposite page*

(and the mining houses not being interested in much less), consolidation since the 1970s has led to the evolution of several supermines. They were formed partly to take advantage of the economies of large scale working and partly because extensions to existing mines or expansions to new ones next door could best be folded into a single unit with the costs of development written off against the profits of the existing parts of the resulting supermine. Thus Gold Fields merged two old and one new mine into Driefontein Consolidated, producing around 60 tonnes a year; and Anglo American stitched together the mines on its Klerksdorp field into Vaal Reefs at 80 tonnes a year, and pulled all five of their Orange Free State mines into Freegold, producing over 100 tonnes a year. There are 34 main underground operations still producing gold in South Africa.

Such consolidation has become more necessary because South Africa, for all its premier position, faces three serious problems. First, rising costs in an industry that is labour intensive; costs rose from \$183 an ounce in 1980 to around \$277 a decade later — the highest by far in a major gold mining country (the US costs are around \$210 an ounce). Second, declining recovered grades, which have fallen from just under 14 grammes per tonne in 1970 to under 5 grammes per tonne by 1990. Third, the technical difficulties of following

The major South African gold mines

Gold mines	Mining house	Approximate date of first declaration of gold	Production 1989 (kg fine)	Grade (grams per metric ton milled)	Metric tons ore milled (1989) (000)	Capex 1989 (R000)	Cumulative production since start of operations (kilograms)	Cumul. ore milled since start of operation (metric tons)	Average grade since start of mining (g/t milled)
ORANGE FREE STATE									
8 St Helena (St Helena Section)	Genmin	Nov. 1951	18715.5	5.23	2048	5 164	777373.8	73564	10.57
3 St. Helena (Oryx)	Genmin	Oct. 1988	198.5	2.21	90	243 507	247.2	112	2.21
7 Free State Cons (North Reg.)	AAC	July 1953	47884.0	4.53	10582	403 300	3867314.6	243141	12.62
6 Free State Cons. (South Reg.)	AAC	April 1954	62989.0	3.96	15333	—	2356674.3	242562	9.57
4 Harmony	Rand Mines	Sept. 1954	29136.0	3.04	9571	34 157	987520.8	163270	6.85
9 Loraine	Anglovaal	May 1955	7908.5	4.99	1585	11 690	316802.0	41350	7.66
5 Unisel	Genmin	Oct. 1979	6384.0	5.99	1053	19 599	79653.4	12131	6.57
1 Buffelsfontein (Beatrix Section)	Genmin	Nov. 1983	13159.3	6.10	2156	73 270	61878.4	10538	5.87
2 H. J. Joel	JCI	Aug. 1988	1288.0	3.18	405	99 662	1492.0	497	3.00
KLERKSDORP									
13 Stilfontein	Genmin	July 1952	4915.0	2.54	1937	277	685679.2	63289	10.83
12 Hartebeestfontein	Anglovaal	July 1955	31157.2	6.48	4805	49 175	939176.1	80479	11.67
10 Vaal Reefs	AAC	May 1956	75455.2	6.91	10920	321 653	1707857.2	179803	9.50
11 Buffelsfontein (Buffelsf'n Sctn)	Genmin	Jan. 1957	14536.0	6.25	2327	10 207	925375.2	86173	10.74
FAR WEST RAND									
23 Venterspost	GFSA	Oct. 1939	6181.0	3.69	1652	37 189	497597.7	65849	7.56
18 Blyyopruitzicht	Rand Mines	Feb. 1942	9491.5	4.24	2239	11 721	1053988.2	70232	15.01
22 Libanon	GFSA	Mar. 1949	7282.7	4.19	1740	27 924	500467.6	56213	8.90
19 Driefontein Cons. (West)	GFSA	Feb. 1952	28790.3	10.12	2820	219 057	1826826.7	82176	22.23
20 Driefontein Cons. (East)	GFSA	April 1972	25581.9	8.97	2852	—	580202.3	40752	14.24
15 Doornfontein	GFSA	Nov. 1953	7932.1	5.08	1560	36 986	540313.5	47061	11.48
24 Western Areas	JCI	Dec. 1961	13352.0	3.55	3760	33 012	511864.4	85708	5.97
17 Western Deep Levels	AAC	Mar. 1962	48568.9	6.16	6584	295 321	1223558.0	96548	12.67
21 Kloof	GFGA	Jan. 1968	26429.3	12.24	2168	303 383	581658.6	39825	14.61
16 Elandsrand	AAC	Dec. 1978	12971.1	6.67	1944	115 946	101646.0	17427	5.83
14 Deelkraal	GFSA	Jan. 1980	9831.6	6.07	1620	73 270	71432.3	13986	5.11
WEST RAND									
26 West Rand Cons.	Genmin	Sept. 1908	2215.2	2.22	996	(823)	689387.9	128786	4.73
25 Randfontein	JCI	Jan. 1974	26901.0	3.06	8700	106 434	365190.0	72004	5.87
CENTRAL RAND									
27 Durban Roodepoort Deep	Rand Mines	July 1898	4947.3	2.45	2018	3 470	693456.2	121012	5.73
EAST RAND									
28 E.R.P.M.	Rand Mines	Sept. 1894	7790.0	2.58	3820	21 242	1386868.7	180691	7.68
29 Grootvlei	Genmin	Sept. 1938	3170.5	3.63	874	(209)	597807.7	98639	6.06
30 Marievale	Genmin	Nov. 1939	759.0	2.19	347	29	271169.1	39502	6.86
EVANDER									
34 Winkelhaak	Genmin	Dec. 1958	11571.0	5.66	2045	71 751	453647.2	56358	8.05
32 Bracken	Genmin	Aug. 1962	2156.0	3.41	633	1 326	230536.5	25870	8.91
31 Leslie	Genmin	Oct. 1962	2868.2	3.30	870	3878	234644.5	36404	6.45
33 Kinross	Genmin	Jan. 1968	12106.0	5.70	2123	31 497	273742.6	37274	7.34

Source: Chamber of Mines of South Africa

the reefs down to greater depths; Western Deep Levels is going down to 4,000 metres but at that depth heat is a problem with rock at 50°C and there are underground reservoirs to contend with. These factors have already meant that the gold mining boom of the 1980s bypassed South Africa. From the peak of 1,000 tonnes in 1970, output fell to between 600 and 700 tonnes a year in the 1980s; the challenge in the 1990s and beyond is to keep production above 600 tonnes annually. Old mines are being extended, new mines developed, but essentially they are providing replacement tonnage for older declining mines. South Africa, nevertheless, will remain the foremost producer, but its share has dwindled to no more than 35 per cent

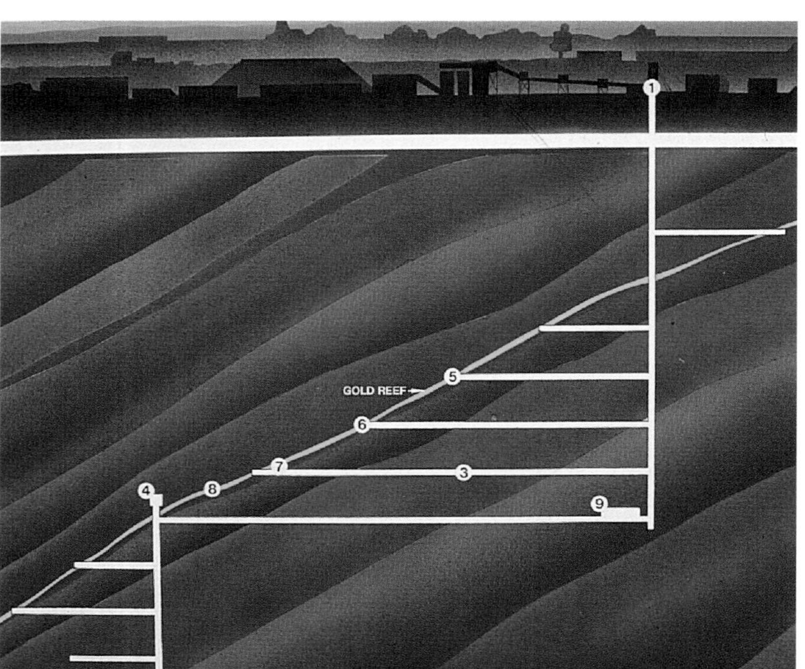

South Africa.

Left:
Cross section of a South African mine, as illustrated below

Below left:
1. Going down a shaft which may be two miles deep;
2. Equipping a new shaft takes several years;
3. Underground trains take workers to the reef.

Below centre:
4. Lower (sub-vertical) shafts have un derground hoists;
5. Drilling the reef in a low-roofed stope;
6. Preparing to blast ore in a stope.

Below right:
7. A boring machine cuts an ore-pass;
8. Wooden supports hold up the stope roof;
9. Refrigeration units cool the deepest mines.

South Africa: Top Twenty Mines

Mine		Major Shareholders	Production (ounces) 1989 (actual)	1990 (estimated)
1	Freegold	Anglo American	3,489,444	3,475,000
2	Vaal Reefs*	Anglo American	2,425,954	2,304,000
3	Driefontein	GFSA	1,740,237	1,660,000
4	Western Deep	Anglo American	1,304,334	1,216,000
5	Hartebeestfontein	Anglovaal	1,001,761	964,000
6	Harmony	Rand Mines	936,752	948,000
7	Buffelsfontein**	Gencor	890,422	888,000
8	Randfontein	JCI	864,894	894,000
9	Kloof	GFSA	849,751	777,000
10	Western Areas	JCI	429,152	425,000
11	Elandsrand	Anglo American	417,031	440,000
12	Kinross	Gencor	389,220	390,000
13	Winkelhaak	Gencor	372,019	412,000
14	St Helena	Gencor	344,498	320,000
15	Deelkraal	GFSA	316,141	309,000
16	Blyvooruitzicht	Rand Mines	305,145	292,000
17	Doornfontein	Anglovaal	255,022	260,000
18	Loraine	GFSA	254,250	230,000
19	ERPM	Rand Mines	250,456	161,000
20	Libanon	GFSA	234,156	226,000

* Includes Afrikaander Lease and Southvaal
** Includes Beatrix

of western mine output and less than 30 per cent if the production of the Soviet Union (q.v.) and China (q.v.) is taken into account.

This has important implications for the gold market, no longer so dependent on South African output. In South Africa the marketing of its gold by the South African Reserve Bank (q.v.) is now managed much more astutely. For many years the Bank, to which all gold must be sold by the mines once it has been through the Rand Refinery (q.v.), simply sold the production more or less as it came in. It now makes much greater use of the forward (q.v.) and options (q.v.) markets to hedge production and will buy back on occasion to support the price.

South African Reserve Bank

The South African Reserve Bank, the central bank, has handled the marketing of South African gold since 1926. Until 1968 the bank used the Bank of England (q.v.) in London, but since then has sold direct to major international market-makers, usually not less than 20,000 ounces (0.6 tonnes) at a time. The bank has increasingly made use of the forward options markets to hedge its sales, and is also prepared to buy back on occasion to support the price. In the management of its own gold holdings, the central bank has also made extensive use of swap (q.v.) facilities with commercial banks.

South African Reserve Bank,
P. O. Box 427
Pretoria 0001
South Africa
Tel: (12) 313 3751
Fax: (12) 313 3749
Telex: 320282

Sovereign

The Sovereign is the traditional English gold coin bearing the likeness of the monarch, or sovereign. Although it is most associated with the period of the gold standard (q.v.) after 1817, when it was the symbol of the pound sterling, the first Sovereigns were struck much earlier. They were minted on 28 October 1489 to confirm the establishment of

Sovereign. *Queen Elizabeth I 'fine Sovereign' of thirty shillings has the enthroned queen on the face and the superbly designed Tudor Rose on the reverse*

the Tudor dynasty of Henry VII. This Sovereign weighed half a troy ounce (15.55 grammes) and was worth 20 shillings or £1. All the Tudor monarchs in turn issued Sovereigns but they had very little circulation, being too valuable for everyday payments. James I suspended their minting. It was not until 1817 that the Sovereign came back, to replace the Guinea (q.v.), when cash payments, that is to say the redemption of notes with gold coin, were resumed after the Napoleonic Wars. This Sovereign was worth £1 and contained ¼ ounce of 916 gold (standard gold (q.v.) as it was then known). It bore the St George and Dragon design of Benedetto Pistrucci. During the next century over 600 million Sovereigns and 90 million Half Sovereigns were issued. They were minted also at branches of the Royal Mint in India and Australia.

Sovereign. *Queen Victoria 'young head', minted in 1872*

After the gold standard was suspended in 1914 the repayment of £1 notes in Sovereigns never resumed and the Sovereign became increasingly an investor's item, with its price based upon its gold content. The Bank of England, however, has continued to order Sovereigns to be struck at the Royal Mint and markets them at a small premium. The market distinguishes between 'old' Sovereigns from the gold standard era, and 'new' Sovereigns, being those bearing the head of Queen Elizabeth II. The Royal Mint also strikes proof Sovereigns annually for collectors and in 1989 issued commemorative copies of the first ones issued 500 years earlier in 1489.

Soviet Union

The Soviet Union is the world's second largest producer of gold; no production figures have been published since the 1920s, but it is estimated to be close to 300 tonnes annually. The major part of this output is sold abroad and, for all its reticence with statistics, the Soviet Union has been an integral part of the international gold market as a trader making full use of forwards, futures and options. As *glasnost* proceeds, more precise information on Soviet output and sales is likely in the 1990s.

Gold production in Russia itself goes back many centuries. Rich alluvial (q.v.) deposits in the Ural mountains yielded gold that passed down ancient trade routes to the Black Sea and the Mediterranean. And a quartz outcrop (q.v.) found at Ekaterinburg in the Urals in 1774 stimulated the Czars to greater exploration. Over the next century prospectors moved steadily east into the Altai mountains and into Siberia along the tributaries of the Yenisei river, locating many alluvial deposits. By the 1840s Russia had become the world's leading producer. In 1847, the year before gold was discovered in California, Russian output was between 30 and 35 tonnes, out of a world total of about 75 tonnes. California, then Australia (q.v.) and later South Africa (q.v.), changed the perspective, but Russian production continued to rise and in 1914 was about 60 tonnes.

After the Revolution Stalin saw gold mining as one way of opening up the vast wastes of Siberia, having noted the effect California had on the development of the American West. He even recruited an American mining engineer, John D. Littlepage, who supervised the birth of a more modern mining industry in the Soviet Union in the 1920s and 1930s. Output increased rapidly to around 155 tonnes annually, almost on a par with Canada and the United States. Thereafter no hard information is available, but it is estimated that by the 1940s the Soviet Union was the second biggest producer (after South Africa), a position retained ever since.

Until the 1970s most Soviet production was alluvial, probably two-thirds of it coming from placer (q.v.) deposits in Siberia. These are concentrated in an area embracing the Lena and Aldan rivers, the province of Magadan, and the Kamchatka and Chukotsk peninsulas, opposite Alaska, where very similar gold deposits are encountered. The harsh climate means the mining is seasonal; even in summer extracting gold from terrain

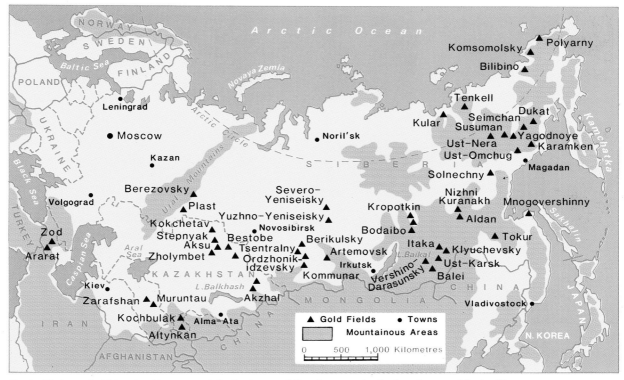

Soviet Union. *Gold is mined in many of the Soviet republics, but most in the Russian republic itself*

locked solid by the permafrost is difficult. Much of the gold is won by huge dredges excavating gold-bearing sands in the rivers once they thaw.

Since 1970 production has been less dependent on Siberia following the opening of a large low-grade quartz gold mine, Muruntau, in the Central Asian province of Uzbekistan between the Aral Sea and the Afghanistan border. The structure of the Muruntau deposit is unique; it is like a tree with branches spreading out near the surface and the trunk plunging deep into the earth. Since the mine opened in 1969 it has been worked partly as a huge open pit excavating the quartz veins or 'branches', while an underground mine has been developed to intersect the 'trunk' 500 metres down. The gold grades at 2.5 grammes per tonne, and is of exceptional purity being 900 fine without any preliminary refining. Muruntau's actual output is disputed; some accounts suggest it has produced 80, even 140 tonnes a year; a more realistic figure is probably between 20 and 30 tonnes — even so a world-class mine. Other Soviet mines have been developed in Armenia, where the Zod deposit yields about 10 tonnes a year,

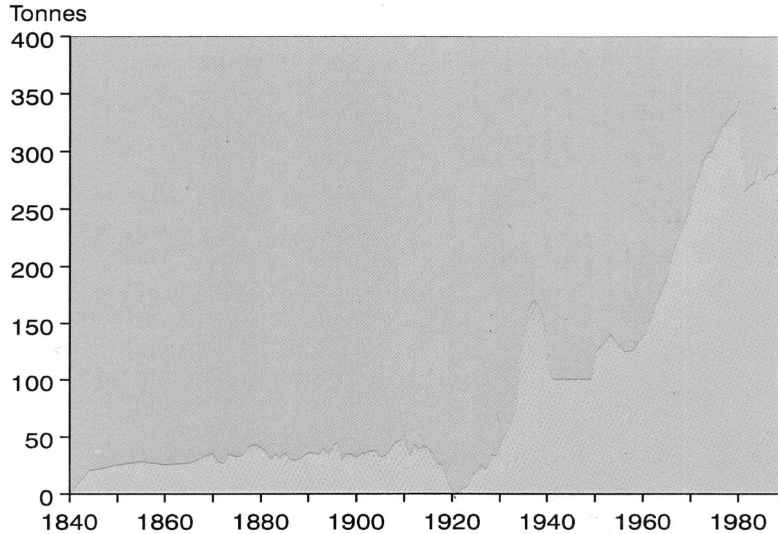

Soviet Union. *The estimated pattern of Soviet output since the 19th century*

Soviet Union. *Core samples from exploration spread out in a Soviet forest*

and in the southern provinces of Kazakhstan and Tadzhikstan. But, as with South Africa, the gold mining boom of the 1980s has largely passed the Soviet Union by. The challenge, as political and economic unrest have spread (especially in the very provinces where gold is mined), has been to maintain output; in fact, since 1985 it may have declined.

Undoubtedly the Soviet Union still possesses enormous gold reserves, and approaches have been made to mining companies in the west for joint-ventures to exploit them. Even if they go ahead it may be the next century before much advance is seen. The task facing the Soviet gold mining industry is to maintain its position as the world's second largest producer; if it slips, the United States, which has come up fast, could overtake it. One test will be whether individual mining groups emerge. Under a centrally planned economy, the Soviet mining industry was handled by a division of the Ministry of Non-Ferrous Metallurgy known as Glavzoloto. Glavzoloto has 14 regional zolotos, or trusts, supervising the far-flung industry. All the gold is sent for refining to the State Refinery in Moscow whose bars, stamped CCCP, with hammer and sickle, are acceptable good delivery (q.v.) on the London market. The refinery has always produced all its bars as 999.9 fine (q.v.), unlike most refineries which make 995 unless specially ordered.

Soviet Union. *Dredge working at night in a winter landscape*

The gold is marketed by the Bank for Foreign Economic Affairs (q.v.), shipping mainly to London, Frankfurt, Tokyo and Zurich. But physical sales have been diversified directly into south-east Asian and Middle East markets offering kilobars. The bank is an active daily market-maker in the international market; it uses forwards, futures and options. Sales figures are not released but in general the bank has marketed about 75 per cent of Soviet production, the balance having been used for domestic requirements (particularly in aerospace and electronics) and, up to 1989, for sale to Comecon partners in Eastern Europe. The amount left for reserve building and the size of those reserves is a matter of much speculation; they are probably in the range of 1,500–2,500 tonnes (about the same as the gold reserves of the Netherlands or Italy). Much debate has taken place in the Soviet Union as to the extent to which they should be sold off or swapped to help to pay for *perestroika*. Outright sale could depress the price; but swaps with commercial and perhaps central banks have taken place. As they do so, the veil of secrecy over Soviet gold for more than half a century gradually lifts.

Special Drawing Rights (SDRs)

This credit unit was created by the International Monetary Fund (q.v.) and originally linked to gold: one SDR being defined as 0.888671 grammes. The gold link was later dropped and the SDR tied instead to a 'basket' of leading currencies.

Specie

Money in the form of coin, usually meaning gold or silver but not necessarily.

Specific Gravity

See **Gold, Properties of.**

Splitting Limits

The agreed limits of difference between a buyer's and seller's assays of gold, which enable them to make a deal without third-party arbitration.

Spoil

See **Overburden.**

Spot Deferred

A long-term funding arrangement, whereby a mine sells gold at the current spot price, for cash. The cash is credited to a deferred account and the cash interest is covered for the period of the arrangement (for example, five years). Gold interest is charged to the account regularly by agreement and with reference to GOFO (q.v.).

Spot Price

Sometimes referred to as the **Cash Price**. The current price in the physical market for immediate delivery of gold. Without specification otherwise, this is normally taken to mean delivery loco London (q.v.) two working days after the date of the deal. In futures markets, spot means the current trading month.

Spread

(i) The difference between a market-maker's bid and offer price.
(ii) In futures markets (q.v.), an investor goes long (i.e. buys a futures contract) in one delivery month and goes short (i.e. sells a futures contract) in a different delivery month, with the intention of balancing out his risk. Because of this the initial (q.v.) margin may be less. This is also known as an 'interdelivery spread', or straddle.
(iii) In options (q.v.), spreads involve the simultaneous holding of puts (q.v.) and calls (q.v.). A 'spread order' is the buying and selling of options of the same type (either puts or calls) with different maturities and/or different striking prices (q.v.).
See also **Bear Spread; Bull Spread; Straddle.**

Square Set Stoping

An underground mining method used in steeply dipping orebodies, under difficult wall rock conditions. Once the ore has been drilled and blasted, the stope is supported with large square timber sets which provide the platform for the next cycle. Seldom used in modern mining due to high cost. Used at Ashanti, Ghana.

Squeeze

In futures markets (q.v.), a squeeze or short squeeze occurs when speculators who have sold the market short (q.v.), anticipating a price fall, have to face margin calls (q.v.) and cover their positions when it rises fast and unexpectedly.

Stamp

Also known as **Chop**. An official mark on a precious metal product.

Stamp Mill

A mill used in early days to break and grind gold-bearing ore. *See also* **Battery.**

Standard Gold

Originally, standard gold meant metal that was 916 fine; this was the usually traded purity until the twentieth century. Thus the sterling price of gold set at £3.17.10½d in 1717 was per standard troy ounce; the price for fine gold (then not refined) was equivalent of £4.4.11½d. The term standard gold is used in all London gold market and Bank of England documents until the beginning of this century when the phrase 'good delivery' (q.v.) for 995 gold replaced it. The term 'standard gold' is still used in India to describe the 916 (22 carat) bars normally traded in the Bombay market. In the United States it refers to an alloy 900 fine, with the balance in copper, used for coinage.

Stockpile

Mined ore which is held at the mine for various reasons before it is sent for treatment. Ore may be stockpiled above ground purely as a strategic reserve against accidents or strike delays in underground working or while waiting for a better gold price.

Stope

An underground excavation resulting from the extraction of ore by mining.

Stoping Width

The distance between the footwall and hangingwall of a stope.

Stop-Loss

A customer's order to his commission house or dealer to liquidate a long position or cover a short position when the price reaches a specified level to prevent further loss. However, there is no guarantee that the order can always be executed at that level because if the market is volatile the price may go through the stop-loss level so fast it cannot be implemented.

Straddle

(i) On futures markets (q.v.), the simultaneous buying and selling of contracts for different delivery months (q.v.).
(ii) In options (q.v.), a speculative strategy of either buying a call (q.v.)

and a put (q.v.), or selling a call and a put each with the same expiration date and the same strike (or exercise) price (q.v.).
See also **Spread**.

Strake/Strake Table

A shallow pit or a wooden box used for washing and concentrating the alluvial (q.v.) gold ore in placer (q.v.) operations.

Strangle

In options (q.v.), a speculative strategy of either buying a call (q.v.) and a put (q.v.), or selling a call and a put, each with the same expiration date but different strike (q.v.) prices. This may vary as a long strangle in which the put is bought at a lower strike price than the call is bought, or a short strangle in which the put is sold at a lower strike price than the call is sold.

Strike

A valuable discovery of ore.

Strike Price/Striking Price

In options (q.v.), the pre-determined price at which the option may be exercised. For example, a gold call option is bought at a strike price of $400 for expiration in June. If the price is above $400 at the end of June, the buyer is entitled to buy gold at $400; that is to say the option is 'in-the-money' (q.v.). If the price is below the $400 strike price, it is 'out-of-the-money' (q.v.) and will not be exercised. The strike price is often also referred to as the exercise price (q.v.).

Stripping Ratio

The ratio between the volume or tonnage of waste and ore which must be removed in an open pit. A lower stripping ratio means that less waste has to be removed to expose the ore for mining and generally results in a lower operating cost.

Sub-Level Caving

An underground mining method used in large, steeply dipping orebodies where the wall rock is of an incompetent nature. Parallel drives are developed in the ore on equally spaced levels. The ore is then drilled and blasted using longholes between levels, often in a circular or fan pattern, on retreat. The weight of the rock is used to assist breakage. The upper levels are mined ahead of lower levels. Broken ore is extracted from the drive before the next blast takes place. The wall rock caves in when the ore is extracted. Used at Renabie, Canada.

Sub-Level (Blasthole) Open Stoping

An underground mining method used in large, steeply dipping orebodies where the wall rock is of a competent nature. Drives are developed in the ore on equally spaced levels. The ore is then drilled and blasted using longholes between levels, often in a circular or fan pattern, on retreat. The ore is extracted at the bottom of the stope on a haulage level. Used at the Williams mine at the Hemlo goldfield (q.v.) in Canada.

Sub-Vertical (Sub-Incline) Shaft

A shaft beginning from underground as a second- or third-stage shaft system to access deeper levels.

Sulphide Ore

An ore whose mineralisation is a compound of sulphur. *See also* **Refractory Ore.**

Sumitomo Corporation

A market maker in gold, silver, platinum and palladium in Tokyo and a member of TOCOM.

Sumitomo Corporation
11-1 Kanda Nishikicho 3 chome
Chiyoda-ku, Tokyo
Japan
Tel: (3) 219 6010
Fax: (3) 294 6180
Telex: J33225 SUMITOMO
Reuters: SCTQ

Support

In technical analysis (q.v.) support is forthcoming at a price level low enough for new buyers to emerge to provide at least a temporary floor. In short, in a bear market, buyers suddenly become more aggressive than sellers.

Survey

A technique used in exploration to determine the presence of a potential orebody.

(i) *Airborne:* a survey made from an aircraft to identify anomalies in the ground that may reflect the presence of mineralisation. Airborne surveys include photographic, geophysical and geological surveys.

(ii) *Geophysical:* the use of geophysical techniques in the search for mineral deposits. The techniques include earth currents, electrical, gravity, heat flow, magnetic, seismic or thermal measurements.

(iii) *Geochemical:* the use of chemical analysis of rocks, soils, sediments, water and plants to identify chemical anomalies which may indicate an orebody.

Sutter's Mill

At the junction of the American and Sacramento rivers where James Marshall noticed gold in January 1848, triggering the Californian gold rush.

Swaps

The word 'swap' has come to have several meanings in the physical gold market.

(i) It can simply mean the exchange of metal in one location for metal in another. For example, gold held in New York with the Federal Reserve may be swapped for gold held in London with the Bank of England; no metal actually has to move.

(ii) But the word 'swap' has increasingly come to describe the simultaneous spot sale of gold with a forward transaction to buy the same amount back at a later date. For governments and central banks it has become a way either of raising cash to meet short contingencies or simply to invest the money on an interest-bearing basis. The swap technique has been used in particular by gold mining nations such as South Africa, Brazil and the Philippines, which market their local production. Instead of selling the gold outright they can swap it to provide immediate liquidity. South Africa, for example, entered into extensive swap programmes from the 1970s onwards, often using part of her reserves in addition to the regular gold production that she was marketing. Swaps, usually for six months, were either rolled over on maturity or, on occasion if the price was high, the gold was partly sold and partly taken back into reserves. At the peak in the mid-1980s South Africa was estimated to have as much as 400 tonnes of gold out on swaps. Central banks usually, though not always, indicate when they have swapped gold by showing a drop in their published reserve figures in the International Financial Statistics; this is sometimes taken as an outright sale; often it is not.

(iii) On futures markets (q.v.) swapping can be used for rolling over or rolling forward contracts.

Sweepings

Fine ore and gold that has remained after mining in cracks and crevices which is 'swept' from the stope. Usually high grade material.

Sweeps

Originally that material in a manufacturing jeweller's plant which was swept up from the floor and sent to a refiner for recovery of precious metals. *See also* **Scrap.**

Swiss Bank Corporation

Swiss Bank Corporation (SBC) has long been a major gold distributor and trader, originally supplying gold to the Swiss watch industry. They were buyers at the third London gold fixing (q.v.) after its inauguration in 1919. In Zurich they are market makers in spot, forwards and options, and members of the Zurich gold pool. In London they are members of the London Bullion Market Association. They are also active traders in Hong Kong, New York and Tokyo. The bank owns the refinery Métaux Précieux/Métalor (q.v.) at Neuchatel.

Swiss Bank Corporation
PO Box 8022, CH 8022 Zurich
Switzerland
Tel: (1) 223 4111
Fax: (1) 223 4805
Telex: 813 451 bvz ch
Reuters: SBCBGL

Switch/Switching

On futures markets (q.v.), the liquidation of an open position and the re-establishment of a similar position for a more distant delivery month (q.v.). It can also be referred to as a rolling-forward or rolling-over.

Switzerland

Switzerland is both the centre for the physical wholesaling of gold and is also synonymous with investment or portfolio holding of gold. There is no tax on gold sales (although this was tried briefly in the early 1980s) and the marketing of gold over bank counters is encountered more than in any other country. Basel, Geneva and Zurich (q.v.) are very important gold trading centres, as also is the Lugano/Chiasso axis in the south near the Italian border. The three main Swiss banks, Crédit Suisse (q.v.), Swiss Bank Corporation (q.v.) and Union Bank of Switzerland (q.v.), have gold trading desks in these centres, although their main international business is run out of Zurich. All three also have their own refineries, Métaux Précieux (q.v.), Valcambi (q.v.) and Argor-Heraeus (q.v.) with acceptable London market status, while a fourth refinery, PAMP S.A., also has London acceptance.

No other nation is so well served with major refineries making bars, especially kilobars for international distribution. Close to 1,000 tonnes of gold passes through Switzerland annually on its way to other destinations — more than through any other country. The prime reason for this is that since 1968 much of South Africa's gold, which had previously been marketed through London, has been sold through Switzerland instead; the Soviet Union has also marketed much of its gold through Switzerland since 1973, where as before this it went to London.

While Swiss banks are major suppliers to such regional gold markets as Dubai (q.v.), Hong Kong (q.v.), Singapore (q.v.) and Tokyo (q.v.), they also have physical business much closer to home; the Swiss watch industry alone requires between 25 and 30 tonnes of gold a year, while Italy (q.v.), the leading manufacturer of gold jewellery (q.v.), is just across the border from Chiasso, where three of the four refineries are located. Even the German jewellery manufacturing centre of Pforzheim is close to Basel.

The physical business is complemented, however, by portfolio investment in gold, notably by the private banks in Geneva, but also those in Basel and Zurich. The two demands for gold tend to be counter-cyclical; when the physical export business is good because prices are low, portfolio managers are usually paying no attention to gold; when prices are beginning to rise the physical business slows down but this is the moment when the private banks increase their clients' portfolio holdings. Switzerland, in fact, acts as a sponge, with its private banks soaking up the metal when business is slow elsewhere.

The image of gold in Switzerland is also encouraged by the Swiss National Bank, which holds 2,590 tonnes, the third largest national holding, and by the Bank for International Settlements (q.v.), the central bankers' bank in Basel which is also active in the international gold market. Even the traditional Swiss gold coin, the Vreneli (q.v.), trades at a premium above most other coins. Over-the-counter options (q.v.) trading was also pioneered in Geneva in the 1970s by Valeurs White Weld (now Crédit Suisse First Boston Futures Trading). *See also* **Zurich.**

Sydney Futures Exchange, Australia

The market opened in April 1978 with a contract for 50 ounces of gold. In 1986, a link was set up between the exchange and COMEX, allowing participants to open futures positions on one exchange and liquidate them on the other. However, the volume of trading remained limited and all gold trading was finally suspended from 29 September 1989.

Tael

Chinese unit of weight in which trading is done on the Hong Kong market and some other centres, such as Taiwan.

1 tael = 1.20337 troy ounce
= 37.4290 grammes.

The nominal fineness (q.v.) of the Hong Kong tael bar is 990 but in Taiwan, 5 and 10 tael bars may be 999.9 fine.

The bars traded are normally 5 and 10 taels, although a 1 tael bar, shaped like a slipper bath, is also sold to investors. The basic contract on the Hong Kong Gold and Silver Exchange (q.v.) is a lot of 100 taels, composed of twenty 5-tael bars. Thirty-three members of the exchange make their own bars but those of Lee Cheong and King Fook are the most widely accepted.

Tael. *The range of tael bars made by King Fook for the Hong Kong market*

Tailings

The waste material from ore after the economically recoverable precious metals have been extracted. However, because of improved processes and a higher gold price, these tailings dumps can often be re-treated to extract more gold. Successful tailings operations have been conducted in South Africa on many of the old dumps from the early days of the mining industry, notably by East Rand Gold and Uranium Co. (managed by Anglo American) at the ERGO operations. In Canada, Eastmaque Gold Mines has a tailings operation in the traditional Kirkland Lake mining camp and in Australia, Elders Resources operates the Mt Morgan tailings operation. There are around 47 operational mines in the western world currently treating or about to treat tailings.

Taiwan

Taiwan became a substantial purchaser of gold in the private and central bank sectors during the 1980s. In the private sector the growing prosperity of the population, who were given little opportunity to travel or invest overseas, meant that money was channelled into both gold jewellery and investment; over 900 tonnes of gold was absorbed in the 1980s. That trend slowed as import restrictions on luxury items eased and foreign investment was permitted in an effort to redress Taiwan's balance of payments surplus. The central bank also bought 246 tonnes of gold in 1987–88 to diversify its reserves and in an effort to reduce its trade surplus with the United States. All the gold was bought for initial delivery in New York, and then sent to Taiwan to offset US imports of Taiwanese goods.

Tanaka Kikinzoku Kogyo KK

Tanaka is a leading Japanese gold trader, refiner and semi-fabricator engaged in almost every aspect of the business in Japan. The firm was founded in 1885. It has also been closely involved in a joint-venture with Johnson Matthey (q.v.) with the development of the platinum market in Japan. Its gold bars are acceptable good delivery on the London gold market. Tanaka also controls the

Yamazaki gold shop on Ginza in Tokyo, which sells everything from gold coins and bars to jewellery (over 20,000 items in stock) including ceremonial 24 carat chopsticks and tea ceremony sets.

Tanaka KK
6-6 Nihonbashi Kayabacho 2-Chome
Chuo-ku
Tokyo 103
Japan
Tel: (3) 668 0111
Fax: (3) 639 5705
Telex: 23563

Taxation

(i) *Mines.* Taxation levels on gold mining vary from one country to another. In Australia gold mines paid no tax until 1991, while in South Africa mines can pay a marginal rate of up to 68.7 per cent. Besides corporate profits tax, mining companies often pay a royalty to the owner of the mineral rights (frequently the State). In most major gold producing countries the 'wasting asset' nature of mining is recognised by a depletion allowance. This amounts to a deduction from gross revenue (or profits) before the assessment of taxable income to compensate for the fact that every orebody has a finite life.

In Australia, gold mines were exempted from corporate profits tax until 1991 provided at least 50 per cent of the mining income was from gold. Mines also pay royalty to most state governments: in Queensland and Tasmania the royalty is between 5 and 7 per cent of profits, in South Australia 2.5 per cent and in New South Wales 4 per cent. Royalty is not levied in Victoria or Western Australia.

In Canada, the corporate profits tax is 46 per cent but mining gets some concessions. The company is initially allowed to deduct 25 per cent of profits arising from mining before assessing taxable income and, further, may deduct one-third of its 'exploration expense' up to a maximum of 25 per cent of profits from that metal. Capital expenditure on shafts is not regarded as exploration costs but may be deducted as current expenditure. Machinery and equipment is written-off at 30 per cent per year and is accepted as an eligible cost for exploration expense depletion. Mining royalties in Canada are usually part of a private treaty and range between 3 and 6 per cent of the ex-mine value.

In South Africa, gold mines are subject to two forms of taxation. Both are calculated by formulae which take into account the various levels of profits, working costs and capital expenditure. Payments vary, therefore, on a sliding scale depending on the level of profitability and capital spending. The State is the owner of all precious metal reserves and leases areas of gold-bearing reef to the mining companies for royalty or lease payment. No lease payment is levied until cumulative profits exceed cumulative capital expenditure; thereafter capital expenditure is treated as an expense as and when incurred. Tax payments are treated in a similar way with the exception that lease payments are included in the formula as an expense. Over and above this, there is a flat rate surcharge, which can vary from year to year. The combined effect of lease payments and corporate tax is that gold mines can be liable for taxation up to 68.7 per cent, far above corporate rates in other business sectors.

In the United States, mining royalties are normally the result of a private treaty and range between 3 and 6 per cent of the ex-mine value. The corporate tax rate is 34 per cent on income over $75,000 per annum. Depletion is earned at 15 per cent on gross mining revenue but is limited to 50 per cent of the taxable income from the property. Mining capital expenditure after 1986 is written off over a seven year period using a 200 per cent declining balance method.

(ii) *Purchase of gold bars and coin*
Taxation on the purchase of gold bars and coin varies widely from country to country, and has had considerable effect in curtailing gold investment (particularly in coins) in many countries, or diverting the purchase to other, tax-free, points. In Europe, gold sales are normally liable to value added tax, except in Austria (where

Tax on retail gold sales

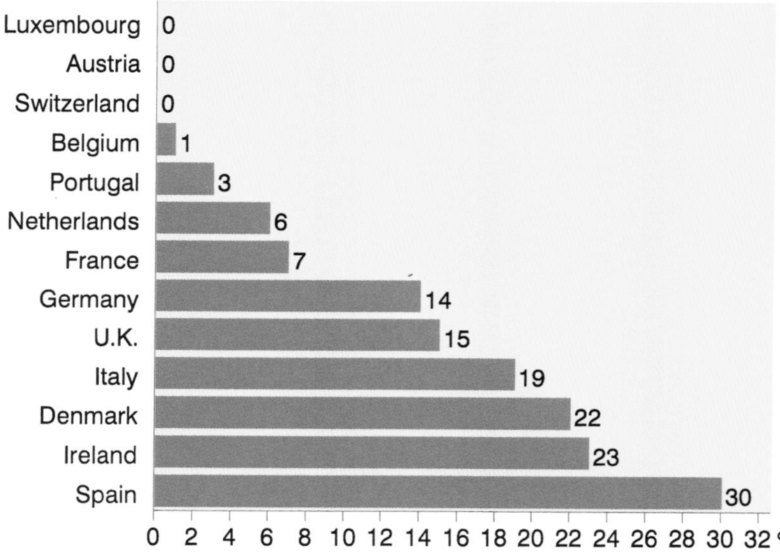

Taxation. *Source: Dresdner Bank*

legal tender coins are exempt), in Luxembourg and in Switzerland. In the United States most states levy sales tax, although this can usually be avoided by taking delivery out of state: in 22 states gold coin sales are not taxed. In Canada, provincial sales taxes vary.

Technical Analysis

Technical analysis, or charting, has assumed great significance in the gold market since the price was freed to find its own level above $35 and, in particular, since the launching of gold futures contracts in the United States in 1975. Technical analysts argue that the price is everything; that scrutiny of the current price and its history will provide the answers. In short, the technician believes that history repeats itself. The market place, he feels, is the combined pool of knowledge of gold miners, bullion dealers, investors, speculators and fabricators; the interplay of their concepts creates the price. Whether or not that is correct, technical charting in gold has become a force, especially in dictating short-term trends, and many market participants invest large sums in their own charts or in subscribing to professional services, which provide graphic visual evidence of the gold market's mood.

Technical analysts chart many aspects of the gold market, from the daily price variations on COMEX (q.v.), to the London fixings (q.v.) and the ratio between the gold and silver price.

To begin any study of charts, therefore, it is important to know what the point of reference is. In the United States, for instance, the high–low–close bar chart of daily COMEX trading is most popular. In Britain and Europe, a chart using the London p.m. fix tends to be more closely observed (the p.m. fix because by then New York is also open). The chart based on COMEX (see Figure i)has a vertical line for each day; the London p.m. chart, naturally, has a single point each day.

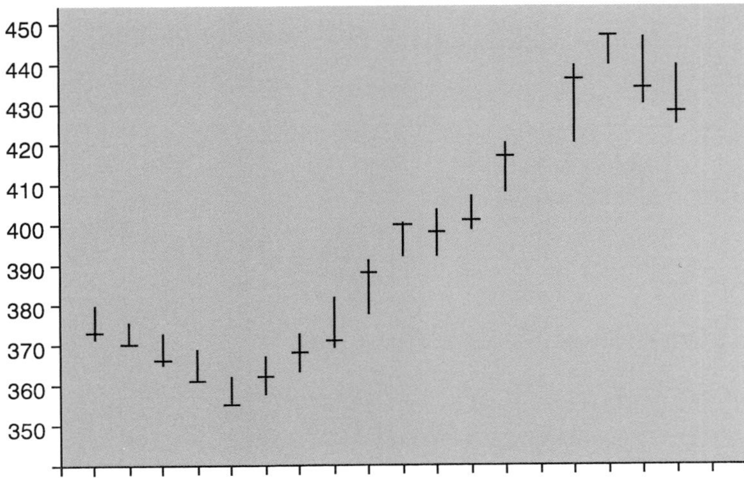

Figure i. COMEX based chart has vertical line for each day

Many charts will also integrate, along with this information, two other lines: Moving Averages of the price, which may be over a one-month, three-month or one-year period, and Momentum Indicators (Oscillators in the US) which measure the volatility or rate of change of the price.

Initially, the chartist will be studying major trend lines by connecting up in a straight line a series of successively higher or lower prices. On a COMEX chart, an uptrend occurs when both the daily highs and lows are at ever increasing price levels; a downtrend is when highs and lows are at progressively lower levels.

If there is no clear uptrend or downtrend and the market is stagnating within a narrow trading range, the chartist notes this as 'congestion', from which there will eventually be a 'break-out' to much higher or lower levels.

When it does break out, the key trend line would be the resistance level if the price went up, or the support level if it went down. The resistance level might be dictated by previous highs that gold has failed to penetrate — in fact, a previous congestion level; the support level would be dictated by a previous low or congestion. The crucial chart point is usually a specific price that was, say, the low last time round. If that was $355.75, and the price falls below that, then the support line is broken and the next support would be an even earlier low, perhaps $335. (Although there is a caveat that you need a 3 per cent penetration, i.e. to $345.07, before the support is truly broken.)

The aim, of course, is to pinpoint a key reversal of a trend, which may signal in a single trading day the end of a bear (q.v.) market or the top of a bull (q.v.) one. To this end, the chartist is looking for a number of patterns or formations which herald such a change.

Charted in tandem with these daily price movements is the moving average of the price; 30-day, three-month and one year are the most common (Figure vii).

In a sense this is standing back, taking a longer-term view of the price pattern compared with short-term fluctuations. The key signpost to watch here is when two lines cross; if in a bear market the one year average of the price, for instance, has been tracking above the line for the daily price but suddenly turns down and cuts below it, then that can be a signal of a key reversal towards a bull market.

Examples of the main patterns of Technical Analysis

Source for all charts: Brian Marber & Co.

Figure ii. Double top formation

Figure iii. Double bottom formation

Figure iv. Head and Shoulders formation

Figure v. Flag or pennant formation

Figure vi. Triangle formation

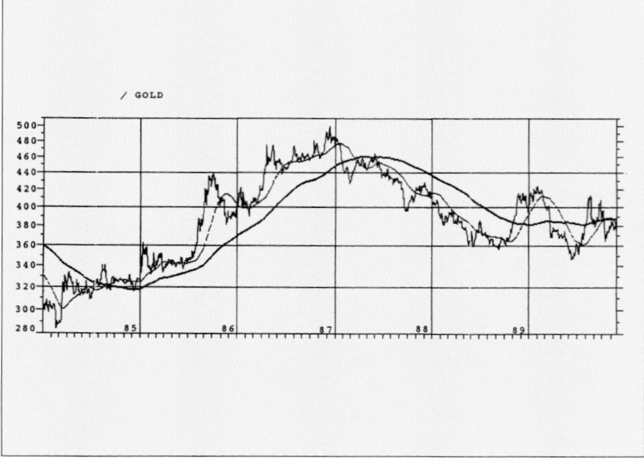

Figure vii. Moving average of the price

Tucked along the bottom of a chart there may be a line, fluctuating above or below zero, which is the Momentum Indicator (Oscillator in the US) measuring the velocity or rate at which the price is moving up or down. In a fast moving bull market it will be rising rapidly above the zero base, in a swift bear market it will be plunging rapidly below; the sign there is to observe how the oscillators, say, slow down, level out almost flat and then perhaps accelerate up. The Momentum Indicator slowing down top or bottom may be another reversal indicator. But the most important factor is the direction of movement — i.e. the actual trend.

The main patterns are:

Double top which is an M formation, when the price makes a new high, meets resistance, falls back slightly, then pushes up close to the earlier high, fails to exceed it and then falls back sharply (Figure ii).

Double bottom is the opposite of this, when the price twice fails to break below a particular support level and then takes off up (Figure iii).

Head and shoulders in which the price makes an initial new high (the line coming up the 'left arm'), slips back slightly, then pushes on to yet another high (the head), falls back again, rises slightly to the level of the initial high, stumbles and falls away abruptly (as it were down the 'right arm'), (Figure iv). This is sometimes known as a *head and shoulders top*; a mirror image head and shoulders bottom may also occur.

Flag or pennant is a short term consolidation in a bull or bear market. In a bull market it occurs when the price rises swiftly to a peak (the flagpole) and then briefly moves slightly lower during a period not exceeding three weeks and then advances to a new rally high. In a bear market a flag occurs after a rapid fall, when prices momentarily rise again (Figure v), consolidating for not more than three weeks and then continue to fall.

Triangles come in three varieties: ascending, descending and symmetrical. An ascending triangle has a horizontal resistance line but the support trend line is rising, indicating a bull market going still higher. The descending triangle has a horizontal support trend line but a descending resistance line — a bear market going yet lower. A symmetrical triangle has a rising support line and a declining resistance trend line suggesting a narrow trading range for a while (Figure vi).

Thailand

Thailand has become an important jewellery manufacturing centre. The jewellery industry employs over 200,000 people and the Thai Gem and Jewellery Traders Association alone has more than 300 members. Modern factories often employ two or three hundred people and use the latest equipment. The export jewellery, however, is chiefly gem-set using 10, 14 and 18 carat gold settings. Gold for these factories is imported through contract holders licensed by the government. The main export destinations are Hong Kong, Japan and the United States.

Thai Gem & Jewellery Traders Association
912/152 Charn Issara Tower, 15th Floor
Rama 4 Road, Bangkok 10500
Thailand
Tel: (662) 2353039
Fax: (662) 2353040
Telex: 84246 NASIMMA TH

Thiourea Leaching

A new process for the chemical leaching of gold involving thiourea (NH)CS, and avoiding the use of cyanide which is environmentally undesirable. It is used for the extraction of gold at the Hillgrove antimony mine in New South Wales, Australia.

Time Value

In options (q.v.) time value, also called **Extrinsic Value**, is the amount by which the premium (q.v.) exceeds its intrinsic value (q.v.) or the amount it is 'in-the-money' (q.v.). If the premium cost $20, the strike price (q.v.) is $400 and the current price is $410, then the time value is $10. It is not worth exercising at this stage but would be if gold rose to $425.

Thailand. *The oldest gold shop in Bangkok, Tang Toh Kang, first opened in the 1880s, has a busy lunchtime clientele*

Tokyo Commodity Exchange turnover

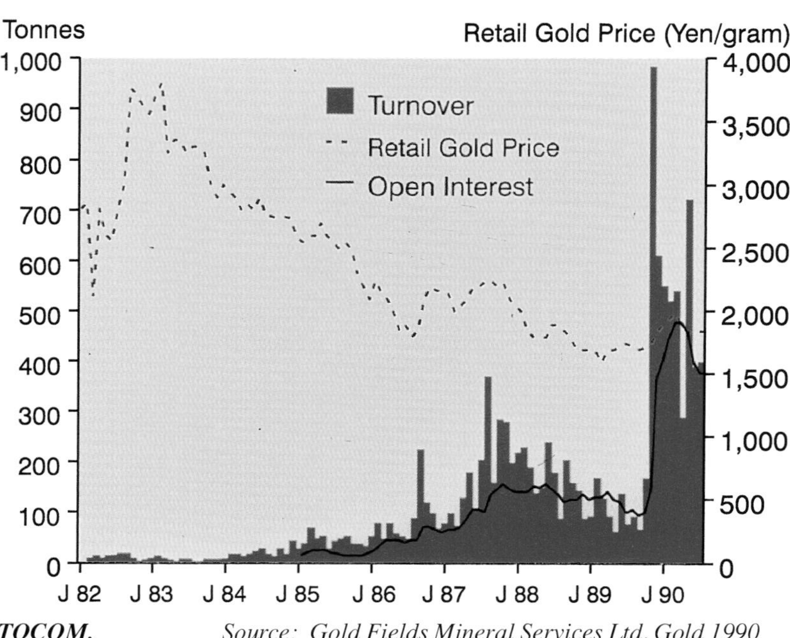

TOCOM. *Source: Gold Fields Mineral Services Ltd, Gold 1990*

TOCOM (Tokyo Commodity Exchange)

The Tokyo Commodity Exchange (Tokyo Kogyohin Torihikijo), or TOCOM, was created on 1 November 1984 by consolidating the Tokyo Gold Exchange, the Tokyo Rubber Exchange and the Tokyo Textile Commodities Exchange. It took over the gold futures contract, priced in yen, originally launched by the Tokyo Gold Exchange in March 1982. The contract traded is for one kilo of 9999 gold. Delivery month: every even-numbered month within the 12-month period after the date of transaction in an odd-numbered current month, and also an odd-numbered month following an even-numbered month. Last day of trading in the current month: the third business day preceding the delivery day. The delivery day is the end of the contract month. During the trading day there are six price calls: 9.10 a.m., 10.30 a.m., 11.30 a.m., 1.10 p.m., 2.30 p.m., and 3.45 p.m.

Initially the exchange attracted only local business because of the difficulty of foreign dealers becoming members and relatively high charges compared with COMEX (q.v.) but from 1987 volume exceeded two million contracts annually and the exchange attracted more international participation by offering associate membership for foreign dealers. The exchange had 31 associate precious metal members by 1990. Commissions and margin requirements have also been lowered.

The Tokyo Commodity Exchange
Tosen Building
10-8 Nihonbashi Horidome
1-chome, Chuo-ku
Tokyo 103
Japan
Tel: (3) 661 9191
Fax: (3) 661 7568
Telex:6502989893

Tola. *Ten tola bars or 'biscuits' are destined mainly for the Indian subcontinent*

Tokuriki Honten & Co. Ltd

Leading Japanese refiner and gold trader, founded in 1727. As a refiner, its bars are acceptable good delivery on the London market. Tokuriki is also a fabricator, wholesaler and retailer of jewellery and small ingots, and a producer of specialist gold products in electronics and dentistry. Tokuriki is a market-maker in gold loco Tokyo.

Tokuriki Honten & Co. Ltd
9-12 Kajicho 2 chome
Chiyoda-ku, Tokyo 1
Japan
Tel: (3) 252 0171
Fax: (3) 258 1233
Telex: 3345

Tola

Unit of weight for gold on the Indian sub-continent. One tola equals .375 ounces or 11.1 grammes of 999 fineness. Usually marketed as ten tola bars (also five tolas). The 999 ten tola bars mainly go to India, but also circulate widely in the Arabian Gulf States; 999.9 ten tola bars are sold in Saudi Arabia. Between 200 and 250 tonnes of ten tola bars are made annually, mainly by Swiss and UK refineries.

Toll Refining

The refining of scrap metal or concentrates for which the refinery is paid an agreed fee and there is no change in ownership of the metal recovered.

Touchstone

A smooth fine-grained, slightly abrasive black stone, usually quartz or jasper, used to assay (q.v.) or test

Touchstone. *Touchstone set used by Mocatta & Goldsmid in London in the 19th century for testing the fineness of gold bars*

the purity of gold by the streak left when it is rubbed with the metal. The colour of the streak can be compared with a standard range of marks. The touchstone was the first method of assaying gold and was used at least as early as 500 BC, the earliest touchstones — long strips of slate — having been found in excavations at the ancient city of Taxila in Pakistan with traces of gold streaks still on their surface. Touchstones are still widely used in the bazaars of India and may be encountered in some other Asian markets.

Trading Limit

(i) On futures markets (q.v.) the maximum change in price permitted in a single trading session.
(ii) The maximum number of futures contracts which may be traded by a speculator during a single trading session in any single commodity such as gold.

Trading Session

The set trading hours of futures and options exchanges such as COMEX (q.v.), Hong Kong Gold and Silver Exchange Society (q.v.), SIMEX (q.v.) and TOCOM (q.v.). Details are given in the entry for each exchange.

Treatment Charge

The charge a refiner makes for handling scrap, usually based on weight.

Trenching

The digging of shallow trenches on the surface to expose potential mineralisation for geological inspection and sampling.

Trend Line

In technical analysis (q.v.), the straight line connecting a series of high prices or low prices to define an uptrend or downtrend in price and to indicate resistance (q.v.) and support (q.v.) levels.

Triangle

An important pattern in technical analysis (q.v.).

Troy Ounce

The traditional unit of weight for gold is the troy ounce, named, it is thought, after a weight used at the annual fair at Troyes in France in the Middle Ages. Although the metric system is used increasingly in mining and the gold business, the troy ounce remains the basic unit in which the price of 995 gold is quoted.

1 troy ounce = 31.1034807 grammes
32.15 troy ounces = 1 kilogramme
1 troy ounce = 480 grains
1 troy ounce = 20 pennyweights (North American jewellery trade)
3.75 troy ounces = 10 tolas (Indian sub-continent)
6.02 troy ounces = 5 taels (Hong Kong)
1 troy ounce = 155.52 metric carats (diamonds/precious stones)

T T Bar (Ten Tola)

See **Tola**.

Tumbago

An alloy of gold and copper that looks like solid gold.

Turkey

Turkey has long been a major market for gold which is fabricated into high carat jewellery and coins. Since 1989 the central bank has had a monopoly on the import of unfabricated gold, keeping consignment stocks from leading bullion banks, which it distributes to authorised wholesalers. The central bank imported 90 tonnes in the first year of this new policy, and 145 tonnes in 1990. Jewellery manufacturers can also import semi-fabricated gold against export orders. The jewellery manufacturing industry broadened its export business substantially in the 1980s, with its designs being popular throughout the Middle East and, increasingly, in the United States. In fact, Turkey is well placed to become an important regional gold market. The Mint in

Istanbul also regularly makes coins from gold supplied by local wholesalers. Five denominations of the 22 carat Ata coins (5,2½,1,½ and ¼) are minted, the basic 1 Ata coin weighing 7.2 grammes.

Tutankhamun

The boy-king of Egypt from 1361 to 1352 BC whose tomb, discovered by Howard Carter in 1922, preserved some of the greatest treasures of the Egyptian goldsmiths' craft. The king's body was encased in a coffin of solid gold sheet two millimetres thick, weighing over 90 kilos. The head of his mummy was shrouded in a great mask of beaten gold. The golden throne nearby was adorned with delicately worked scenes showing the young king being anointed by his queen. The treasure of Tutankhamun is normally on display in the Cairo Museum but has drawn crowds of several million when exhibited in Europe and America. It is a symbol of the magnificence achieved in gold from ancient times.

***Tutankhamun.** Detail of the golden throne of the Egyptian boy king*

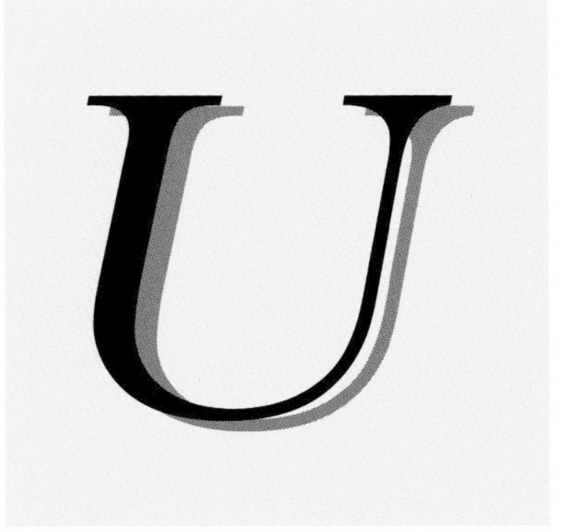

Umpire

An independent accepted assayer who will act as arbitrator in any dispute between a refiner and his client about the assay of ore or gold bullion. The conditions of employing an umpire are part of many contracts.

Unallocated Gold

Gold held for clients by a bank or bullion dealer as part of a general 'pool' or stock. Individual bars are not assigned to each owner, who is not a secured creditor. Opposite of **allocated gold** (q.v.).

Uncovered

An open futures or forward market position; compare also with naked options (q.v.). *See also* **Short/Short Position.**

Union Bank of Switzerland

Union Bank of Switzerland (UBS) is a market-maker in spot, forwards and options in Zurich and Geneva; also a member of the Zurich gold pool, and of the London Bullion Market Association. They are also active traders in Hong Kong, New York and Sydney. UBS also has 75 per cent participation in the Argor-Heraeus SA refinery (q.v.).

Union Bank of Switzerland
Bahnhofstrasse 45
Zurich CH 8021
Switzerland
Tel: (1) 235 4320
Fax: (1) 235 6876
Telex: 814239 ub ch
Reuters: UBZE

United Kingdom

See **Bank of England; Britannia; Fixing; Goldsmiths' Company; Guinea; Hallmarking; Loco London; London Bullion Market Association; London Good Delivery; Sovereign.**

United States of America

The United States is the third largest producer of gold, after South Africa and the Soviet Union, with output of close to 300 tonnes in 1990. That position was only won back in the 1980s but is likely to be retained for the rest of this century.

In the second half of the nineteenth century, the United States was the world's leading gold producer. Since the liberalisation of private gold holding and trading in the United States from 31 December 1974, after a generation from 1934 in which citizens could not hold gold, New York has become the centre of futures (q.v.) and options (q.v.) trading on COMEX (q.v.). The United States has the largest official gold reserves of any nation, with just over 8,100 tonnes or nearly 23 per cent of all officially declared reserves worldwide; it is also more than double the

United States gold mine production

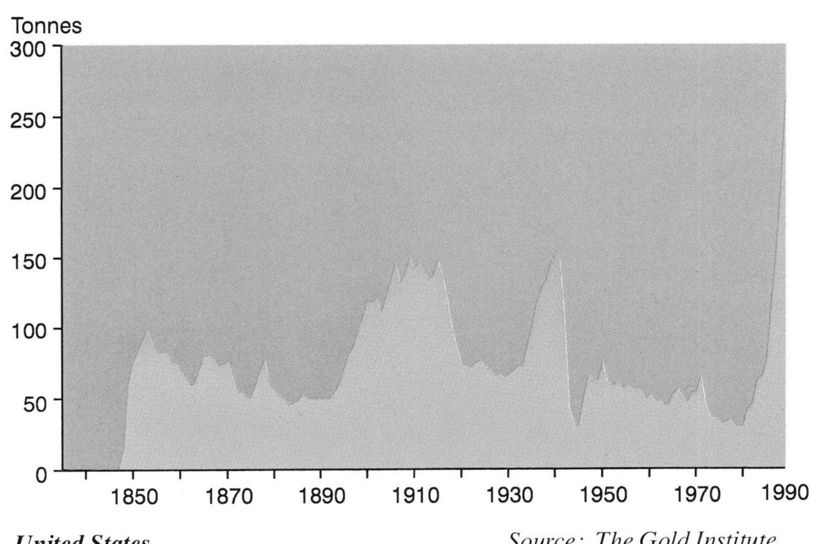

United States. *Source: The Gold Institute*

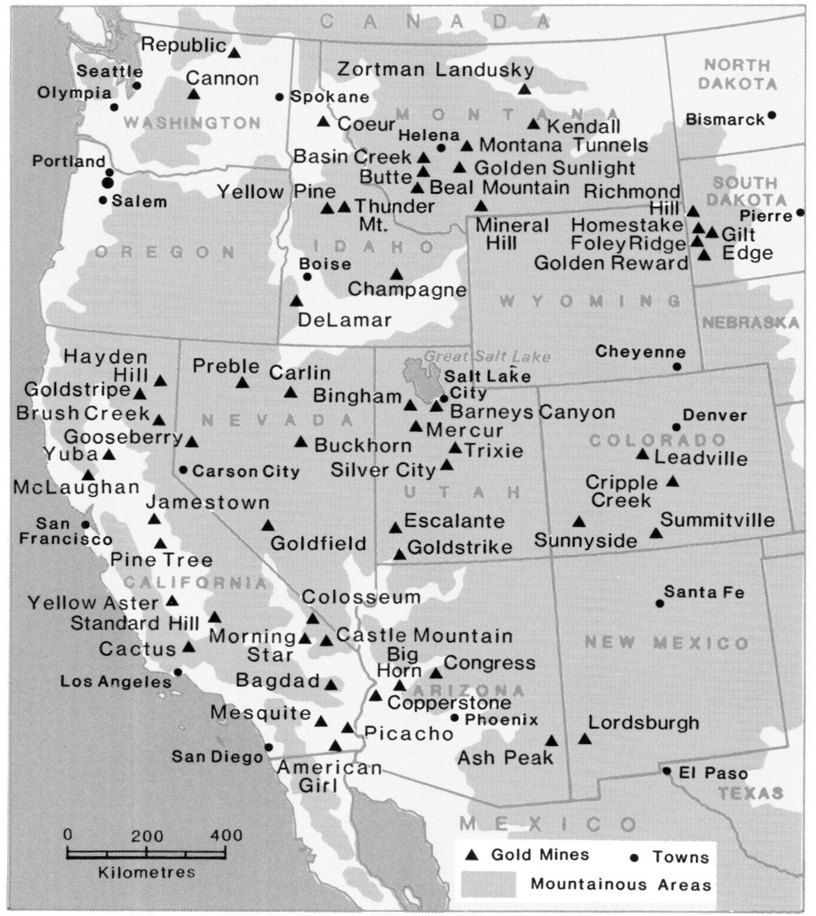

United States. *The main gold mines in the western United States*

reserve of the second largest holder, Germany.

Although 1848 and the symbolic Californian gold rush (q.v.) stand out as a landmark in the history of gold, ushering in an entirely new dimension in world gold output, gold had already been discovered in the United States in the foothills of the Appalachian mountains in North Carolina in 1799, starting a small gold industry there, and later in Georgia that produced about 3 tonnes a year for many years.

The discovery of gold in the tailrace of John Sutter's mill near the junction of the American and Sacramento rivers in January 1848 ushered in a new era and saw the start of the Californian gold rush. In a few short years, output soared, reaching 77 tonnes in 1851, and peaking at 93 tonnes in 1853 when the best of the California gold had been worked out.

California not only provided much of the gold that eventually enabled most of the world to shift from a silver to a gold standard (q.v.) within a few years, but the effect of hundreds of thousands of prospectors trekking to the gold rush had the most profound influence on the opening up of the American West.

Although California was past its prime in six years, and output there fell back to around 30 tonnes a year, prospectors kept looking throughout the west for the rest of the century, coming up with the Comstock Lode at Virginia City, Nevada, at Pike's Peak and other areas of Colorado, to Boise in Idaho and to Montana, where a rich quartz lode at Whitlatch helped push the new territory's output to over 30 tonnes in 1866. Thence on to the Black Hills of South Dakota, where America's foremost gold mine, the Homestake mine at Lead, opened in 1877; it is still producing. In well over a century the Homestake mine has created more than two hundred miles of tunnels and shafts to a depth of 7,400 feet beneath the Black Hills, yielding well over 1,000 tonnes of gold, close to 10 per cent of all the gold ever mined in the United States.

Such diversification throughout the west kept America as the leading producer until 1898, when it was overtaken by South Africa. Although first place was briefly regained during the Boer War in South Africa, it did mark something of a turning

United States. *The joint mill for Echo Bay's McCoy and Cove open pits in Nevada*

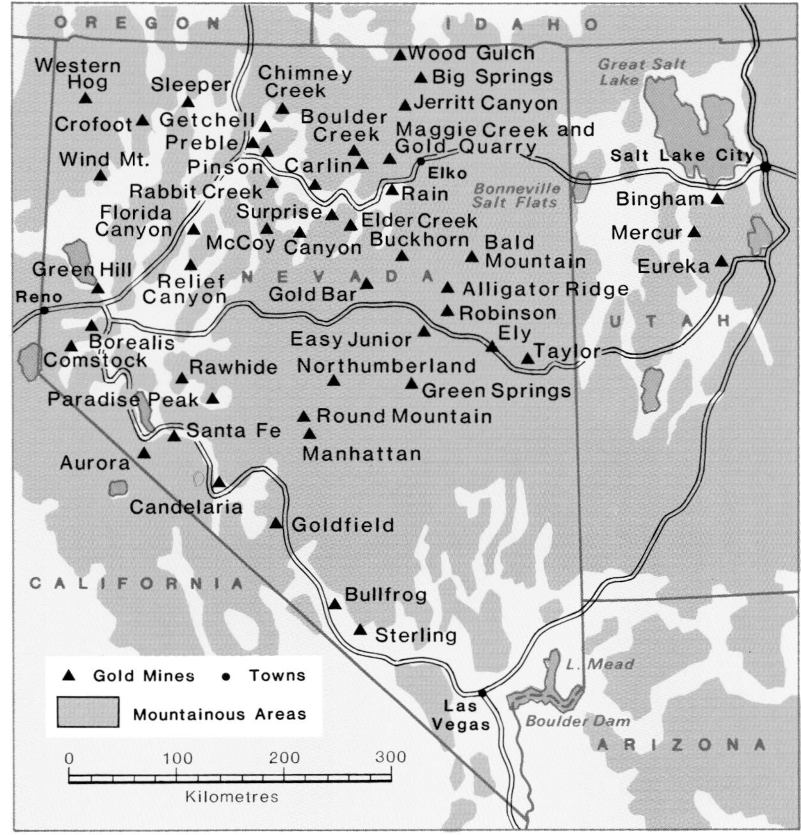

United States. *Nevada is the major gold producing state, contributing nearly 60% of output, virtually all from open-cast pits*

point. Through much of the twentieth century American gold mining declined. The short, bright recovery came between 1934 and 1940, after President Roosevelt had put gold up to $35 an ounce; a mining boom ensued in which US production more than doubled to 155 tonnes in 1940, an all-time record until 1988. Thereafter, for forty years it was in decline. The United States, unlike its neighbour Canada (q.v.), did not subsidise gold mining, so miners went after more profitable base metals. Only the Homestake mine at Lead kept going, along with by-product from such operations as the huge open-pit copper/gold mine at Bingham Canyon in Utah.

By 1980 American production was down to a mere 30.5 tonnes. Gold at $850 changed that. In less than a decade the industry was revitalised, pushing output up over 250 tonnes. Actually much of that had to do with new technology, as well as the rising price. The first signpost actually came rather earlier. Two geologists from Newmont Mining (q.v.) found a high grade deposit (11 grammes per tonne) of very finely disseminated gold north of Elko, Nevada. It was the first sighting of what became known as the Carlin Trend (q.v.), a huge, usually low grade, epithermal (q.v.) gold deposit spreading out through a vast area of north–central Nevada. An open-pit mine started in 1965 yielded over 100 tonnes of gold in the next twenty years; Carlin pioneered the concept of the open-pit mine, soon to be aided by heap-leaching (q.v.), carbon-in-pulp recovery (q.v.), and, of course, a higher price. Gold mining, almost literally, became fashionable again, bringing in many new mining groups who found that Nevada contained not just the Carlin Trend, but was peppered with disseminated epithermal orebodies. Newmont, as the originators, pushed their production with other open-pits to well over 30 tonnes a year; they were joined by American Barrick

United States. *Gold Strike mine, operated by American Barrick, will be America's largest*

United States: Top Twenty Mines

	Mine	Major Share holders	Output (000 oz) 1989 actual	1990 estimated
1	Newmont Carlin	Newmont Gold 100%	1,467,800	1,700,000
2	Bingham Canyon	RTZ Corp. 100%	507,000	500,000
3	Homestake	Homestake Mining 100%	381,788	400,000
4	Round Mountain	Echo Bay 50%/Homestake 25% /Case, Pomeroy 25%	318,616	440,000
5	Jerritt Canyon	FMC Gold 30%/Minorco 70%	296,900	380,000
6	McLaughlin	Homestake 100%	283,843	270,000
7	Sleeper	Amax Gold 100%	256,219	252,000
8	Battle Mountain Complex	Battle Mountain 100%	251,000	252,000
9	Chimney Creek	Hanson 100%	230,000 (e)	230,000
10	Paradise Peak	FMC Gold 100%	228,100	190,000
11	McCoy/Cove	Echo Bay 100%	214,566	320,000
12	Goldstrike	American Barrick 100%	207,264	330,000
13	Mesquite	Hanson 100%	197,000 (e)	195,000
14	Ridgeway	RTZ Corp. 52%/Galactic 48%	172,505	169,000
15	Cannon	Asamera 51%/Breakwater 49%	150,420	130,000
16	Getchell	FirstMiss Corp. 100%	121,124	189,000
17	Mercur	American Barrick 100%	117,536	110,000
18	Golden Sunlight	Placer Dome 100%	111,589	89,000
19	Jamestown	Sonora 70%/COGEMA 30%	111,300	110,000
20	Florida/Relief Canyon	Pegasus Gold 100%	109,200	84,000
	Also of note:			
	Copperstone	Cyprus Minerals 100%	60,000	100,000
	Robinson	Echo Bay 40%/Alta Bay 60%	78,828	100,000
	Barney's Canyon	RTZ Corp. 100%	25,000	114,400
	Bullfrog	Bond Int. Gold 100%	56,771	230,000

(q.v.) whose Goldstrike mine will be the biggest in the US; by Battle Mountain Gold; by Echo Bay Mines (q.v.) and many others. Nevada was the focus, producing over 60 per cent of US output in the late 1980s. But other new mines came in, notably Homestake Mining's McLaughlin mine in California. The test for most of them was low-cost. Because they are open-pit, capital costs are relatively low and operating costs are kept down by the new technology.

The average working costs on most of these new American mines are around $210 per ounce (compared with South Africa pressing towards $280); a few, like Chimney Creek in Nevada, have working costs under $120.

The test for this new generation of American mines is to control those costs, particularly once the more accessible oxide ore in the open pits is worked out, and they may have to go underground and mine refractory (q.v.) ores which are more difficult to treat. Environmental controls, already very strict in California on such mines as McLaughlin, also restrain expansion. The renaissance, however, will not be short lived; in Nevada alone even the parameters of the Carlin Trend are not yet fully defined. Much of Nevada is a goldfield that will be developed into the next century.

Just as South Africa is still a major producer more than a century after its main reefs were found, so the United States now has a goldfield to work into the twenty-first century and its role as a long term leading producer is confirmed.

See also **California; COMEX; Eagle Coin; Taxation; American Barrick; Battle Mountain Gold; Echo Bay Mines; Newmont Mining.**

United States Mint

The United States Mint was established in Philadelphia, Pennsylvania in 1792 and produced the first $5.00 Half Eagle gold coins in 1795. The modern Mint, completed in Philadelphia in 1969, strikes the current Eagle gold bullion coins (q.v.) and other special commemorative coins in gold and silver. The Mint's bars are acceptable good delivery on the London market. A branch of the US Mint also operates in Denver, Colorado, where it was originally established in 1862 to produce gold coinage from new gold discoveries in the region.

United States Mint,
Fifth St at Independence Mall,
Philadelphia, PA 19106,
USA.

Unwrought Gold

Gold cast as bars before it is fabricated.

Upgrading

To improve the purity of gold by smelting or refining. For example, upgrading 995 gold by electrolytic refining to 999.9.

USSR

See **Bank For Economic Affairs; Chervonetz; Soviet Union.**

Valcambi

Valcambi SA was founded as a refinery in 1961 and became a fully owned subsidiary of Crédit Suisse (q.v.), Zurich, in 1980. The refinery, located at Balerna, is active in gold, silver, platinum and palladium refining and recycling. It is a leading manufacturer of gold watch cases and bracelets and produces a wide range of specialist gold products including dental alloys, coins, medals, galvanic salts, and small Crédit Suisse ingots. Its bars have acceptable London good delivery status.

Valcambi SA
Via Passeggiata, CH 6828
Balerna, Switzerland
Tel: (91) 43 5333
Fax: (91) 43 0808
Telex: 842456 vlbi ch

Value Added Tax (VAT)

See **Taxation.**

Variation Margin

On futures markets (q.v.), variation margin is the additional margin for which an investor may be called upon by the clearing house (q.v.) on a daily basis if the price moves against him. *See also* **Margin.**

Vega

In options (q.v.) the sensitivity of an option's theoretical value to price volatility.

Vein

A seam or lode (q.v.) of gold-bearing or other metallic ore through rock. *See also* **Mining.**

Venezuela

Venezuela experienced a considerable gold rush in the 1980s, mainly to placer deposits along the Caroni and Paragi rivers and down towards the border with Brazil. Production rose to about 20 tonnes annually, much of which was bought by the central bank, which established its own gold buying unit, and was then sold abroad. Mining companies attempting to follow up and develop operations have been hampered by restrictive mining laws.

Vermeil

A thin plating of gold, not less than 100 millionths of an inch thick, overlaying solid sterling silver

Vertical Crater Retreat (VCR)

An underground mining method in which vertical longholes are drilled from drives developed in the ore between two levels. The ore is then blasted using a charge which occupies a relatively small length of the hole, some distance from the bottom face. The blast creates downward facing craters and the broken ore drawn from the stope on the lower level. The method has a low explosive consumption. Used at the Homestake mine in the United States.

Vibrating Table

A concentration device for the separation of gold and other heavy minerals. Often used in placer mining (q.v.) and occasionally in conventional gold operations.

Vicenza Fair

Jewellery fair held at Vicenza in Italy (q.v.) in January and June.

Details from: Ente Fiera Vicenza
CP 805, I-36100 Vicenza
Italy
Tel: (0444) 969 111
Fax: (0444) 563954
Telex: 481542 FIERVII

Volatility

The volatility or rate of change of the gold price from day to day is important in two main areas:

(i) In options (q.v.) it is one of the factors built into the Black-Scholes (q.v.) formula for calculating the cost or premium of an option.

(ii) In technical analysis (q.v.) it is the basis of momentum indicators (oscillators) on charts. Volatility appears to attract speculative activity and increased trading interest generally.

Volume

The volume or number of contracts traded each day on futures exchanges such as COMEX (q.v.), TOCOM (q.v.) or the Kam Ngan (q.v.) is an important indicator of market mood. High volume in gold on a particular day or for a month will indicate extra speculative or hedging interest. Volume on COMEX is usually around 10 million contracts annually (with a gold equivalent of over 32,000 tonnes) and on TOCOM is around 2 million contracts. Options (q.v.) volume on COMEX is also an indicator of activity in that sector, with usually just over 1.5 million contracts traded annually. Volume on other markets, such as loco London, where there is no Open Outcry (q.v.), cannot be assessed.

Vreneli. *Nearly 60 million of these Swiss coins were minted*

Vreneli

A 20-franc Swiss gold coin, fine gold content 0.1867 troy ounces, 900 fine, with a portrait of a girl on the face, which first appeared in 1897 and was minted until 1949. In all 58.6 million of these coins were struck. The Vreneli remains an important investment coin with Swiss investors and often trades at a significant premium of 20% or more to the gold price.

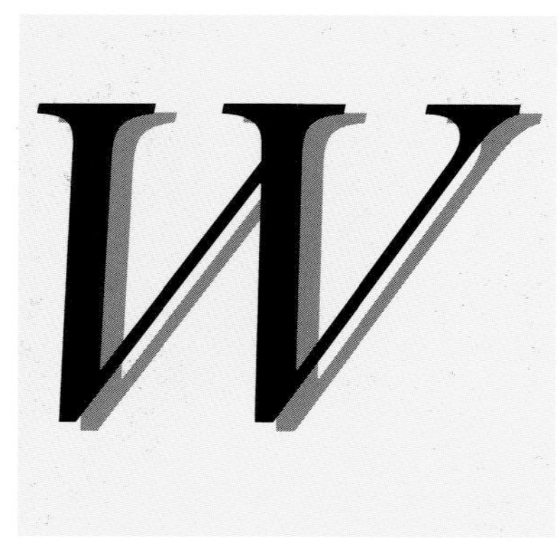

Wafer

A thin gold bar, such as 1 gramme rolled gold, popular in the Middle East, south east Asia and Japan. Also used generally to describe gold bars of less than 50 grammes troy, especially in the United States.

Wall Rock

A rock mass adjacent to a fault zone or lode (q.v.). *See also* **Country Rock.**

Warehouse Receipt

A warehouse or depository receipt is issued when delivery is taken on a futures contract. It specifies the quantity and fineness of the gold held there.

Warrant

See **Gold Warrants.**

Waste

Rock lacking sufficient grade and/or other characteristics of ore to be economic.

Western Australian Mint

See **Perth Mint**.

Western Mining Corp.

Western Mining is a major diversified mining company, and the largest gold producer in Australia. Other significant mining interests include aluminium and nickel. Gold currently accounts for about 35 per cent of earnings, and for the year to June 1990, the company produced an attributable 927,635 ounces (28.8 tonnes) of gold. Western Mining has interests in gold mining operations in Australia, Fiji, North America and Brazil. The largest single gold operation is Kambalada in Western Australia which produced 203,447 ounces (6.3 tonnes) in the year to June 1990.

Western Mining Corporation
360 Collins St
Melbourne, Victoria 3001
Australia
Tel: (3) 602 0300
Fax: (3) 670 4969
Telex: AA 30250

White Gold

A gold alloy containing either nickel or palladium or a combination of the two as whitening agents, often used as a setting for diamond jewellery.

Width

Also known as **Reef Width**. The actual thickness of the gold-bearing rock layer, exclusive of waste.

Winnipeg Commodity Exchange

The Winnipeg Commodity Exchange in Canada pioneered gold futures contracts in North America, when American citizens were still forbidden to hold or trade gold privately. The 400 ounce contract, denominated in US dollars, was launched in November 1972. The first trade was at $62.50. Delivery on the futures contracts was effected by tendering gold certificates of 400 ounces fine, issued by the Bank of Nova Scotia or the Canadian Imperial Bank of Commerce. An additional 100 ounce contract was launched in 1975. Winnipeg also introduced exchange traded options (q.v.) on futures contracts in 1979. The most active year in gold was the fiscal year August 1974 to July 1975 when 108,891 futures contracts were traded. But Winnipeg was eclipsed thereafter by COMEX (q.v.) and the other American exchanges; gold trading finally ended in April 1988.

Winze

See **Ramp.**

Witwatersrand Basin

The Witwatersrand Basin is the heartland of the South African gold mining industry. Within it a great area of gold-bearing reefs stretches from forty miles east of Johannesburg to ninety miles west, and then swings south-west into the Orange Free State. *See also* **South Africa.**

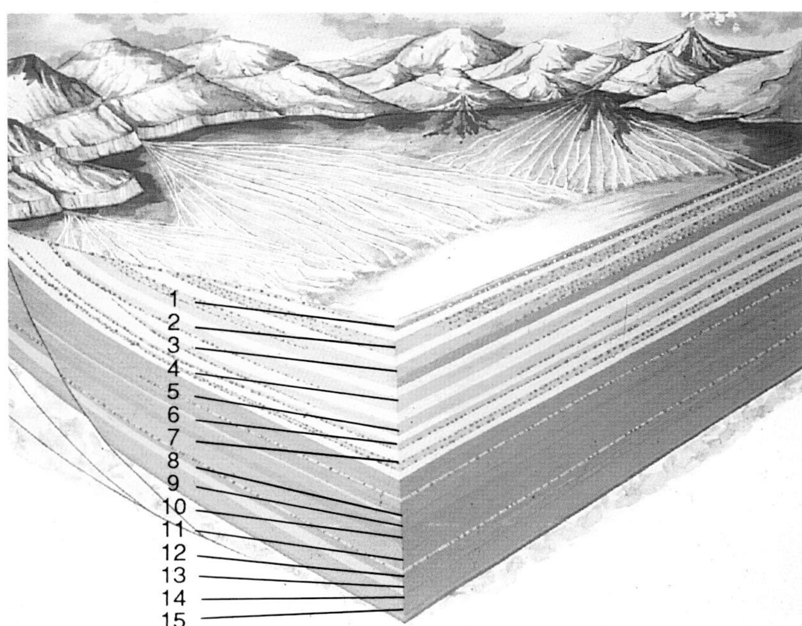

Witwatersrand Basin. *Cutaway of the multi-layered gold-bearing reefs (listed below)*

Reef or formation	Areas where mined
1 Ventersdorp Contact Reef (VCR)	West Wits Line and Klerksdorp
2 Mondeor Conglomerate Formation	West Wits Line, West Rand and Southern OFS
3 Kimberley Conglomerate Formation	Evander, East Rand, Klerksdorp and Southern OFS
4 Bird Conglomerate Formation	West Rand, Klerksdorp and Southern OFS
5 Livingstone Conglomerate Formation	West Rand
6 Johnstone Conglomerate Formation	West Rand
7 Main Conglomerate Formation	East, Central and West Rand, West Wits Line, Klerksdorp and Southern OFS
8 Crown Formation	
9 Veldschoen Reef (inner basin reef)	Klerksdorp
10 Magnetic horizon in lower Jeppestown shale	
11 Buffelsdoorn (outer basin reef)	Klerksdorp
12 Boulders Reef	
13 Magnetic shale in Witpoort Jie Formation	
14 Magnetic West Rand shales	
15 Rietfontein tillite	

Wohlwill Process

The electrolytic method of gold refining was first developed by Dr Emil Wohlwill of Norddeutsche Affinerie in Hamburg in 1874. Dr Wohlwill's process is based on the solubility of gold, but the insolubility of silver, in an electrolyte solution of gold chloride ($AuCl_3$) in hydrochloric acid. The impure gold is cast into anodes of about 100 ounces each, which are suspended in porcelain cells, while the cathodes are thin strips of pure gold. By passing an electric current from anode to cathode through the electrolyte solution, the anodes are gradually dissolved and the gold therein is deposited on the cathodes; any silver, not being soluble in the solution, is precipitated to the bottom of the cells. The sequence takes about two days, following which the gold-coated cathodes are removed, melted and cast into bars. The initial process can produce gold up to 999.5 fine, with further treatment bringing it up to 999.9. The disadvantage of the Wohlwill process is the time that the gold is 'locked up'. Initially this led to most gold being refined by the quicker Miller (q.v.) chlorine process, which can take gold to 995; as long as gold was essentially a monetary metal that was all that was required. But the modern demands of jewellery, industry, coin, and investors in many regional markets for gold that is at least 999, if not 999.9, has led to the extension of electrolytic facilities at many refineries. *See also* **Electrolysis.**

World Gold Council

A Geneva-based organisation of over seventy gold producers from eleven countries, formed in 1986 to promote gold, and which replaced the International Gold Corporation (Intergold). The jewellery division works mainly with the jewellery trade and industry to co-ordinate promotions and increase direct involvement by the trade in special projects. The investment division has promoted schemes such as gold accumulation plans in Japan and Europe, and the bullion coin market. The Council also seeks to educate mining companies to a full understanding of the gold business.

World Gold Council
1 Rue de la Rotisserie
1204 Geneva, Switzerland
Tel: (22) 21 96 66
Fax: (22) 28 81 60
Telex: 428471

Writer

In options (q.v.) the writer or grantor is the one who sells the option, sets the premium (q.v.) and receives that premium income.

Year Mark

The hallmark (q.v.) stamped on a piece of jewellery by one of the four assay offices in the United Kingdom includes the date letter indicating the year in which it was approved. The letters of the alphabet are run through in a sequence; 1990 was R.

Yellow Gold

An alloy (q.v.) of gold, copper, silver and sometimes zinc, which looks yellower than gold itself.

Yield

Also known as **Recovered Grade**. The actual gold grade realised at the mine mill. *See also* **Grade.**

Zaire

Zaire is the scene of considerable unofficial placer gold mining, which accounts for over 10 tonnes a year, most of which leaves the country through the neighbouring state of Burundi on its way to European refineries. A little official mining continues at the Kili-moto mines.

Zimbabwe

Traces of quartz mining in Zimbabwe go back to ancient times, and it may well have been one of the earliest sources of gold, even for the Egyptians three thousand years ago. Today Zimbabwe has a production of around 16 tonnes annually, from a number of small mines operated by Lonrho, RTZ (q.v.) and Cluff Resources (an entrepreneurial British company that has invested in the Royal Family, Freda and Rebecca mines). For many years Zimbabwe gold was refined in South Africa, but in 1988 the central bank, the Reserve Bank of Zimbabwe (q.v.), which also markets the gold, opened its own refinery in Harare, Fidelity Printers & Refiners (Private) Limited, which has acceptable London good delivery status.

Zurich

Zurich is both the centre of the gold business in Switzerland (q.v.) and the world's premier physical gold market. The three main Swiss banks, Crédit Suisse (q.v.), Swiss Bank Corporation (q.v.) and Union Bank of Switzerland (q.v.) all operate their main international gold trading operations from here. They also have their own broker, Premex (q.v.), and operate an informal gold pool among themselves.

The pool has its origins in the three Zurich banks' successful bid to capture South African gold sales in 1968, when the London market was closed for two weeks. By then the Zurich banks had become London's largest clients for physical gold, having cultivated the Middle East and Far East markets assiduously since the late 1940s. Their united front won them South African sales which they retained for much of the 1970s. They also persuaded the Soviet Union to market much of its gold through Zurich when it resumed large-scale sales in 1972. While South African and Soviet sales have since become more diversified, Zurich still exports

Zimbabwe. The mill for Cluff Resources Freda and Rebecca open-pit mines

close to 1,000 tonnes of physical metal to regional markets around the world each year, most of it bearing the marks of their own refineries. Their overseas relationships are aided by offices, not only in London and New York, but in regional markets like Bahrain, Singapore, Hong Kong and Tokyo. The close co-operation between the three pool banks, which was always flexibly adapted to the requirements of the market, has been a major element in maintaining Zurich's role in the gold business through all the structural changes in the market in the last three decades.

Bank Leu, one of the oldest Swiss banking houses (in which Crédit Suisse now has a controlling interest), is also a major coin dealer, noted particularly for its auctions of numismatic coins (q.v.).

Zimbabwe. *The Rebecca mine which has given a substantial lift to Zimbabwe's output*

Bibliography/Sources

Books

T. E. Anin, *Gold in Ghana,* Selwyn Publishers Ltd, London 1987.

Robert Beale, *Trading in Gold Futures,* Woodhead-Faulkner Ltd, Cambridge 1985.

W. H. Dennis, *Metallurgy in the Service of Man*, Macdonald, London 1981.

C. P. Dyer, *The Royal Mint,* Llantrisant 1986.

C. E. Fivaz and R. P. King (eds), *Extractive Metallurgy of Gold,* South African Institute of Mining and Metallurgy, 1986.

John Kenneth Galbraith, *Money,* Andre Deutsch, London 1975.

Gold, Alpine Fine Arts Collection, New York 1981.

Gold Dealers Luxembourg a.s.b.l., *Guide to Precious Metals, 1990*

Timothy Green, *The New World of Gold,* Weidenfeld & Nicholson, London 1985.

Timothy Green, *The Prospect for Gold: the View to the Year 2000,* Rosendale Press, London 1987.

Guido Gregorietti, *Jewellery Through the Ages,* Hamlyn, London 1970.

Philip Grierson, *Numismatics,* Oxford University Press 1975.

Graham Hughes, *The Art of Jewellery,* Peerage Books, London 1972.

R. W. Jastram, *The Golden Constant,* John Wiley & Sons, New York 1977.

Pierre Lassonde, *The Gold Book,* Penguin Books 1990.

Alfred G. Lock, *Gold: Its Occurrence and Extraction,* E. & F. H. Spon, London 1892.

E. H. MacDonald, *Alluvial Mining,* Chapman & Hall, London and New York 1983.

Mase Westpac Ltd, *The Winning of Gold,* London 1990.

Terry Mayer, *Commodity Options: a User's Guide to Speculating and Hedging,* New York Institute of Finance, 1983.

W. P. Morrell, *The Gold Rushes,* A. & C. Black, London 1968.

Sheldon Natenberg, *Options Volatility and Pricing Strategies,* Probus Publishing Co., Chicago.

Jeffrey A. Nichols, *The Complete Book of Gold Investing,* Dow Jones-Irwin, New York 1987.

Paul Sarnoff, *Trading in Gold,* Woodhead-Faulkner Ltd, Cambridge 1989.

Swiss Bank Corporation, *Gold,* Zurich 1981.

Journals

Aurum, The International Review for Manufacturers, Designers & Retailers of Gold Jewellery, published quarterly, 1979–1989, by the World Gold Council, Geneva, Switzerland. Notably Jochem Wolter's four-part series 'Gold Chains and Mesh', in Autumn issues 31–34, 1988–1989

Gold Bulletin, International Gold Corporation, Marshalltown, South Africa:

Vol. 5, no. 1, January 1982, Guilia Bologna, 'Gold in Book Binding';

Vol. 15, no. 2, April 1982, Susumu Tomiyama and Yasdo Fukui, 'Gold Bonding';

Vol. 15, no. 2, April 1982, 'Wire for Semi-conductor Applications';

Vol. 15, no. 2, April 1982, Alan J. Foster, 'Electro-deposited and Rolled Gold';

Vol. 15, no. 3, July 1982, Aram Papazian, 'Liquid Golds';

Vol. 15, no. 3, July 1982, David Buckton, 'Enamelling on Gold';

Vol. 15, no. 4, October 1982, Guy Bacquias, 'Bright Gold Electroplating Solutions';

Vol. 15, no. 4, October 1982, Gregory J. Higby, 'Gold in Medicine';

Vol. 16, no. 2, April 1983, S. L. Cantor, 'Gold Filled Products in the USA';

Vol. 16, no. 2, April 1983, Andrew Oddy, 'Assaying in Antiquity';

Vol. 18, nos 1, 2, 3, 1985, George B. Kauffman, 'The Role of Gold in Alchemy';

Vol. 19, no. 1, January 1986, Blaine M. Sutton, 'Gold Compounds for Rheumatoid Arthritis';

Vol. 19, no. 1, January 1986, Andrew Oddy and Susan la Niece, 'Byzantine Gold Coins and Jewellery';

Vol. 19, no. 3, July 1986, Peter Wilkinson, 'Understanding Gold Plating'.

Gold Bulletin and Gold Patent Digest, World Gold Council, Geneva, Switzerland:

Vol. 21, no. 1, 1988, David Brown, 'Oral Golds';

Vol. 22, No. 4, 1989, Geoffrey Bafner, 'The Development of 990 Gold — Titanium'.

Gold 1990, Gold Fields Mineral Services, London

Goldsmiths Technical Digest, The Worshipful Company of Goldsmiths, London 1988/89

Gold Gazette, published fortnightly, Resource Information Unit, Subiaco, Western Australia

L'Orafo Italiano, Milan, Spring 1990

Jewellery News Asia, Hong Kong

International Gold Mining Newsletter, monthly, Mining Journal Ltd, London

The Australian Gold Conference 1990, speakers' papers:

Kenneth Yeung, 'Hong Kong and China as a Market for Gold';

William Scarson, 'Papua New Guinea';

Joel Muyco, 'The Philippines Gold Mining Industry for the 1990s';

Ross Louthean, 'Prospects for the Australian Gold Mining Industry'.

Acknowledgements

Maps
created by Christopher Elliott

Charts & diagrams
created by Alistair Powell

Picture credits
A: page 1, The Hulton Picture Company; page 3, courtesy Anglo-American Corporation; page 4, Timothy Green; page 6, Timothy Green

B: page 10, *Illustrated London News;* page 11, courtesy PAMP SA; page 12, courtesy American Barrick; page 13, MAGNUM; page 14, World Gold Council; page 16, (top) MAGNUM; (bottom) MAGNUM; (right) World Gold Council

C: page 21, Daniel Wiener for Echo Bay Mines; page 23, (top right), Robert Harding Picture Library; (bottom right) courtesy MTB Banking Corporation; page 25, courtesy Tanaka Kikinzoku Kagyu KK; page 26, courtesy Uno e Erre; page 28, courtesy King Fook Finance Co. Ltd.; page 31, courtesy MTB Banking Corporation; (bottom) courtesy Comex; page 35, courtesy The Austrian Mint

D: page 39, World Gold Council; page 40, (bottom left) Timothy Green; (top right) Spink & Son Ltd.; page 41, (left) World Gold Council; (top) Novosti; page 42, Spink & Son Ltd

E: page 43, courtesy MTB Banking Corporation; (right) World Gold Council; page 44, (top) World Gold Council; (bottom) courtesy PAMP SA; page 45, World Gold Council; page 46 (top) Bayerische Museum, Germany; (bottom) World Gold Council; page 47, Spink & Son Ltd; page 48, Timothy Green

F: Page 49, courtesy Wartski; page 50, World Gold Council; page 51 (bottom), courtesy N.M. Rothschild; page 53 (top), World Gold Council; page 54 (bottom), courtesy Chamber of Mines of South Africa; page 54 (top), courtesy PAMP SA

G: page 57, Robert Harding; page 60, World Gold Council; page 61, courtesy The Royal Bank of Canada; page 62, Hulton Picture Co; page 65, Spink & Son Ltd

H: page 67, Timothy Green; page 68 (top), Timothy Green; page 68 (bottom), World Gold Council; page 69, PAMP SA; page 70, Novosti; page 71, World Gold Council

I: page 73, World Gold Council

J: page 77, courtesy Tanaka Kikinzoku Kogyo KK; page 78 (top left to right), Hutchinson Picture Library; World Gold Council; World Gold Council; page 78 (bottom left to right), Kuntshistorisches Museum, Vienna; Hutchinson Picture Library; World Gold Council; page 80, all World Gold Council

K: ; page 82 (left), courtesy King Fook Finance Co. Ltd; page 82 (right), World Gold Council

L: page 84, World Gold Council; page 86, World Gold Council

M: page 88, courtesy The Royal Canadian Mint; page 91 (top), courtesy The Chamber of Mines of South Africa; page 91 (bottom), Timothy Green; page 92, Timothy Green; page 95, Hutchinson Picture Library

N: page 96, Spink & Son Ltd.; page 97 (top), courtesy *Gold Gazette*, Perth; page 97 (bottom), Timothy Green; page 98 (left), Timothy Green; page 98 (top), courtesy Goldcorp, Australia; page 98 (bottom), Spink & Son Ltd

O: page 100, courtesy Newmont Gold Company; page 103, World Gold Council

P: page 105 (top), MAGNUM; page 105 (bottom), World Gold Council; page 106, courtesy Placer Pacific; page 107, courtesy The Austrian Mint; page 109, World Gold Council

R: page 114, courtesy PAMP SA; page 116, Bridgeman Art Library, courtesy Guildhall Library

S: page 121, Timothy Green; page 122, Timothy Green; page 126, courtesy The Chamber of Mines of South Africa; page 128 (top), Spink & Son Ltd.; page 128 (bottom), Spink & Son Ltd.; page 130 (top), Novosti; page 130 (bottom), Novosti

T: page 135, courtesy King Fook Finance Co. Ltd.; page 136, courtesy Dresdner Bank, Frankfurt; page 139, Timothy Green; page 140, courtesy PAMP SA; page 141 (top), Michael Freeman; page 141 (bottom), Hutchinson Picture Library

U: page 144, Daniel Wiener for Echo Bay Mines; page 145, courtesy American Barrick

V: page 149, courtesy Bank Leu

W: page 151, courtesy The Chamber of Mines of South Africa

Z: pages 153 and 154, courtesy Cluff Resources